Unbroken Communion

Unbroken Communion

The Place and Meaning of Suffering in the Theology of Edward Schillebeeckx

Kathleen Anne McManus, O.P.

ROWMAN & LITTLEFIELD PUBLISHERS, INC.
Lanham • Boulder • New York • Oxford

ROWMAN & LITTLEFIELD PUBLISHERS, INC.

Published in the United States of America
by Rowman & Littlefield Publishers, Inc.
A Member of the Rowman & Littlefield Publishing Group
4501 Forbes Blvd., Suite 200, Lanham, Maryland 20706
www.rowmanlittlefield.com

P.O. Box 317, Oxford OX2 9RU, United Kingdom

British Library Cataloguing in Publication Information Available

Library of Congress Cataloging-in-Publication Data

McManus, Kathleen Anne, 1959–
    Unbroken communion : the place and meaning of suffering in the
theology of Edward Schillebeeckx / Kathleen Anne McManus.
        p.   cm.
    Includes bibliographical references and index.
    ISBN 0-7425-1402-1 (alk. paper)—ISBN 0-7425-1403-X (pbk. : alk.
paper)
        1. Schillebeeckx, Edward, 1914—Contributions in Catholic doctrine of
suffering.   2. Suffering—Religious aspects—Catholic Church.   I. Title.
    BT732.7 .M3   2003
    233—dc21   2002009328

Printed in the United States of America

The paper used in this publication meets the minimum requirements of
American National Standard for Information Sciences—Permanence of Paper
for Printed Library Materials, ANSI/NISO Z39.48-1992.

To
My Parents, Ann and John McManus,
Whose love has nurtured in me the ground of trust

In Memoriam

Monsignor James S. Conlan,
Whose preaching healed multitudes

And

Neil Boyle,
Whose suffering and death illumined the bonds
of communion among us

Contents

Acknowledgments

This book comes out of my research for my doctoral dissertation. For its publication, therefore, I remain indebted to the many persons, communities, and institutions that contributed to the completion of my doctoral project. I want to express gratitude to the members of my Dominican Family in the United States and in Toronto who provided encouragement and inspiration along the way. In particular, I thank Mary Catherine Hilkert, O.P., for my earliest and most inspiring introduction to the theology of Edward Schillebeeckx. I am deeply grateful, also, to the Sisters of St. Joseph of Toronto, who provided a supportive "home-away-from home" during the time of thesis writing. Sr. Dorothy O'Connor, C.S.J., was a source of wisdom and courage in more ways than can be named, even as she negotiated the challenges of her own increasing frailty. Loving mentor of mind and heart, Dorothy went home to God on the Feast of St. Joseph this year. Though I grieve her passing, I rejoice in her liberation into the fullness of life.

The communities of St. Michael's and Regis Colleges provided companionship and guidance at many levels. Margaret O'Gara's advisement in my beginnings at St. Michael's, Jean-Marc Laporte's availability for directed readings and fruitful conversations along the way, and Ellen Leonard's quietly insightful accompaniment stand out in what was for me a thoroughly supportive and life-giving experience at the Toronto School of Theology. I am especially grateful to my director, Daniel Donovan, for his constancy, his wisdom, and his generous sharing of his own rich stores from "the great Christian tradition."

For the marvelous opportunity to "breathe the air that Schillebeeckx breathes" for six weeks in the summer of 1995, I am indebted to my director (for the idea and inspiration!), and to the Dutch Dominicans for their warm hospitality. Ted Schoof, O.P., and Erik Borgman were helpful with their insights and sharing of bibliographic material. Most especially, I thank Hadewych Snijdewind, O.P., for her generous, sisterly sharing of her home with me. I thank Edward Schillebeeckx for his kind attention and interest in my project. Above all, I am grateful for his great Dominican heart and his steadfast faithfulness to the God who chose to be among us as human.

I cannot express the depth of my gratitude to my Blauvelt Dominican Congregation for the opportunity to study, for the witness of my sisters among the poor, and for our heritage of preaching an enfleshed Word. Mary Ann Collins and M. Timothy Cunningham, O.P., consistently embodied my congregation's nurturing involvement in this process; the sisters of Rosary Community lovingly provided my New York home-base, and Ann Lovett and Mary Reddy-Reichley shared each stage of my journey even through their own changing paths.

Finally, I am aware that I could not have met the diverse challenges of the Toronto years without the close accompaniment of loving family, faithful spiritual guides, and precious friends. For God's own companioning in and through them, I am unspeakably grateful.

Introduction

The world in the third millennium possesses unprecedented capabilities for advancing the quality of human life, transforming social structures, and restoring the damaged balance of nature. As inhabitants of this world, we who understand ourselves as creatures have unprecedented power to realize our role in the divine/human partnership in creation and salvation. At the same time, we have unprecedented power to destroy creation and each other—all that God has entrusted to us. The former is what we hope for; here and there, in fragmentary ways, we see and experience the realization of such hope, and we rejoice. Too often, however, we see and experience hope thwarted, salvation opposed, the *humanum* threatened. Sorrow takes the place of rejoicing in too many human lives. The scarlet thread of suffering woven through our human history gains texture and density in proportion, it seems, to human progress. The reality of suffering is the greatest challenge to faith in the goodness of creation and the possibility of salvation. Edward Schillebeeckx not only takes this into account, but dialectically incorporates the reality of suffering into the construction of a theology generally defined by its focus on the interrelated themes of creation, salvation, and eschatological hope.

Schillebeeckx has spent his life as a theologian proclaiming God's commitment to human flourishing, and he has done this in a world more schooled in suffering than in joy. The promise of humanity's positive potential that I have here evoked is captured by the Latin *humanum,* a word that Schillebeeckx frequently employs to express the not-yet-seen fulfillment of all that it means to be human,[1] the promise of humanity's positive potential. Schillebeeckx grounds his entire theological project in the promise of a divine/human future made visible in creation and entrusted to human freedom. If Schillebeeckx gives a privileged theological locus to the human experience of suffering, it is on the basis of an originally good creation and against the horizon of the eschatological promise. But because suffering is so tangibly present in human experience, it provides the means, dialectically, of imaging the horizon of our hope. Schillebeeckx demonstrates that salvation can only be articulated in counterpoint to the concrete real-

1

ity of suffering. This, in fact, is the essence of the notion of "negative contrast experience" that emerges in his later theology.[2] In other words, Schillebeeckx's method of doing theology corresponds to the content of his theological message. The dialectic of human suffering and salvation is most identifiable after Schille-beeckx's dramatic shift wherein human experience assumes center stage in his theology. The fundamental elements of this dialectic are, however, present even in Schillebeeckx's earliest work. This study, therefore, will engage the reader in an analysis of how suffering operates as a formative factor throughout the whole of Schillebeeckx's theological development.

WHAT KIND OF SUFFERING?

Human suffering in all its forms confronts ordinary people with the essential questions of life's meaning and purpose. And this raises the question of just what the term "suffering" really means in this discussion. Suffering constitutes the raw and immediate challenge to countless concrete lives running desperately short of hope. Rawness. Immediacy. Dearth of hope. These may be taken as the defining characteristics of the term "suffering" in this study. It is this quality of agony, this experience of affliction, that must be understood by this use of the term. And the cause of affliction may be internal or external, emotional or physi-cal, social or economic. The suffering I speak of may be the result of natural disaster, international violence, political injustice, or subtle personal oppression. It may be one person's excruciating battle with terminal illness, and another's agonizing loss of a loved one to sickness and death. The term "suffering" con-jures up the unfathomable civil terror of Rwanda and Kosovo, ongoing starvation from India to the Sudan, and the ravaging of societies by earthquakes and hurri-canes. "Suffering" evokes the increasing scourge of homelessness throughout North America. In the drug and crime-ridden streets of our inner cities, suffering is exacerbated by society's brutal stripping of basic human services from the most destitute among us. It cries out in the overwhelming spectrum of human rights abuses in China, and in the exploitation of women and children by multiple industries throughout the world. The many facets of the AIDS crisis give rise to suffering in all of its physical, psychic, and spiritual dimensions. Suffering sim-mers in the seasoned, principled hatreds of centuries in the Middle East, in East-ern Europe, and in Northern Ireland. It is evident in the solemn devastation of Guatemalan and Salvadoran peasants digging up loved ones from the mass graves of the disappeared. Worn by now-stilled violence, these weary ones seek merely to entrust the dead to God by name in Christian burial as they take up life again under what they know to be a false and corrupt civil peace. There is something in the concrete, trusting simplicity of this act that evokes what will emerge here as central to Schillebeeckx's theology: Suffering challenges us humans to resist its causes on every front, but when our earthly efforts fail we are held by the mystery of a hidden God in whom life is stronger than death, in whom human acts of truth triumph beyond earthly limits.

But what "suffering" means in Schillebeeckx's and my usage is still not exhausted (nor will I exhaust it here). Suffering is at once more immanent and more ambiguous in its existence under the contradictory signs of modern comfort and success. The most common suffering is no less painful for being invisible. It is hidden away in middle-class homes. It hovers beneath the polished facade of the affluent. The immediacy of loneliness, the rawness of broken relationships, the incomprehensible pain of mental illness, the dearth of hope when the fulfillment of earthly desires leaves unnamed emptiness unassuaged, the slow relinquishing of life with the years: This only begins to name what is indicated by Schillebeeckx's comprehensive references to "suffering."[3] What remains constant in all the myriad scenarios of suffering is the human experience of affliction.

THE EXPERIENTIAL CONTEXT OF SCHILLEBEECKX'S THEOLOGY

Schillebeeckx's writing is marked by his engagement with history, with varied philosophical disciplines, and his own religious tradition, Dominican and Catholic. Amidst many streams of influence, his theological project is consistently shaped by suffering as mystery and as challenge. These two dimensions are equally present in Schillebeeckx's fundamental engagement with both the concrete experience of suffering men and women and the religious and philosophical approaches to this experience. Indeed, in the course of Schillebeeckx's development, the practical and the theoretical become one in the ground of his *own* experience. It is this ground of Schillebeeckx's own experience that becomes, necessarily, the place of synthesis for his theology. This is what Schillebeeckx means when he says that his theological method arises from the narrative structure of experience. Thus, the historical situatedness of Schillebeeckx's own understanding is the experience from which to trace the development of his theology and the role of suffering as a formative factor in that development. With this in mind, my analysis will be directed according to the widening and deepening spiral emanating from the center point of Schillebeeckx's own concrete experience as a Dominican whose life and work have passed through the crucible of the Second Vatican Council and its aftermath.

I will lay the groundwork of Schillebeeckx's methodological development in the first chapter. An initial biographical sketch will reveal the personal roots of the incarnational faith that informs his life project at every turn. Schillebeeckx's early intellectual training in philosophical phenomenology and historical theology provided the framework for his appropriation of the thought of Thomas Aquinas. Most importantly, Schillebeeckx appropriates Thomas's *method* as a theologian who brings doctrinal theology and human experience of the God of salvation into a synthesis. Human experience of the God of salvation incorporates not only everyday experience, but also the intellectual currents of the time. The most significant currents shaping Schillebeeckx's later theological development are hermeneutics, critical theory, and modern Biblical exegesis. I will examine how these disciplines interface with the role of suffering in Schillebeeckx's thought and, in so doing, will show that Schillebeeckx's manner of incorporation and his principles of selection are guided by the pervasive force of suffering in the world.

The question of suffering leads inevitably to questions about the nature of good and evil and, ultimately, original sin.[4] In Thomas Aquinas's teaching on this subject are seen the patterned roots of Schillebeeckx's anthropology. The goodness of God and the fundamental goodness of humanity are basic to Thomas's thought. Thomas's discussions of the nature of evil and sin frequently evoke what Schillebeeckx will come to speak of as "experiences of negative contrast." That is, God is to be found on the underside of even life's darkest, most threatening experiences. Over and over again Schillebeeckx proclaims that, when all worldly evidence attests to the malevolence of reality, God is to be found as mercy at the heart of reality. This sense of God on the underside of the negative reality of evil and suffering is central to Thomas Aquinas's system. In chapter two, under the title "Roots of Developing Contrast," I will examine the Thomistic paradigm of original justice and original sin as it is evidenced in key works of Schillebeeckx's early theology.

What Schillebeeckx retains from the classical Fall construct is the sense that it is only obedience to God that can sustain us through the experiences of suffering, sin, and evil. "Obedience" here has the relational connotation of committed trust and unbroken communion. Christians cannot think away suffering or the "surd" of evil damaging God's good creation. They can only look to Jesus, in whom God has the last word over the very real and destructive experience of suffering. Ultimately it is the gospel, the life praxis and proclaimed message of Jesus Christ, that becomes the norm and criterion for living and proclaiming the truth of salvation amidst suffering.[5] Chapter three, where I will deal with Schillebeeckx's christology, reveals the sense of "obedience" as "trust," born out in Jesus' own relationship of unbroken communion with God through suffering and death. This is the element of mysticism at the core of Schillebeeckx's engagement with suffering. The inseparability of this mysticism from the concrete immediacy of human experience is evident in Schillebeeckx's pervading conviction that incarnational faith reveals humanity as a fundamental symbol of God. He speaks of a hermeneutic of humanity from which we must interpret the gospel, and vice versa: "In the light of Jesus Christ, the gospel itself is a hermeneutic of fundamental human experience."[6] My approach here, following Schillebeeckx, will reflect the profound incarnational insight from Thomas that undergirds the whole of Schillebeeckx's theology: Simply stated, the humanity of Jesus is the *mode of existence* of the Son of God in the world.[7] The discussion of christology is therefore grounded in soteriology, beginning with the vision of the *humanum* arising from Schillebeeckx's system of anthropological coordinates. This will lead, through reflection upon the humanity of Jesus, into a discussion of the "Mysticism of the Cross and Negative Contrast Experience" in the second part of this third chapter. The mysticism of the cross experienced in each personal "turning" or *metanoia*[8] is at the core of the human solidarity in grace that becomes manifest in ethical, political praxis. The fourth chapter will explore the significance of political mysticism in Schillebeeckx's theology,[9] the social and political ramifications of the original human solidarity in grace and sin elaborated in chapter two. If the imperative to social action dominates Schillebeeckx's later work, it is because the imperative to personal conversion in his early work has intensified and developed in the face of increasing global suffering. My examination of the reciprocal relation between solidarity and metanoia will reveal the mystical centrality of trust throughout the major shifts in Schillebeeckx's work. Trust is key to the success or failure of our human vocation as mediators of grace, which highlights the human need for reconciliation. My discussion of reconciliation as both gift and task in the latter part of chapter four will explore Schillebeeckx's realization that God's fullest self-revelation occurs precisely where we least expect it—in experiences of human sinfulness and vulnerability.

The experience of metanoia in this dynamic of salvation is, as I have said, integrally bound up with experiences of negative contrast. And these intertwined realities depend upon the power of story for their meaning and efficacy. The saving narrative begins on the sure ground of God's graced creation and promised future.[10] It proceeds with the bold naming of suffering, sin, and evil in concrete human situations. This negative theology of protest issues in concrete political praxis to recreate human structures in the image of divine justice proclaimed by the gospel. The crisis of meaning and faith enters in when the praxis of justice is thwarted, and, more critically, when radical, gratuitous suffering renders the presence of evil more evident and potent in the world than the presence of God or goodness. At the place where human effort or understanding reaches its limit, at the place where God seems absent, there is evoked a praxis of solidarity.

In the fifth and final chapter this praxis of solidarity becomes, inescapably, the crucial substance of Schillebeeckx's implicit theology of suffering. It has different manifestations in accord with the vastly different types of individual and communal suffering. The praxis of solidarity is manifest in transformative action as well as in resistance and protest. In situations of the most extreme suffering, it appears as faithful waiting: attentive love in a "now" that belies the very promise that sustains us. The praxis of solidarity is a contemplative, relational praxis rooted in Jesus' intimacy with God, an intimacy that sustained the cross and issued in resurrection. It is manifest in the most hopeless situations by the courageous, ministering human presence that alone witnesses to God's final word over suffering, sin, and death.

Edward Schillebeeckx has absorbed the pervasive reality of suffering into the motive, method, and content of a theology that unflinchingly insists that God's deepest desire is the happiness of human beings: God is committed to the human cause. This is the message that men and women long to hear but can hardly believe. Out of the real experience of suffering arises the divine summons to participate in mercy at the heart of reality. This entails trust in the God who has so designed human nature that *we are each other's happiness.*

NOTES

1. Rosino Gibellini observes that Schillebeekkx's theology has "a lively sense of the integrity of the *humanum* in its anthropological, social and cultural, theoretical and practical, utopian and religious dimensions. It is a theology which develops a soteriology in a modern key, in that it is guided by two preoccupations: in the negative sense, by what Bloch calls the 'threatened *humanum*' and by the stories of the suffering and death of men and women; and in a positive sense by what Ricoeur calls the '*desirable humanum*,' the fullness and integrity of the *humanum.*" In Schillebeeckx, *I Am a Happy Theologian* (New York: Crossroad, 1994), xii.

2. Human suffering appears in stark contrast against the horizon of the eschatological promise. "Negative contrast experience" is a term that emerged after Schillebeeckx opened himself and his theology to the impact of Marxist-based critical theory. The term refers to those experiences of injustice, oppression, suffering that give rise to protest and the ethical imperative toward active transformation. Schillebeeckx emphasizes that "these contrast experiences show that the moral imperative is first discovered in its immediate, concrete, *inner* meaning, before it can be made the object of a science and then reduced to a generally valid principle. . . . The initial creative decision which discovered the historical imperative directly in its *inner* meaning in the very contrast experience *is,* for the believer, at the same time the charismatic element of this whole process." See "Church, Magisterium, and Politics," in *God the Future of Man,* trans. N. D. Smith (New York: Sheed & Ward, 1968), 155–56. A nuanced analysis of the development of negative contrast experience as it pertains to suffering will follow in this volume.

3. Schillebeeckx notes that beyond those areas where human efforts can effect healing, we are still constantly confronted with the fundamental suffering of the human person: "suffering from love, suffering as a result of guilt, because of our finitude and mortality, suffering through failure and inadequacy, and finally suffering over the invisibility and hiddenness of God. No human techniques of healing or emancipating practices can ever remove or diminish this suffering." *Christ: The Experience of Jesus as Lord,* Dutch, 1977; trans. John Bowden (New York: Crossroad, 1980); British title: *The Christian Experience in the Modern World* (London: SCM Press, 1980), 764. Later, Schillebeeckx speaks of the culmination of the authority of experiences in the particular authority of human stories of suffering: "stories of suffering over misfortune and failure, the suffering of pain, the suffering of evil and injustice, the suffering of and in love, sorrow or guilt. Here lie the great elements of the revelation of reality in and through finite human experiences." *Church: The Human Story of God,* trans. John Bowden (New York: Crossroad, 1990), 28.

4. A plethora of studies on original sin published in the 1950s testifies to the struggle of theologians to come to grips with new currents of biblical interpretation altering the reading of Genesis. (See, for example, a series in the *Downside Review* from 1953 to 1958,

volumes 71, 72, 75, and 76, that feature articles on original sin, paradise, pain, and the mystery of evil.) Commenting in 1975 on the constant stream of Roman Catholic publications on original sin since the early fifties, George Vandervelde notes that "in the last decade alone, one can count at least seventy titles." Vandervelde, *Original Sin: Two Major Trends in Contemporary Roman Catholic Interpretation* (Washington, D.C.: University Press of America, 1981; Amsterdam, 1975), 42. Tracing the roots of this phenomenon, Henri Rondet recalls how LaGrange's ground-breaking 1897 publication on innocence and sin, initially controverted, was canonized by Pius XII in *Divino afflante spiritu* (1943). The work of Protestant exegete Hermann Gunkel, among others, similarly had a profound impact on the interpretation of Genesis. Though the 1950 encyclical, *Humani Generis,* seemed to close doors to unrestricted interpretation, it actually allowed some room for formerly rejected theories and for the utilization of the sciences. See Henri Rondet, *Original Sin: The Patristic and Theological Background,* trans. Cajetan Finnegan (New York: Alba House, 1972), 218–30.

5. Explaining how Jesus in his own person presents God as salvation for suffering men and women, Schillebeeckx writes: "Jesus is about God's business, and the business of humanity, the *humanum,* is to search after God 'for God's sake.' Jesus is the man whose joy and pleasure is God himself. God's lordship is God's mode of being God; and our recognition of that engenders the truly human condition, the salvation of humankind. For that reason God's lordship, as Jesus understands it, expresses the relation between God and humanity, in the sense that 'we are each other's happiness.'" *Jesus: An Experiment in Christology,* Dutch, 1974; trans. Hubert Hoskins (New York: Crossroad, 1979), 142.

6. Edward Schillebeeckx, *Christ: The Experience of Jesus as Lord,* 76.

7. Philip Kennedy asserts, "In much the same way as Schillebeeckx's entire theological corpus, with its governing preoccupation of explaining religious knowledge, can be described as an extended excursus on a single text of Aquinas (*Summa Theologiae,* I, q. 1, a.7, ad 1, Schillebeeckx's Christology . . . can also be understood as a gradually unfolding commentary on yet another passage of Aquinas . . . (ST III, q. 2, a. 10)." Kennedy explains that, over against the Leonine text, which speaks of "Christ in whom human nature is so assumed as to belong to the person of the Son *(in quo humana natura assumpta est ad hoc quod sit personae Filii Dei).* . . . [t]he majority of manuscripts reflect Thomas's intention of indicating that the humanity of Jesus is itself a manner of being of the Son of God. Most manuscripts speak of Christ, 'in whom human nature is so assumed as to be the person of the Son of God *(sit persona Filii Dei).'*" *Deus Humanissimus,* 297–99.

8. *Metanoia* is generally understood as the biblical term for conversion (Greek "change of mind"). Schillebeeckx himself, in a glossary of technical terms at the end of his *Jesus* book, defines it as follows: "This means repentance and conversion in the sense of making a right-about turn. In a context of faith in God it entails radical self-criticism. *Metanoia* is the consequence and implication of the coming of God's kingdom." Schillebeeckx, *Jesus,* 747.

9. During the period of his conscious development of "political mysticism," Schillebeeckx defines "mysticism" as "an intensive form of experience of God or love of God," and "politics" as "an intensive form of social commitment." See Schillebeeckx, *On Christian Faith: The Spiritual, Ethical, and Political Dimensions,* trans. John Bowden (New York: Crossroad, 1987), 71–72.

10. Schillebeeckx emphasizes that the fundamental human "no" to evil discloses a more fundamental, though unfulfilled, "open yes," which is the positive condition for opposition. See *Church: The Human Story of God,* trans. John Bowden (New York: Crossroad, 1990), 6.

Chapter One

Schillebeeckx's Methodological Development: An Overview

BIOGRAPHICAL SKETCH

Edward Schillebeeckx may be characterized as a living father of the Church. Indeed, his entire life as a theologian has been given to the struggle to birth a new church order, one that makes visible in the world the fullest implications of God's incarnation in humanity. The labor of that struggle, fraught with pain, has yet to bring forth the fullness of the long-awaited birth. The light is waning on Schillebeeckx's life, and many of those who have labored with him have entered their own eschatological fulfillment. A new generation of theologians in a rapidly changing world takes up the struggle. This generation includes increasing numbers of women as well as men from diverse cultures around the globe. The work of these theologians makes it possible to hear the voices of the suffering human communities they represent. Through those voices the thread of the *threatened humanum* running through Schillebeeckx's lifework is configured in flesh and blood, in bone and breath. Out of the dark stream of suffering in human history arises, through hope and longing, a vision of the *humanum*—that full human flourishing that fulfills the divine will at the heart of creation. This is revelation-in-word and in experience. This is the meaning of "salvation coming from God in Jesus Christ."

The life of Edward Schillebeeckx literally bridges the modern and postmodern worlds. It has been observed that through the complexity of our postmodern era the very best elements of the declining modern age are straining to finally take form. Modern ideals of freedom, social reform, and individuality find their authentic meaning when defined in relation to the needs and demands of the "other" whose inexorable presence dominates postmodern consciousness.[1] Increasing modern focus on human experience as the locus of revelation in theology consistently referred Schillebeeckx to experiences of suffering. The suffering

8

"other," personally proximate or politically and geographically distant, became for him the measure of authentic Christian proclamation.

Schillebeeckx himself does not appear to be giving voice to the suffering "other" in the way that a black, Asian, feminist, womanist, or Latin American liberation theologian does. Indeed, he is a white, male, European theologian. But it is precisely as such that he has prepared the way for these new voices to be heard. And he could only do that by being faithful to the historical particularity of his own life. It is to that particularity that this discussion now turns.

Family Life

Edward Schillebeeckx, the sixth of fourteen children in a Flemish, Catholic family, was born on November 12, 1914. The texture of Edward's life cannot but have been deeply woven through with the effects of two world wars. Though he grew up in the town of Kortenberg, Belgium, Edward was born in Antwerp as his parents journeyed back home after a brief exile to the Netherlands during the German invasion.

An atmosphere of family faith and devotion permeated Edward's growing. It may be surmised that the mutually challenging relationships that his parents promoted among his brothers and sisters nourished a naturally democratic temperament and shaped his spirituality and theology. The Schillebeeckx children learned from one another through play and dialogue, all in relation to the profoundly traditional background presence of their father, whom Edward has affectionately described as "a true patriarch," and "the high priest of the family." Indeed, Edward's earliest memories of Christmas revolve around his father's explanation of the manger scene, culminating in the pronouncement, "that baby is God!"[2] This childhood impression of the incarnation was to bear itself out in the central theme of Schillebeeckx's developing christological assertions.

At the age of eleven, Edward went off to the Jesuit boarding school at Turnhout, where he was steeped in the classics. Here, under the mentorship of an admired Jesuit teacher, Edward began to develop the commitment to social issues that would come to the fore in his later work. Despite this positive experience, the priestly vocation that Edward had contemplated since early childhood did not lead him to join the Jesuits. At the age of nineteen, while intentionally exploring the lives of the founders of the great religious orders, he read the life of Saint Dominic and decided to become a Dominican. It is significant that the young Edward was attracted by the joy and human warmth that balanced Dominic's intellectual commitment to truth. From the beginning, there was a relational basis to Edward's pursuit of truth. For the young serving boys at Turnhout who had little opportunity to learn, Edward created "newsletters" to aid their understanding. Later, as a lecturer in theology to Dominican students, he would create a journal of spirituality for their formation. The human need to understand the deep things of the soul has always been the motivation firing his ceaseless theological work. Clearly, it is not coincidental that the young Edward should have been captured by his encounter with Dominic, nor that his relationally based, experience-centered theology should have developed in the context of Dominican common life. The Dominican charism of seeking and preaching truth is centered on the immanence of the Word-made-flesh. The decidedly incarnational force of this charism is borne out gradually and systematically in the nature and trajectory of Schillebeeckx's theology. How is this so?

Early Intellectual Influences

In 1937–1938, during his initial years of Dominican formation in Ghent, Schillebeeckx came under the tutelage of Dominic DePetter for his philosophical training. DePetter set his student to a project which, according to Philip Kennedy, resulted in Schillebeeckx's enduring interest in the concept of experience.[3] Under DePetter, Schillebeeckx studied the phenomenology of Husserl, Merleau-Ponty, and Heidegger from a Thomistic perspective. His encounter with the thought of Maurice Merleau-Ponty was to permanently influence the shape and development of his work. Here are revealed the philosophical roots of the concrete, incarnational quality that pervades Schillebeeckx's theology. The phenomenological centrality of the body in perceiving and expressing the world and its reality is preeminently incarnational. And this sensory apprehension of reality echoed, for both Schillebeeckx and his teacher, DePetter, the Thomistic construct of human participation in/experience of the divinely created world.[4]

In its simplest terms, "phenomenology" is defined as "the setting forth and articulation of what shows itself."[5] The field of phenomenology is concerned with an exploration of the intentionality of consciousness and a description of phenomena as they give themselves, free from cultural, ontological, and philosophical bias.

Phenomenologists such as Merleau-Ponty and DePetter consciously distanced themselves from the Cartesian dualism dominating the (modern) philosophical tradition. They returned to the starting point of the embodied human person as perceiver of a world "already there." The body is "our point of view on this world, the locus of our experience with visible phenomena and the visible form of our intentions." Merleau-Ponty, who views flesh as an element of being in the same sense as "air," "fire," "water," and "earth," "claims that there is no word in traditional philosophy to designate "flesh": "this visibility, this generality of the sensible in itself, this anonymity innate to myself."[6] In contrast, Merleau-Ponty "describes flesh in its 'intertwining' with the world and consciousness, and so undermines the accepted meanings of all of these: the body, the mind, and the world."[7]

It is easy to see how Schillebeeckx's reading of Merleau-Ponty and Thomas Aquinas would have been mutually reinforcing. In the Thomistic and Dominican tradition, an incarnational view of the human person as participant in the divinely created order, a knower and lover of God precisely in and through the flesh, was second nature to Schillebeeckx. And, though Dominic DePetter was responsible primarily for Schillebeeckx's philosophical formation, it was he who introduced Schillebeeckx to theology. Schillebeeckx's indifference to theology as a closed system of dogma lacking the intellectual challenge and freedom of philosophy was cured forever, beginning with his exposure to the writings of Karl Adam. For the first time, Schillebeeckx's mind was opened to the implications of culture and the contemporary relevance of theology. After a year of military service, Schillebeeckx went to Leuven for the theological studies leading to his ordination in 1941. He remained at Leuven for further theological study in a classically Thomistic vein at the Dominican House of Studies, where he was then appointed lecturer in theology for two years. Balancing his intellectual tasks, he was also responsible for the spiritual formation of Dominican students.

As early as 1945, while still at Leuven, Schillebeeckx attempted to elaborate a "culture-theology." Erik Borgman notes that, "although this term no longer appears in his work after the '40s, all his writings, however diverse, can be viewed as contributions to a theology of and about present day culture."[8] And Philip Kennedy insists that the basic foci of Schillebeeckx's theological thought can be gleaned from six articles he published in 1945.[9] The very title of Schillebeeckx's first published article, "The Sense of Being a Creature as the Basis of Our Spiritual Life," indicates the phenomenological Thomism underlying the whole of his theological development. The reality of the human person as both created and creating is certainly the prerequisite of culture in all its manifestations. Schillebeeckx's engagement with culture thus necessarily translates into engagement with the ambiguity of human experience overwhelmingly marked by suffering.

Later in this same year, Schillebeeckx went to France to begin his doctoral studies. He pursued his interests with professors at Le Saulchoir, the Sorbonne, and the École des Hautes Études. Among the great thinkers to whom he had access, Marie Dominique Chenu's influence upon Schillebeeckx was to equal the formative effects of DePetter in parallel ways. Chenu—theologian, worker-priest, and principal agent of *ressourcement*—held that God's word in the world extends and completes the incarnation of Christ. According to Chenu, "incarnation means that God and the world can no longer be received separately, which implies that faith—and theology as reflection upon faith—can only exist in a creative interaction with the culture in which one lives."[10] This view emerged naturally from Chenu's restoration of the real Thomas Aquinas in historical context. Thus restored, Aquinas was for Chenu the model theologian: one who brings doctrinal theology and human experience of the God of salvation into a synthesis. Borgman stresses that this synthesis cannot be copied, but must be achieved anew in every age. Clearly, this was the "Thomas" Schillebeeckx learned from Chenu. Inspired by this Dominican confrère and teacher, Schillebeeckx similarly incorporated first the thought, and later, more accurately, the method of Aquinas.

As fervently as Schillebeeckx emulates the spirit of Chenu in his early, Flemish period, Borgman notes that his work is already distinguished from that of the older Dominican. "While Chenu expresses his plea of freedom in theology charismatically, wishes to be a full part of the present-day culture and views this as his place as a theologian, Schillebeeckx rather wants to clarify this culture philosophically and theologically."[11]

Schillebeeckx's own definition of theology as reflection upon faith might be elaborated this way: Faith is an *experience* in the context of historically situated life in the world. It is, in other words, mediated by culture. An element of that faith experience is contained within the cognitive dimension. Faith is, in fact, a way of knowing. What Schillebeeckx states in his "Memoriam" for Chenu reflects the character of his own theological method:

> I learned from Chenu that "to think" is sacred: "it is the intellectual which contains the spiritual." Indeed, most of all, I am still surrounded by the great communicative warmth of Fr. Chenu. He was a man of hope, an optimist of grace. So he was a Thomist through and through.[12]

"A man of hope, an optimist of grace"—Chenu was rooted in the world and engaged in human, political struggles. And though Schillebeeckx's engagement with those human, political struggles was not as immediate as Chenu's, his consciousness of the human suffering they entailed increasingly shaped the direction of his thought and the development of his theology. Beyond even his appropriation of Chenu's historical theological method, Schillebeeckx's identification with Chenu's persona fit squarely with his own philosophical grounding in phenomenology.

In 1947, Schillebeeckx returned to Leuven and taught dogmatic theology for the next ten years. In addition to related pastoral responsibilities as spiritual director and confessor to Dominican students and communities of religious sisters, and as editor of the spiritual journal *Tijdschrift voor Geestelijk Leven,* Schillebeeckx also engaged in prison ministry during those years. Presumably the students, the sisters, and the prisoners, respectively, were experiencing the effects of the aftermath of World War II. It is also presumable that, as individuals, they were suffering the exigencies of the particular circumstances of their lives at a critical moment in European history. Assuredly, Edward Schillebeeckx absorbed and responded to these sufferings as confessor and spiritual director. In fact, it is clear that, in his own life, Schillebeeckx was already experiencing the hidden suffering that was to perpetually accompany his authentic efforts as a Dominican theologian obedient to truth. That suffering is evident in his own account of the continuing conflicts with his Dominican superiors over his critical resistance to the oppressive discipline of Dominican student life. During his own formation, Schillebeeckx had submitted to the structures that were in place. Deeply secure in the "rightness" of his Dominican vocation, and in that sense happy, he simply moved through experiences that may have been harsh. As *magister spiritualis* of students, however, he quietly and matter-of-factly abolished oppressive disciplines. Relationship was the natural source of his authority in the lives of the sixty students entrusted to his spiritual care. Rather than "master," Schillebeeckx felt himself to be an "elder brother" to the young men with whom he sought to form genuine community. The sense of community was reinforced through his academic teaching of theology. It was precisely this reality of integration that disturbed Schillebeeckx's superiors, for he simply did not fit into his hierarchical "slot" as professor and spiritual master. He did not conform to the conventions of "community" amongst his "equals" who were "superiors."

Thus, Schillebeeckx's "praxis" with regard to his students reflected the theoretical grounding of the theology he taught. This theology also met with academic critique from some quarters. He was not only teaching, but also living from the theological renewal engendered in him by masters like Chenu. Even in those early days, he knew firsthand the pain involved in liberating truth from structures that have forgotten the purpose of their existence. Though he was not yet employing the language of "praxis," Schillebeeckx recognized that any significance religious life (or the committed Christian life) was to have would arise from the concrete instances in which men and women lived their vocations out of authentic human depths. Indeed, those lives would have to somehow make visible the personal nature of the fundamental human encounter with God in Christ.

History, Phenomenology, and Sacramental Encounter

Schillebeeckx's twofold grounding in historical method and phenomenology gave rise in the 1950s to the development of a sacramental theology that has permanently impacted the Church's praxis. Schillebeeckx's first major book appeared in Dutch as *De sacramentele Heilseconomie* in 1952. The 1958 publication of *Christ: The Sacrament of the Encounter with God,*[13] which emerged from this original work, proved influential around the world. Schillebeeckx shattered the prevailing mechanistic understanding of grace and sacraments and introduced the person of Christ as the underlying, universal means of encounter with God. In so doing, he established the human basis of Christ's mediation of God, and posited the incarnation as the fundamental or "primordial" sacrament.

It is important to note that *Christ: The Sacrament* significantly predates the major shift effected in Schillebeeckx's work by the forces of hermeneutics, critical theory, and the new biblical exegesis. Yet, elements of this book reveal contrasts and continuities relative to the formative role of suffering in Schillebeeckx's theology. On the one hand, Schillebeeckx's christology underwent a major reversal between the writing of this book and the writing of *Jesus: An Experiment in Christology.*[14] The former clearly emerges from a doctrinal starting point, taking the Chalcedonian formula as something to be translated and brought into the realm of common human experience and language. Though still working out of an old paradigm, what Schillebeeckx achieves here is noteworthy even for us today. First of all, it is a demonstration of his fundamental instinct that theology must respond to the deep human need to understand faith in the context and language of ordinary experience. Secondly, though still working deductively, Schillebeeckx gives evidence of his intuition that both faith and cognition have a relational basis.

On the other hand, the most important qualities of *Christ: The Sacrament* are those elements that have continued in evolving ways to be earmarks of Edward Schillebeckx's theology. The first of these is the Thomistic principle that all creation, having come from God, continues to live, move, and have its being in God. Human beings encounter God's personal, intimate presence in and through all creation. And that presence continues to be a *creating* presence by being a *saving* presence. In this still-early work, Schillebeeckx states that "God's saving activity 'makes history' by revealing itself, and it reveals itself by becoming history."[15] Speaking further of revelation as grace-made-visible, he notes that life in the world "belongs to the content of God's inner word to us," and that "human bodiliness is human interiority itself in visible form."[16]

Other instances evoking continuity abound. What Schillebeeckx later speaks of as Jesus' "Abba experience" is present here in his description of the "intimacy of life between the Father and the Son."[17] It would seem that Schillebeeckx's fundamental continuities are due to the permanence of his phenomenological roots. These are evident in his explanation of sign causality in his theology of sacrament. In a telling departure from the standard way of speaking about sacrament, Schillebeeckx speaks of human nature not as instrument, but as mode of existence.[18] And, in his early working out of Thomistic principles in a DePetterian phenomenological framework, Schillebeeckx already shows intimations of leanings that will later open him to the influence of hermeneutics. Schillebeeckx's combined elucidation and critique of Thomas's distinction between sign value and causal value touch upon this leaning. Schillebeeckx wants to emphasize that a sacrament causes salvation as a sign in the full human sense, and not merely as an indication of "something beyond." And yet he is careful to maintain that it is, indeed, God who is the cause of grace.

Schillebeeckx prefers to speak in terms of "the instrumental causality of the symbol" as a means of maintaining the "organic unity of 'sign' and 'instrumental and efficient cause of salvation.'"[19] It is vital to him to make clear that the humanity of Christ is the *mode of existence* of the Son of God in the world.[20] And, though the earthly Church has a separate concrete existence, its sacramental rites become the outward embodiment of the risen Christ's ongoing saving activity. It is in this sense that Schillebeeckx emphasizes the efficacy of Christ's *humanity* in the work of salvation. As Schillebeeckx's theology develops, so too will the implications of this point.

What is perhaps most significant about Schillebeeckx's method in *Christ: The*

Sacrament is the manner in which he incorporates human experience during this phase of his theology. His understanding of the significance of relationality has a contemporary quality. Yet, his method at this point is to draw upon human experience for examples to illustrate the way that Christ operates through the sacraments in the economy of salvation. The operation of grace, God's activity in creation, in Christ, and in the sacraments, is already doctrinally established. Schillebeeckx's concern here is to clarify for ordinary believers how this is so. His urgency to help people to understand, to make connections between their faith and their lived experience, is at work here. He wants to render Christ and the sacraments real, as well as assert the real importance of people's lived experience for understanding God's ways with them. This is a vital step in a deepening incarnational theology, but it is clearly a middle step. Schillebeeckx is, at this point, still giving priority to theory over praxis. His starting point is the Church's christological and sacramental dogmas. He adverts to human experience to help people understand, by analogy, God's ways with human beings. At this early stage, the role of human experience is one of response to revelation, which lies on God's side of the equation (in this case, expressed in sacramental rites). That human response is telling; it is important—even "history-making." But it is not in itself the locus of revelation. The centrality of the body in Merleau-Ponty's phenomenology has not yet found its full theological implications in Schillebeeckx's thought. Before arriving at the point where he can trust human experience itself as a locus of revelation, Schillebeeckx will move through a series of transforming dialogues. Simultaneously, increasing consciousness of global and historical human experiences of suffering will foster the development of Schillebeeckx's early, Thomistic insistence that humanity is God's mode of being in the world.

HERMENEUTICAL SPIRAL

This biographical sketch is by no means complete. Suffice it to say that 1958 marks not only the publication of *Christ: The Sacrament,* but also Schillebeeckx's assumption of a professorship at the Catholic University of Nijmegen in the Netherlands. Since then, Schillebeeckx has been a member of the Dutch province of the Dominican Order, has lived with the Dominican community at Nijmegen, and has identified himself with the Dutch Church. Since his formal retirement in 1985, he has retained the title of professor emeritus. What is important here is that Schillebeeckx's major work has emerged out of this context. The details of that context are biographical as much as they are theological, and so it is appropriate at this point to introduce the hermeneutical spiral that will guide the movement of this work. This will provide the framework that will show how his biographical history and his evolving theological method are intertwined.

Recently, Schillebeeckx has explained in simple and straightforward terms the method that has always been implicit in his theology:

> My theological method is based on human and Christian experience, communal and personal. I apply it to tradition, which is an experience that becomes extended. Individuality is included in this communal experience. In my theological reflection I continue to apply the method of experience.[21]

Schillebeeckx applies the "method of experience" in a way that corresponds to his own image of the hermeneutical spiral. At the beginning of his appropriation of hermeneutics Schillebeeckx described the movement of human understanding as an initially circular process that deepens into a spiral:

> All understanding takes place in a circular movement—the answer is to some extent determined by the question, which is in turn affirmed, corrected, or extended by the answer. A new question then grows out of this understanding, so that the hermeneutical circle continues to develop in a never-ending spiral. . . . The hermeneutical circle thus has its basis in the historicity of existence and therefore all human understanding.[22]

This explanation appears in the 1967 (Dutch) publication that marks the decisive turning point in Schillebeeckx's theological project. An analysis of the factors leading to this major shift will follow. Noteworthy here, however, is our earlier reference to the task Schillebeeckx undertook as a student of DePetter in 1937, when he examined the interplay between question and answer in his search for a nonconceptual component of knowledge. At this early stage, the intuition at the heart of his later hermeneutical development is already evident. The historically situated nature of understanding is the foundational premise upon which Schillebeeckx will ultimately assert the primacy of praxis over theory. The primacy of praxis presumes the primacy of experience, and the historical situatedness of Schillebeeckx's own understanding is the "experience" from which to trace the formative influence of suffering upon the development of his theology.

Mysticism is central to Schillebeeckx's engagement of suffering; it has also been shown to be the internal element of continuity throughout his work.[23] For this reason, Schillebeeckx's evolving personal experience of the world and the Church in a history of suffering and salvation is important. My method here will thus follow the hermeneutical spiral of Schillebeeckx's own method, sharing with Schillebeeckx the concrete starting point of the exigency of human suffering; from this center, each of the spiral's deepening turns will be directed by the question of how suffering is a formative factor in the development of his theology.

RECIPROCAL INFLUENCE OF SUFFERING AND SCHILLEBEECKX'S APPROPRIATION OF HERMENEUTICS, CRITICAL THEORY, AND MODERN BIBLICAL EXEGESIS

Given the context of Schillebeeckx's early personal, spiritual, and theological formation in his Flemish period and his natural willingness to allow his theology to be shaped by dialogue with the philosophical, historical, and cultural realities that engage him, it is evident that until 1958 and the beginning of his life in the Netherlands, Schillebeeckx is solidly rooted in historical method. Like so much of what shapes this theologian and his work, historical method (and phenomenology, for that matter) will not give way before the pressure of new theories, but will expand and develop in the deepening and widening spiral that history, after all, is. And so the inquiry confronts the "hermeneutical spiral."

Hermeneutics

Critical Faith Communities, History, and the Hermeneutical Task

The Catholic Church in the Netherlands was experiencing the bracing winds of change significantly before the opening of the Second Vatican Council. And the movement did not begin with the theologians, but with the Dutch people themselves. Concern for pastoral praxis in the Catholic community began to emerge among the laity engaged in such professions as journalism and the social sciences. Holland saw the rise of its now famous "critical communities" before Vatican II was visible on the horizon. Theologians followed the ferment, reflecting upon emerging praxis and working to interpret what was happening in the light of the tradition.[24] A Dominican journal called *De Bazuin,* while in some tension with the order, "became the heritage of the greater part of Dutch Catholicism." As Schillebeeckx recalls, " *De Bazuin* was basic in the preparation of the Council."[25] At the beginning of 1961, two years after Pope John XXIII had announced the council, a pastoral letter signed by all the Dutch bishops appeared. Schillebeeckx effectually wrote this letter, which arose from the activity of the critical communities in conjunction with the bishops, who fostered the ferment amongst them. In Schillebeeckx's words: "The letter caused pandemonium, outside the Netherlands as well, and was translated into many languages. From then on the Holy Office began to take an interest in me."[26]

It is generally understood today that the Council did not initiate a new theology. It confirmed what had been achieved by the work of such theologians as Marie Dominique Chenu, Yves Congar, and Karl Rahner in the 1930s, 1940s, and 1950s. These and others suffered persecution by the Holy Office and, in some cases, exile from teaching posts. In the end, their theology triumphed at the council. However, the backlash against the reforms of Vatican II that started assuming new vigor in the late 1990s began in the Netherlands immediately after the council. For the critical communities in the Netherlands, the theology of the council was merely a compromise of the innovations they were already beginning to implement. In the aftermath of the council, the progressive Dutch bishops were gradually replaced by conservative appointments. The critical communities that had brought new life to the church found themselves struggling in resistance to an increasingly disapproving hierarchy.

Schillebeeckx's involvement in the critical communities continued, and his grassroots engagement in social analysis opened him to the impact of new philosophies on the development of theology. Writing in 1970, Ted Schoof notes that Schillebeeckx's articles since the Second Vatican Council trace his "progressive discovery of contemporary approaches to hermeneutics and his position with regard to influential theological movements like the death-of-God theology, Moltmann's theology of hope, Pannenberg's theology of history, Metz's political theology and related tendencies to describe theology mainly as critique of society."[27]

Even during the dogmatic phase of his writings, as M.C. Hilkert observes, Schillebeeckx understood the theological task as a hermeneutical task.[28] His own experience of the Church in Holland was a concrete experience of the hermeneutical character of history that opened him to new fields of thought and set him irrevocably on the road from a dogmatic to an experiential starting point for theology. And, indeed, the experience of the critical communities in which Schillebeeckx shared was an experience of suffering that would prove to be ongoing.

In 1966, Schillebeeckx began to teach a course in hermeneutics, and his preparation exposed him to the German schools of Bultmann and the post-Bultmannian "new hermeneutics," Gadamer, Pannenberg, and Habermas; to Paul Ricoeur and the structuralist movement in France; and to linguistic analysis and analytical philosophy in Britain, Scandinavia, and the United States. A lecture tour through the United States jolted Schillebeeckx into an awareness of secularization. Conversations with "death-of-God" theologians in the United States and university chaplains in France left Schillebeeckx in a fruitful tension between American pragmatism and French *spiritualité*. Ultimately, his own impulse to render faith understandable and meaningful to believers was coldly checked: Many people did *not* believe; skepticism ran deep. The new challenge was to search the very experience of the secular world that gave rise to such skepticism in an effort to discern God's Word precisely there. This was the identifiable moment when theory and praxis reversed places, and praxis assumed unassailable priority in Schillebeeckx's work. While he did not abandon DePetter's phenomenology, he abandoned its ideological starting point in metaphysics. The only tenable starting point now was the concrete experience of human beings in the world, and that required social analysis.[29]

The prioritizing of praxis over theory signaled a major shift in Schillebeeckx's methodological basis from deductive to inductive reasoning. This was his shift to an explicitly hermeneutical method, marked by the 1967 article "Towards a Catholic Use of Hermeneutics."[30] Here Schillebeeckx explicitly explored distinct approaches to hermeneutical theory and critiqued them from the point of view of gospel praxis. The very language of hermeneutics emerged in Protestant theological and philosophical circles in which Schillebeeckx was actively engaging, but it corresponded to what in Catholic realms was termed "the development of dogma." Traditionally, it had been held that dogma did not "develop." Rather, the indefectibility of the Christian message was maintained by distinguishing between the "essential dogmatic affirmation" and its "mode of expression."[31] The latter could undergo change through the influences of culture, but the "deposit of faith" remained intact. In contrast, Schillebeeckx asserted that the "deposit of faith" could, in fact, *only* retain its essential truth through transformation congruent with the transformations of culture and history through time. The content of faith and its expression cannot be separated from one another, any more than content and form in the act of writing can be separated. Faith's identity exists in its reinterpretation.

Schillebeeckx maintained that the greatest danger to faith and theology was the loss of reality. Human beings, even as early as the late sixties, had created a situation of alienation and meaninglessness through the construction of a technological and scientific world that they now regarded as their only and ultimate reality. Genuine reality requires a living historical context. Modern humanity had alienated itself from just this context, and Catholic teaching, in a different way, had isolated itself from the living effects of culture. Human beings are historical beings; our faith, too, Schillebeeckx asserts, "subsists in history."[32] In his attempt to articulate the living force of faith, Schillebeeckx takes pains to emphasize the objectivity of truth as divine and historical reality. Dealing specifically with the central mystery of the Eucharist, Schillebeeckx declares the indivisibility, as it were, of horizontal and vertical views of revelation. "What comes to us from heaven—grace—in fact comes to us *from the world,* from human history with its secular environment."[33] The image of the hermeneutical spiral necessarily includes the interpreter, the historical situation and philosophical environment conditioning understanding, and the object that is to be understood. Faith, then, as an object of understanding, is an event—a human, historical event with roots in the past, contemplated in light of the present and open to the transforming pull of the future. Truth is, however, more than a historical expression that changes in each period. While Schillebeeckx engaged the developments of the "new hermeneutics," he cautioned against its dangers. He especially critiques Bultmannism, for instance, as limited by a one-sided lapse into pure existentiality.[34]

Schillebeeckx appreciated Gadamer's development of hermeneutics from the classical tradition, but found the German philosophical school too limited to aesthetics, and Gadamer, in particular, too focused on the contemporary process of

understanding the past. Gadamer's principle concern was the restoration of the
authority of retrieved traditions, to the exclusion of critical reflection followed by
changes in distorted praxis.[35]

Biblical Hermeneutics and Incarnation as Event

While Bultmann brought an essential theological perspective to hermeneutics, he
and his followers were concerned with interpretation of the kerygma, or Word of
Revelation, rather than with what actually *inspired* the kerygma. Schillebeeckx
saw this approach as leaving the reality of the event of Jesus outside the sphere
of criticism. He judged the work of these theologians as phenomenological in the
sense that it was gradually distancing him from the starting point of DePetter. In
this case, it was the Biblical reality that, like DePetter's metaphysical starting
point, was being assumed as the "given" that did not warrant exploration in terms
of its relationship to human experience.

Schillebeeckx viewed the more fundamental hermeneutical problem to be the
interpretation of the human event of Jesus as God's act of revelation in history.
He was impressed by Wolfhart Pannenberg who, rather than restricting hermeneutics to a theological interpretation, had entered into an interpretation of history itself, to which scripture bears witness. In *The Understanding of Faith,*
Schillebeeckx elaborates his developing method of critical interpretation. Summarizing what is fruitful for him in Pannenberg's approach, he writes:

> The concept of an external authority, of scripture or of the Church's teaching office
> plays no part in Pannenberg's program of fundamental research; what is involved is
> the inner authority of the event itself which, because of its meaning, understood by
> us, demands our understanding and our adhesion.[36]

Schillebeeckx's impatience with a purely theoretical hermeneutics gives rise
to his insistence upon a relationship with lived experience as the criterion for the
meaning of theological interpretations.[37] As Ted Schoof presents it, for Schillebeeckx, only the essential reality inspiring the kerygma is worth a human being's
total surrender.[38] What Schillebeeckx means by this will later be borne out in the
first volume of his christological trilogy, *Jesus: An Experiment in Christology.*[39]
Here he will assert that underlying the kerygmatic tradition preserved in the
scriptures is the original faith community's historical experience of relationship
with the living Jesus of Nazareth. That event, that movement initiated by the One
who would come to be recognized as the Christ, is the reality that evokes and
deserves our personal surrender as it continues to address us. Treating hermeneutics explicitly, Schillebeeckx notes that "the past, though unrepeatable in its factuality, also contains an element which transcends factuality."[40]

Schillebeeckx's understanding and theological employment of hermeneutics is
developed through dialogue with the theologies of Moltmann and Pannenberg on

the one hand, and Paul Ricoeur and the French structuralists on the other. Moltmann's theology of hope introduced eschatology as having hermeneutical significance. Pannenberg's theology of history similarly evoked the power of the
future in a way that intensely engaged Schillebeeckx. Schillebeeckx joined Moltmann and Pannenberg in protesting the failure of German philosophical hermeneutics to question future possibilities—a failure which seems a logical outcome
of the failure to adequately critique the past.

This seems to be the point at which scripture took on new, hermeneutical significance for Schillebeeckx. He saw that, from a biblical point of view, it is the
future which is of primary importance. The Bible reveals that both the present
and the past exist within the sphere of God's Promise. Thus, dogma must be
oriented toward the future if it is to be true, if it is to be faithful to the scriptures
that authentically norm the tradition. Dogma becomes, therefore, the proclamation of the historical realization of God's Promise, which of its very nature
implies an openness to the future and to new historical realization.[41]

The growth of secularism and the startling decline of belief simultaneously
intensified Schillebeeckx's focus on human activity in history and opened him to
the pluralism of Divine revelation in the religions of the world. And this movement only served to increase the incarnational quality of his theology. As a necessary consideration of any concretely embodied faith, the approach to the reality
of suffering became the litmus test for truth in any system of belief, including
Christianity. The Christian revelation, while definitive for Christians, is but one
manifestation of God's universal being. And yet, if God's *logos* is expressed in
human self-understanding, then, Schillebeeckx believes, human activity is *divine*
activity.[42] In this light, the Christian belief in God's incarnation in Jesus Christ
provides an unparalleled model of revelation amongst the diversity of religions.
Or (and this requires infinite sensitivity) perhaps an incarnational theology gives
to human experience a revelatory primacy that is seminal throughout the plurality
of world religions.

Human self-understanding is rendered in the context of privileged historical
events, that is, human events expressing the ultimate meaning of human existence. "It is possible for all human speaking and activity to become God's activity in the privileged sense, just as it is possible for the opposite to happen."[43] It
is possible for divine being, the ground of reality, to be manifest precisely in and
through human activity. And, because of the role of human freedom combined
with the limitations and sinfulness inherent in the human condition, it is possible
for human activity to hinder the presence and action of God, or to actively effect
evil. That is the mystery of God's power in human potential and in human frailty.
Schillebeeckx will come to speak of God's "risk" in creating us free and respect-
ing our partnership in responsibility for the development of the world. Human
agency in cultivating the conditions for authentic human flourishing will become
the criteria for forming a common ground in the diversity of world religions.
Schillebeeckx reminds us that all religions are "an answer to something older

and more original than they are."[44] In some sense, then, every religion is an institutionalized religious response to original Being. Revelation is larger than Christian revelation. The truth of God is larger than all the systems of religion that struggle to articulate Truth. The one, Divine Truth can never be contained in one "authentic tradition," nor in all the faith traditions taken together. Yet all reveal something of God, in fragmentary ways.[45]

Privileged historical events are revelatory of the divine ground of all human being. Christians have come to identify themselves in the context of a history of salvation, and thus, in a particular way, to identify God as Creator and Redeemer. Schillebeeckx maintains that "God's activity in history therefore means, in an interpretation that is both Christian and secular, that there are certain human words and actions in which the characteristic activity of God, as creator and redeemer, is revealed in a very special way."[46]

This interpretation is "both Christian and secular" because what in Christian terms is named as revelatory of God is, in secular terms, recognizable as the full expression of human goodness in actualized truth, justice, and love. Christians believe that the paradigm for human authenticity is to be found in the historical person and life of Jesus of Nazareth. In this supreme actualization of authentic humanity Christians recognize the definitive manifestation of God. As members of a historical and global community of faith who recognize themselves in a common scriptural story, Christians receive the revelation of God in Jesus as the culmination of a series of "revelations-in-experience"[47] that have become part of their collective experiential memory. Schillebeeckx asserts: "Revelation and interpretation are correlative, and no historical event can be a decisive act of God for us unless we accept and understand it as something that determines our understanding of ourselves and of reality."[48]

Thus, the secular basis of revelatory experience is nonnegotiable in a theological hermeneutics. The ontology of language that is the basis for all religious speech assumes the universality of the pre-understanding, the pre-reflective reality of those special human experiences that take on revelatory significance in the language of faith. From his now-established phenomenological and hermeneutical perspective, Schillebeeckx believes that theology can be seen as "the rational and meaningful unfolding of what shows itself in history."[49] Theology as a discipline thus can enter into dialogue with many other interpretations of reality in this world. While religious experience does indeed require a language of its own, it must be a language that corresponds to the ordinary human experience variously expressed in these disciplines. Theology, of course, approaches the dialogue not only as a discipline in its own right, but out of a context of belief. It is this common context of belief that has shaped the interpretation of history from the Christian perspective to start with.

The identification of specifically Christian experiences of revelation depends upon the authority of scripture as another form in which the historical community's experience of God is articulated: "The believer acknowledges the authority of scripture not so much on the basis of its inspiration, but rather on the basis of the authentic witness that it bears to an event and its meaning and because he understands that event as normative."[50]

Schillebeeckx's theological appropriation of a neo-Heideggerian hermeneutics equipped him with the language to discuss the historically conditioned character of all human activity.[51] The textual authority of the Bible for the Christian community emerges from precisely this understanding of the historical, secular reality in which it concretely shares: "For Christianity, the foundation, norm, and criterion of every future expectation is its relationship with the past, i.e., with Jesus of Nazareth and what has taken place in him."[52]

Christian Orthodoxy and Human Meaning

Even as he forges a theology that seriously engages secular culture, Schillebeeckx's insistence that "the Lord is prior to every Christian community"[53] breaks through the intellectual morass of the interminable "How do you know?" and the unending distinctions between "what is said" and "what is meant"[54] in which a purely theoretical hermeneutics can leave us mired. The question of meaning, Schillebeeckx acknowledges, demands an answer to the question of the *criteria* for meaning. And, for the Christian community, the criteria for meaning are the criteria for orthodoxy. Orthodoxy, for Schillebeeckx, is discerned according to the criterion of the proportional norm.

Orthodoxy cannot be verified except by eschatological faith, which "sets our theological interpretive understanding of faith within the hope which transcends all rational evidence or doubt, assurance or alarm."[55] Indeed, this context of hope and promise, the context of all Schillebeeckx's theologizing, is progressively strengthened by increasing awareness of the multiple dimensions of suffering. The hermeneutical development that transformed Schillebeeckx's understanding of scripture and opened him to the impact of critical theory simultaneously illuminated the centrality of the biblical promise negated in suffering human experience. It is from precisely this place of tension and contradiction that Schillebeeckx would forge his major theological work.

Orthodoxy, then, arises from the inseparable realities of orthopraxis and revelation. True interpretations of faith are reflections upon embodied, enacted Christianity. Concepts and formulations of faith are correlative not only to the mystery of Christ, but also to the deeper intentionality of the act of faith. "What one believes can never be separated from the fact that one believes."[56] The continuing authority of God's Word thus consists in "the relationship between the intentionality of faith and a given (and changing) referential framework."[57] Theory, essential to praxis, is tested according to the criterion of the proportional norm, fashioned by the word of scripture. "This criterion," Schillebeeckx emphasizes, "always refers to something other than itself; in it is revealed the transcendence of mystery over pure theory."[58]

Culture, Secularization, and Theology

While the "criterion of the proportional norm" may suffice within the critical community of faith, Schillebeeckx acknowledges the problem of the intelligibility of the Christian message for modern secular society. The very renewal of a sense of eschatology that Schillebeeckx hearkens to in the theological sphere was engendered by the radical impact of future-consciousness in secular culture. If, in fact, society is unable to find meaning in the religious rendering of the Christian message, it is in some way due to the malfunctioning of the "proportional norm," creating a gap between religious language and secular reality. And, the loss of faith's intelligibility in the secular realm faces the Christian with the relentless challenge "to make a defence to anyone who calls us to account for the hope that is in us (1 Peter 3:15)."[59] And there is no place from which the call to give account is issued with greater exigency than the place of suffering. Schillebeeckx understood that faithful response to this challenge in modern society requires the Christian to take seriously the secularization of culture: "There is a correlation between what we say about God and what we say about human beings. Religion, as a living, human reality in the world, is also a visible social factor and therefore implicated in all the great social changes that occur."[60]

As always, Schillebeeckx is sensitive to language that would seem to separate religious and cultural reality. Thus, he speaks broadly of a "radical religious change" taking place in society, of which secularization is only one aspect. True to the fundamental incarnational nature of his theology, Schillebeeckx is concerned with the revolutionary transformations affecting the lives of modern men and women. In the midst of the maelstrom, the natural human quest for meaning must also be disrupted, sometimes frustrated, but always revolutionized as well. What is happening in society does not merely affect religion; it profoundly affects the deep, experiencing core of human beings, believers and nonbelievers alike. For believers, this profound inner revolution gives rise to new religious symbols—a new concept and image of God.

The crisis of identity so palpable in the Christian churches is a religious rendering of the crisis of identity afflicting men and women throughout a society experiencing a change in orientation from past to future. As human beings embrace their capacity through modern technology and knowledge to construct the future, they experience to an unprecedented degree the burden of human freedom and responsibility. The cultural anxiety manifest in "secular" forms also has its counterpart in the religious anxiety at work in the churches. It is the same human phenomenon that is experienced in both arenas. As Schillebeeckx takes pains to emphasize, "secularization" only applies to one purifying aspect of a radical change in humanity's experience of religion which takes place as soon as believers really want to take an active part in the present cultural transformation."[61]

From a positive perspective, as modern men and women assume responsibility for the construction of a human future, as they take seriously the imperative to act in the face of injustice and oppression, to correct the imbalances that give rise to the situations that degrade human dignity, they are carrying out the gospel mandate in secular culture. Christians engaged in this world-transforming activity will name it in gospel terms, gradually creating a new language for religious human experiences and giving shape to a new image of God. People engaged in transformative praxis recognize God as the one who comes in the liberation of captives, the healing of alienation, the restoration of human dignity, and the renewal of the face of the earth. Thus Schillebeeckx examines the possibilities of an experience of God that is really integrated into the new culture, and of a new concept of God that has roots in this culture. He then investigates whether, "on the basis of this, we can perhaps speak of the secularization of faith in an entirely new, theologically justified sense."[62] Schillebeeckx goes on to pose the question as to whether this new concept of God has anything to tell us about the existential anxiety of humanity faced with a future unknown and needing to be constructed.[63]

The New Concept of God and Negative Theology

The existential anxiety of secular culture is the other side of the experience of hope of the Christian community, which partakes in that same secular culture. The new concept of God changes the function of theology and the nature of Christian identity in the world. The new concept of God as "the One Who is to come" brings about a new concept of Christians as "the community of those who hope." Schillebeeckx leaves no doubt as to where the burden of responsibility lies: "Believers themselves will have to show, in their total commitment to life, where the richest springs are that can overcome the evil that deprives man [*sic*] of his joy and improve the world by really caring for humanity."[64]

The theological importance of secularization lies in its formation of an attitude that recognizes the presence of God in our human history and can help to bring about a future of salvation for all. It is thus that our faith in God becomes secular. Popular theological literature since Vatican II makes frequent use of the image of the Church, particularly in its concrete social manifestations, as "leaven" in the world. This is a dimension of "secularization theology" with which many ordinary believers are familiar.

The "new concept of God" emerging from secularization theology's eschatological faith gives rise to a "negative theology." Following his own criterion for orthodoxy (the proportional norm), Schillebeeckx observes that "the identity of the new concept of God with the original Christian message will have to come indirectly to light in the activity of Christians themselves."[65] This is because the positive content of the eschatological promise is available to Christians only in hope. Much more readily evident in concrete form is the content of suffering, of disaster, of what Schillebeeckx calls "anti-history." This negative force of reality is what contributes to existential anxiety in the face of an unknown future. For those who belong to the community that hopes, however, the eschatological promise becomes "a powerful 'symbol that makes us think,' a call to transcend what we have made—war, injustice, the absence of peace, the absence of love."[66]

Schillebeeckx's serious engagement with hermeneutics and the resulting mutually critical correlation of theology with contemporary culture naturally and necessarily opened him to a transforming dialogue with critical theory, beginning in the early 1970s. William Portier refers to the period that led up to this development as merely a "brief flirtation with the theology of secularization and the over-identification with modern Western culture it implied."[67] It would seem, though, that the immersion in culture that Schillebeeckx and his theology underwent was an absolutely essential and deeply formative element of his developing methodology. As God entered fully into the flesh and blood of humanity, with its limitations and its sin, so too must theology take on the form and substance of modern culture if it is to have any effective meaning at all. Theology must, however (and in this regard Portier is right), emerge from the familiar solidarity with culture and, using the power of this shared experience, level a critique where critique is needed.

Critical Social Theory

The eschatological promise, that "powerful symbol that makes us think," is ever the ground of Schillebeeckx's theologizing, the horizon against which he contemplates the too-tangible history of human suffering. Retaining this positive ground and horizon, he opens himself and his theology to the impact of Marxist-based critical theory.

Schillebeeckx's experience of hermeneutics gave him a language and construct with which to engage theology and secular culture. The scriptural ground from which he forged that engagement of its own nature illumined what was lacking both in theology and in culture. Neo-Heideggerian hermeneutics can discover breakdowns in communication in the historical dialectic when these come from original differences in the sphere of understanding. They cannot, however, uncover breakdowns arising from "repressive and violent power structures that already exist as givens in any society."[68] Against the horizon of the eschatological promise, the human suffering inflicted by such structures emerges as a stark expression of contrast. It is the forceful reality of such experiences of negative contrast that takes hold of Schillebeeckx and shapes all of his subsequent theology. And yet, "negative contrast experience," despite its permeating significance in Schillebeeckx's thought, remains a difficult and elusive concept.

Schillebeeckx himself does not know its origin or how he developed it. Erik Borgman notes that it emerged in Schillebeeckx's writing just after Vatican II, though in different terms. It is present as a concept in Schillebeeckx's movement in the direction of Moltmann and others who were writing a theology of hope.[69] "Negative contrast" is named as a sphere of meaning in his elaboration of the image of the *humanum* as the universal basis of human pre-understanding that he absorbed from the work of Ernst Bloch and Paul Riceour.[70] However, it assumes an unmistakable, active presence when Schillebeeckx begins to explicitly incorporate the work of the critical theorists of the Frankfurt School.

Schillebeeckx's contact with the political theology of Johann Baptist Metz directed him toward the study of the Frankfurt School. (It was Metz, in fact, who first employed the term "orthopraxis," which was to become so central to Schillebeeckx's theology.)[71] This engagement marked the turning point in what Philip Kennedy calls Schillebeeckx's evolution from *implicit intuition* to *negative contrast experience.*[72] Of significance is the fact that Schillebeeckx is still talking here about the cognitivity of faith, albeit in a new mode.

Schillebeeckx was already being guided by the critical function of eschatological faith. His own recognition of the peculiar, elusive knowledge gained only through the experience of contrast was, one may say, the "pre-understanding" of his dialogue with critical theory. Critical theory itself is a complex, evolving discipline. Schillebeeckx engaged the thinkers of the Frankfurt School, especially Theodor Adorno, but was specifically influenced by the early writings of Jürgen Habermas. The pattern of Schillebeeckx's engagement is best traced from the perspective of his own experience as a theologian. Recall his exposure as a young Dominican to the worker-priest movement in France under the mentorship of Chenu. There he was affected by the real social struggles of men and women. At the same time, his earliest theological formation was marked by a return to historical sources as modeled by Chenu and by Yves Congar. Introduction to both the person and the writing of Albert Camus at this time made a permanent impact. All of this blended with his original philosophical phenomenology, and, with the added influence of linguistic analysis, would later lead him to engage in a hermeneutics of history. This hermeneutical development took place in direct relationship with his involvement in the critical base communities in the Netherlands. And then, of course, there was his exposure to secularization theology and the impact of U.S. culture. All of these experiences of the theologian Edward Schillebeeckx were continually being absorbed, critiqued, refined according to the living force of the gospel's eschatological promise.

Certain elements of critical theory's original manifestation in the Frankfurt School[73] bore an affinity to Schillebeeckx's own deepest intuitions. A review of these elements will illumine the ways in which the human experience of suffering gains priority for Schillebeeckx—not only as ultimate concern, but as integral component of an authentic theological method. Theodor Adorno's negative dialectics and the sustained protest of the Frankfurt theorists had a profound impact in this regard. With equal force, Jürgen Habermas's "turn to language" captivated Schillebeeckx. Ultimately, however, Schillebeeckx's fundamental intuition of gospel praxis cuts a path through the evolving dimensions of critical theory. In the face of human suffering under structures of domination, there is a need for praxis adequately addressed by neither the Frankfurt theorists nor Habermas.

Negative Dialectics and Resistance

The exaltation of reason in the history of Western culture had not succeeded in redeeming humanity from domination and oppression. To be sure, it contributed in some ways to the alleviation of many forms of suffering and alienation, particularly through medicine and psychology. It had not, however, universally restored human dignity or removed alienation and suffering. To the contrary, it had produced new forms of domination and, with the advance of technology, deepened and multiplied human experiences of alienation. This double-edged failure of human reason was what the Frankfurt theorists sought to expose through their negative critique. Looking back from a vantage point on the cusp of the twenty-first century, it is clear that what they exposed then is present today in new and heightened manifestations. At the same time, the critique they undertook has developed in evolving paradigms parallel to the increasingly negative realities of dominant Western culture. And, while the Holocaust functions for many as the symbol of the beginning of the postmodern era, we can see the seeds of postmodern thought being planted by the Frankfurt theorists in between the two world wars—in the very land from which the Holocaust sprung. This exemplifies what Edward Schillebeeckx counterposes as "the history of human disaster" and "salvation history." As he repeatedly cautions, this "negative dialectic" is neither static nor black and white. The history of human experience is ambiguous, characterized always by the inextricable entwinement of good and evil. Too often, it is this very entwinement that forms the substance of an excruciating moral suffering for the most intensely conscious inhabitants of any age.

Like their counterparts in our own day, Adorno, Horkheimer, and the others shared the prevailing perspective of the intellectual avant-garde that the established (bourgeois) culture was in ruins. Adorno, in particular, was formed in the tradition of Marx, but with a major difference. He rejected the notion of the proletariat, of a collective revolutionary subject, in favor of the unique primacy of the concrete individual. Adorno maintained that valid intellectual activity was revolutionary in itself. He argued for the non-identity of theory and political praxis, drawing upon Marx's own argument that "work—not only manual labor but intellectual labor as well . . . was concrete social praxis."[74] And here we have echoes of Schillebeeckx's learning from Chenu that "to think is sacred," that "the intellectual contains the spiritual." The two, Adorno and Chenu, merge in those strains of Schillebeeckx's synthesis that point to a world where the dignity of human beings is paramount, and where critical intellectual work can aid in the restoration of dignity. There is no split between spiritual and temporal truth. Ultimately, for Schillebeeckx, the notion of "praxis" will never be something set over against theory, but rather the concrete reality that participates in theory— which in and of itself is concrete praxis.

Schillebeeckx shares with Adorno a debt to the philosophy of Ernst Bloch. Adorno's opposition to identity thinking and his development of negative dialectics was influenced in particular by Bloch's view of "the creative possibilities of disintegrating forms."[75] Bloch invited philosophers to venture beyond the safe bounds of formal logic and "confront, as religion and art confronted, the "unformulatable question" of utopian realization."[76] Thus Adorno developed his notion of history as discontinuous. There was danger in the glorification of history as a structural whole: the danger of rationalizing the suffering and violence that had been inflicted on human beings in the course of history's progress.[77] Adorno and others of the Frankfurt school "develop the antithetical or inverse insights into how scientific reason is mythic, how enlightened liberal morality is barbaric, and how technological progress is regression."[78]

The acceptance of dualistic patterns that made possible the development of structures of dominance originated then, as now, in the dynamic of human fear.[79] Adorno confronted dualism by attacking the identification of subject and object in his theory of negative dialectics:

> When the tree is no longer approached merely as Tree, but as evidence for an Other, . . . language expresses the contradiction that something is itself and at one and the same time something other than itself, identical and not identical. Through the deity, language is transformed from tautology to language. The concept, which some would see as the sign unit for whatever is comprised under it, has from the beginning been instead the product of dialectical thinking in which everything is always that which it is, only because it becomes that which it is not.[80]

Imbedded in such dialectical thinking is the silent assumption of mystery, of the expansive unknown that makes paradox not only possible but necessary. The impoverishment of the Enlightenment is its conditioning of a humanity that imagines itself free of fear when there is no longer anything unknown. It seeks to ensure that nothing remain outside known boundaries, "because the mere idea of outsideness is the very source of fear."[81] A certain willingness "not to know," a capacity where comprehension is not possible to apprehend, a comfortability with the seeming chaos that mystery often wears: all of these are stances toward reality that seem prerequisite to negative dialectics. And, in new and changing forms, yet unmistakably, they are today the hallmarks of postmodernism. And what concerned Adorno then, and Schillebeeckx since then, is still a concern: the unintentional truth that surfaces in non-identity.

Thus, Adorno went beyond the Frankfurt Institute's exposition of the untruth of identity to state the converse as well: "non-identity was the locus of truth."[82] Adorno was always fascinated by the breaks in logic; thus, truth was most eloquently expressed in the fissures, the inconsistencies, the unwitting contradictions of bourgeois thinking. And it was this quality of Adorno that so clearly contributed to Schillebeeckx's all-important notion of negative contrast experience.[83] The unintentional truth that surfaced in non-identity is akin to the truth known by contrast in concrete experiences of negativity.

For the Frankfurt theorists, the contradictions of conventional thought lay precisely in society's overriding emphasis on the creation of a unity that was more truly uniformity, achieved through techniques of domination. As a result, not only were people reduced to objects; the weight of the system crushed their capacity to imagine life differently. With the abandonment of thought required by domination, Enlightenment "relinquished its own realization."[84]

Such total abandonment of thought is, ultimately, an abandonment of human beings. If the totalitarianism and untruth of the Enlightenment resided in the fact that it turned thought into a "thing," an "instrument,"[85] and perceived the process of reality as "always decided from the start,"[86] then it followed that human beings were also "things" and "instruments" whose lives were determined by the dominant order.

Suffering, Imagination, and Redemptive Memory

The subjectivity of the whole, concrete, and transitory human being that was the concern of the Frankfurt theorists is the concern of Edward Schillebeeckx. The act of knowing involves the whole person and thus has to encompass the reality of human suffering.[87] Any system's attempt to restrict authentic knowledge is also the attempt to repress recognition of suffering and the restless indignation such suffering brings. Because the Enlightenment had pressed the structures of religion and popular art into its service in the perpetuation of dualism, Adorno could see no possibility of redemption except in certain examples of "true" art. True art held together the knowledge of sense and intellect, body and soul. Real art "has a redemptive capacity that religion has lost. . . . As an expression of totality, art lays claim to the dignity of the Absolute."[88]

Schillebeeckx would counter that real, authentic *faith* also holds together the knowledge of sense and intellect, body and soul. He, too, acknowledges the complicity of religious institutions in the perpetuation of dualism and domination— even to this day! But Schillebeeckx's image of authentic humanity entails critical grappling with worldly forces in the ongoing work of redemption that encompasses secular and religious structures. The Frankfurt theorists' work began and ended in the task of critical negation. It was not theirs to construct a future. Nevertheless, they offered tools for the work of construction.

If Adorno had "faith," it was invested in art's potential to heal and transform imagination atrophied by cultural repression. One dimension of art in which he was actually willing to invest hope was language. He perceived language as an expression of "the longings of the oppressed and the plight of nature," and proclaimed that "the need to lend a voice to suffering is the condition of all truth."[89] With Horkheimer, Adorno drew upon the ancient concept of mimesis to arrive at an understanding of truth as the power of calling things by their right names.

The power of calling things by their right names becomes the power of praxis when what is named is the injustice and irrationality of the status quo. This theme, expressed in Marxist terms by Adorno, had a markedly mystical, even overtly theological quality in the writings of Walter Benjamin. Benjamin's capti-vation by the power of naming was rooted in his Jewish adherence to the scrip-tural tradition from Genesis. The power of God's Word to call creation into being was in some way shared with human beings through the gift of language. Benja-min's brand of critical theory is marked by a mysticism that emerges from con-crete, particular, historical reality. He was convinced that historical materialism would be successful only if it took theology into its service.[90] While Adorno criti-cized Benjamin for his redemption theme with its tendency to slip into positive theology, it has been noted that Adorno's own later writings bear the marks of redemption and the language of naming in connection with the newly emerging concept of reconciliation.[91]

Along with its powerful negative critique, perhaps the strongest *positive* force in the Frankfurt School's contribution to the theology of Edward Schillebeeckx is this understanding of "redemptive memory" arising primarily, though not exclusively, from the thought of Walter Benjamin. Redemptive memory, how-ever, presses toward and feeds upon redemptive praxis in the concrete, particular present for the sake of a promised and named future. The Frankfurt School lacked such a notion of praxis. Adorno, in particular, never squarely faced the problem of the relationship between individual intellectual transformation and social transformation. Adorno may have been able to ignore this question because his concept of experience lacked a theory of inter-subjectivity.[92]

Nevertheless, the Frankfurt School's enduring contribution lies in its passion-ate insistence that suffering be given a voice and that other voices be raised in a solidarity of urgent protest against all structures of oppression and domination. Adorno's negative dialectics and Benjamin's intuition of the power of the Word and of redemptive memory become fruitful for Schillebeeckx when he weaves them together with their counterparts in the Christian tapestry. To this weaving Schillebeeckx adds threads of the work of Jürgen Habermas, whose contribution begins in the gap left by the Frankfurt School's lack of a theory of intersubjectiv-ity. Filling this gap, Habermas retains some elements of the quality of redemptive memory; however, he lacks the underlying mysticism which is the dark inspira-tion of the Frankfurt School.

Habermas and Transformative Praxis

The critical social theory of Jürgen Habermas is constructed upon a negative cri-tique of the Frankfurt School. If the Frankfurt theorists brought the Enlighten-ment into the first order of reflectiveness, Habermas took upon himself the Enlightenment's "second order of reflectiveness." That is, he analysed ideology critique itself and found it empty of any truth of its own, bereft of reason or potency. He concludes that the Frankfurt theorists leave themselves no path but the path of determinate negation on an ad hoc basis in protest against the omni-present fusion of power and reason.[93] Habermas rejects this option as inferior to the rigorist tactic of confronting defective structures "with an idea they cannot match up to."[94] Ultimately, he accuses the proponents of negative dialectics of a negativity that blinded them to all existing traces of communicative rationality in cultural modernity and left them groundless.[95]

Habermas's contribution to Schillebeeckx's development lies precisely in his offering of a communicative action theory as a means of transformative praxis. In his dismissal of his predecessor, however, Habermas fails to notice the positive contribution of negative dialectics. That is: The strokes of negative dialectic produce by contrast an underside tapestry in which is woven, against the grain, an alternative vision for the future. This negative weaving is itself an essential, creative component of transformative praxis. It is the foundational response to the senselessness of suffering engendered and sustained by the common fabric of society. It is precisely this intuition of the unintentional truth that emerges from experiences of radical contrast that Edward Schillebeeckx shares with the Frankfurt theorists. Discussing negative experiences of contrast as the substance of a basic experience accessible to all human beings, Schillebeeckx states: "So the human experience of suffering and of evil, of oppression and unhappiness, is the basis and source of a fundamental 'no' that men and women say to their actual situation of being-in-this-world."[96] This is the "no" of the original critical theorists. Schillebeeckx embraces the foundational truth of this protest, but not merely as an ideology critique. At the same time, he shares Habermas's impulse toward active construction of alternatives to the defective structures of society. What he does not share, however, is the idealist abstraction of both views. The reason for this, which we cannot state often enough, is that Schillebeeckx's starting point is always the eschatological promise.

Schillebeeckx's Critique and Appropriation of Critical Theory

First of all, it is important to keep in mind Schillebeeckx's own pattern of absorbing from various disciplines what is fruitful for his theological project. Though he read widely in the area of critical theory, he is not concerned with distinctions.[97] He was profoundly, if amorphously, influenced by Adorno's sensitivity to the dark stream of suffering in humanity that took shape in negative dialectics. Yet, his most direct and oft-quoted dialogue partner in this field is, in fact, Habermas. All of this is usable background for Schillebeeckx's passionate focus on his mission as a theologian in a suffering age. And this mission is a concrete mission enfleshed in a historical community with a past, a present, and a future. That the mission's source is the Word Incarnate makes communication as essential a component as historical embodiment. Thus, Schillebeeckx's particular attraction to Habermas lies in the latter's unique engagement of hermeneutics *as* critical theory.

In "The New Critical Theory and Theological Hermeneutics," Schillebeeckx asserts that critical theory takes place within the hermeneutical circle.[98] True to form, he goes to the roots of the divergent strands of critical theory that have influenced his own thought, and gives consideration to the original work of Marx. Contemplating Marx's famous statement, "Philosophers interpret the world, and the point is to change it" in conjunction with Heidegger's assertion that Marx "denies what is implicitly presupposed in the second half," Schillebeeckx offers the judgment that

> critical theory is not based exclusively on scientific analysis. It depends in the first place on a fundamental ethical option in favor of emancipation and freedom. I personally can only applaud this choice. The decision to oppose all kinds of manipulation and to defend human freedom is an ethical action of the first importance and is quite independent of the question of what we are to do with this freedom in the world once it has been divested of all compulsion.[99]

Thus, Schillebeeckx avows that a hermeneutic of humanity, or an interpretation of the human condition, is implicit in a critical theory of society. In this, he is already at odds with the evolvers of critical theory who hold fast to the tenet that the espousal of any positive philosophy or vision poses the threat of ideology. In the above statement, we see Schillebeeckx's absorption of the value of negative dialectics as well as concrete scientific analysis. He joins the Frankfurt theorists in their unmitigated "no" to all structures responsible for human suffering, and yet shares Habermas's critique of their despairing rejection of any hope in human techniques of communication and praxis. He embraces Habermas's reconciliation of theory and praxis in which praxis determines theory, yet finds it necessary to move beyond the scientific limitations of Habermas's program. Ultimately, Schillebeeckx's great wisdom is evidenced in his ability to allow what is fruitful in a discipline to stand in its integrity as he incorporates it into his own project in critical relationship to other disciplines in the context of his own vision.

What has been most fruitful for Schillebeeckx in Habermas's work has been his contribution of a renewed understanding of *praxis*. Drawing upon Fichte, Habermas worked out a unity between theoretical and practical reason based on the priority of human emancipation. Schillebeeckx appreciated Habermas's blending of Marxist influence with a conviction of the real meaning and necessity of reflection. Unlike Marx, Habermas knew that praxis was more than practice, that methods of human knowing had to be rooted in human interests, and that the foundational human interest is freedom. Thus, epistemology has to be rooted in social theory.[100] Schillebeeckx affirms Habermas's assertion of the "inner bond between theory and praxis, in which praxis determines theory."[101] He elaborates: "In Habermas's opinion, praxis determines the conditions by which man [*sic*] may come to knowledge yet is also dependent on these processes."[102] In many ways, Habermas's concrete efforts to reconcile theory and praxis create the space where hermeneutics and critical theory come together. This is evident in his development of a "'theory of communicative competence,' according to which positive political proposals should aim at the enhancement of the 'ideal speech situation' implied in the very structure of language itself."[103] Many contemporary theorists who appreciate Habermas's efforts in this regard nevertheless critique him for his own particular brand of idealist abstraction.[104]

Schillebeeckx developed his own critique of Habermas in response to the very theologians of contestation who drew him into dialogue with Habermas in the first place. These theologians, some under the tutelage of Metz, were related to critical communities in the Netherlands and Belgium in the late sixties and early seventies. They were the ones who had issued a challenge to secularization theology's uncritical alignment with Western culture, at the same time dismissing traditional theology as ideology. Schillebeeckx took up the challenge, which led him into serious development of the notion of *orthopraxis* to which he had given "a passing nod" in his 1968 essay on hermeneutics.[105] Critically engaging Habermas on their account, Schillebeeckx at the same time critiqued these theologians for reducing theology to critical theory. One of these, the Belgian Dominican Marcel Xhaufflaire, Schillebeeckx exempted from this critique. Xhaufflaire had written a book on theology in a post–Ludwig Feuerbachian context which called for precisely the revolution in theology that Schillebeeckx undertook when "he affirmed in 1971 that 'orthopraxis' must be 'an essential element of the hermeneutic process.'"[106] Portier cogently summarizes the elements of this "revolution" resulting from Schillebeeckx's encounter with critical theory in three points.

The first of these elements is the reformulation of theology's task as "the self-consciousness of Christian praxis." The second involves the shift of emphasis from past experience to reflective consideration of present experience as the theologian's main concern. Experience becomes invested with new and ultimate authority, as borne out in Schillebeeckx's explicit reflection upon the "authority of experiences" in the *Christ* book. Human experiences of suffering bear special authority and "exercise a corrective function against ideological distortion."[107] It is here, Portier notes, that Schillebeeckx reveals the particular contribution of Christianity to a critical theory of society. Certainly, critical theory and Christianity share a common concern for the redemption of the world. The negative dialectics of the Frankfurt School become pivotal *vis-à-vis* both memory and the present experience of human suffering. But a positive dimension is also required, and in a more fundamental way than Habermas's communicative speech theory provides. Portier notes Schillebeeckx's judgment of Habermas's notion of freedom as merely an abstract utopia. Here we are reminded again that Habermas lacks a concrete subject of history to enact a program of social change. In contrast, Schillebeeckx cites Christian faith as "a basis for political proposals which have both a specific direction and a concrete subject or carrier group."[108] We find this direction in the Christian narrative, which includes the narrative of human suffering.

Finally, Portier observes that the third result of Schillebeeckx's dialogue with critical theory is "the move to expand traditional compassion for those who suffer to include an evangelical call to think and act politically on their behalf."[109] Ultimately, this fusion of mysticism and politics that becomes so consuming for the remainder of Schillebeeckx's theological career is biblically and christologically based. It is the scriptural and christological grounding of Schillebeeckx's methodology that will occupy the rest of this chapter.

Modern Biblical Exegesis

Contemporary New Testament Exegesis: Another Level of the Hermeneutical Spiral

Schillebeeckx's incorporation of hermeneutics and critical theory achieves "practical and critical effect" when he turns his attention again to the substance of Christian faith in contemporary times. This next turn in the hermeneutical spiral of the theologian's own cumulative experience brings into view the person of Jesus Christ through a spectrum of Church traditions nuanced by modern disciplines. Urgent concern for genuine human liberation is the horizon against which Schillebeeckx engages contemporary New Testament exegesis. The real experience of human beings in the modern world, in all of its ambiguity, is now the starting point for his scriptural reflection.

Jesus, the Story of a Living One

The publication of Schillebeeckx's *Jesus* book was hailed as a watershed contribution to Christian ecumenical dialogue in a Roman Catholic voice. The importance of serious exegesis in doing systematic theology was just beginning to be recognized. For an exegetical project of this magnitude to be undertaken by a Catholic systematician signaled a dramatic dissolution of stereotypes and evoked new possibilities for communication. This alone was a major achievement in the opinion of supporters and critics alike. And critics there were. Schillebeeckx was taken to task for errors in technique, for what some considered to be embarrassing gaps, and for questions of orthodoxy. Even the most stringent critics, however, express awe at Schillebeeckx's dedication of several years to the strict study of exegesis in preparation to write a book about Jesus. Details of the aforementioned criticisms will surface here, but the focus of this discussion will remain on the formative, reciprocal dynamic between exegesis and the reality of suffering in the development of Schillebeeckx's theology. In the pervasive context of suffering, exegesis impacts Schillebeeckx's method in reciprocal relation with hermeneutics and critical theory.

The literal translation of the original Dutch as rendered above provides an accurate "hermeneutical key" to Schillebeeckx's purpose and method in writing the *Jesus* book. We have stated that Schillebeeckx's starting point for reflection is the experience of men and women in the contemporary world. Schillebeeckx himself also repeatedly emphasizes that the man Jesus, as a historical human person, is the starting point of all his theological reflection. There is no contradiction here; this is demonstrated in the title as well as in Schillebeeckx's articulation of the challenge he has undertaken:

> As a believer, I want to look critically into the intelligibility for man [*sic*] of Christological belief in Jesus, especially in its origin. Face to face with the many real problems, my concern is indeed to hold a *fides quaerens intellectum* and an *intellectus quaerens fidem* together: that is, in a like regard for faith and for human reason I want to look for what a Christological belief in Jesus of Nazareth can intelligibly signify for people today.[110]

The central christological assertion in Schillebeeckx's earliest, phenomenologically and Thomistically influenced works still holds. That is, the very humanity of Jesus is God's chosen manner of being in the world. That makes our experience and understanding of what it is to be human critical to our understanding of Jesus as the Christ, and vice versa. And it makes the personal experience of the theologian a vital hermeneutical ingredient. In a profound admission, Schillebeeckx acknowledges that the "why" of belief in Jesus is ultimately a matter of faith. *This* has been the "growing certitude" throughout his theological labors. This unassailable core of experienced faith he calls the "storm-free zone." While belief contains within itself its own sure justification, this must be defended as soon as faith is expressed. Once expressed, faith leaves the "storm-free zone" and must enter the fray of critical dialogue. Implicit here is faith's incarnational character. While we can speak of its inviolable nature theoretically, faith's very existence demands—no, *entails*—expression and embodiment. It is then that believers are required to give an account for the hope that is in them. And then they "become vulnerable to the exigencies of critical rationalism." Schillebeeckx continues: "This is why the book has been written: In deference to the unique and irreducibly original character of believing, of exercising faith, and out of respect for the demands of critical rationality. Each can help protect the other from becoming totalitarian and detrimental to freedom."[111]

This single statement of intent reveals the inextricable intertwining of hermeneutics and critical theory in Schillebeeckx's exegetical approach to the question of Jesus for people today. Experience, individual and communal, is the unspoken core of this intent. The experience of faith occurs within the substance of ordinary human experience in the midst of the world. Faith's linguistic expression is characterized by the culture out of which it emerges in tension with the scriptural formulations of the past. (Those scriptural texts are themselves culturally formed expressions of the faith of the earliest Christian communities.) And, underlining this statement of intent is Schillebeeckx's increasingly central concern with human emancipation. The need to guard against totalitarianism is not merely a societal need. Because it has to do with fundamental human interests, it has to do with faith and its ongoing expression in the Christian community.

The suffering human need for justice and liberation in relation to the question of Jesus is Schillebeeckx's true guiding passion. The *Jesus* book, however, turns out to be only an approach to a substantive address of this central concern. Schillebeeckx calls it a *prolegomenon* to a christology. (Interestingly, the *Christ* book that follows focuses on experiences of grace and emancipation within contemporary culture, and Schillebeeckx calls this, too, a *prolegomenon.*)[112]

Describing the method and scope of his study in *Jesus,* Schillebeeckx notes: "I confine myself here to a consideration of the 'course taken by dogma' from the start of primitive Christianity up to the formation of the Gospels and the books of the New Testament."[113] From his earliest works, Schillebeeckx has been concerned with the humanity of Jesus. He has also consistently employed a historical-critical theological method, gradually nuanced by the overlapping disciplines of hermeneutics and critical theory. The new development here is his emphasis on precisely the historical nature of the man Jesus and the community of his followers. The concrete, historical particularity of Jesus is precisely what has theological import.

The historical Jesus is the starting point. But this concrete person who lived in an identifiable place and time can only be accessed through the concrete community enfleshing his memory and mission. History is accumulated human experience; therefore, our understanding of the historical nature of experience and the experienced nature of history will determine our understanding of christological faith. The authority of history is, in fact, the authority of experience. Further, as Schillebeeckx noted in his earliest work on hermeneutics and further elaborates in the *Christ* book, all experience is interpreted experience.[114] The other dimension of experience that keeps surfacing in Schillebeeckx's work is its relational character. What the New Testament provides, Schillebeeckx tells us, is the story of a people who found salvation in Jesus.[115] Christianity's origin is constituted by both Jesus and the earliest community together as offer and response.[116] In fact, what the New Testament provides is, more precisely, an "echo" of primitive Christianity: itself a response to the person and life of Jesus of Nazareth.[117]

In the elements of history and experience with their relational underpinnings, we see the effects of the merging impacts of hermeneutics and critical theory on Schillebeeckx's exegetical reflection. In his focus upon the "incubatory period" between the life of Jesus and the formation of the first Gospels, Schillebeeckx employs principles of hermeneutics to explore the pluralism of christologies in the early Church. Who Jesus was for the earliest believers had much to do with their expectations of salvation in the first place. For them, as for people of any age, concrete experience formed the only context from which expectations of salvation could be projected. Instrumental in this context of expectancy (then and now) are negative experiences, accumulated through centuries, reflected upon, and punctuated by fragmentary experiences of well-being.

Here Schillebeeckx's dialogue with critical theory comes to the fore: "From its ideas of what constitutes salvation one can . . . glean the story of a people's sufferings, even when it is no longer possible for us to trace from other sources the precise course those sufferings have taken."[118]

Notably, Schillebeeckx's own appropriation of critical negativity is manifest in his accent on the positive. (And this remains the case in spite of what has been called his "almost obsessive preoccupation with the presence of evil and suffering in the world. . . .")[119] The value of negative experiences lies precisely in the positive ground and horizon that they illuminate by contrast. Fragmentary experiences of well-being provide images of a future promise that nourish hope in the present. Hope for salvation in turn unmasks evil and suffering and probes its origins. Thus, the hermeneutical function of critical negativity issues in positive revelation through experiences of contrast.

Despite the importance of the first Christians' expectations of salvation for constructing early christologies, Schillebeeckx acknowledges the existence of both continuity and discontinuity between the questions people were asking about salvation and the historically concrete answer that is Jesus.[120] The identity of Jesus for the earliest believers was formed, it seems, as much through the illumination of mistaken hopes as through the vindication of accurate ones. More truly, we might say it was formed in the tension of real contrast between the two. Much of the memory of Jesus behind the New Testament accounts was shaped in this space of experienced contrast. And, christology, if we are to believe Schillebeeckx, is really reflection upon the New Testament interpretation of Jesus.[121] This is one of many points with which critics take issue. One of them notes that, throughout the *Jesus* book, "Schillebeeckx demonstrates his awareness that the fundamental underlying issue, peculiar in some senses to Christian theology, is the problem of history."[122] The acuteness of this perception crystallizes in the breadth of responses to Schillebeeckx's own work. Clearly, an appreciation of Schillebeeckx's nuanced hermeneutics of history is necessary for a sympathetic reading of his approach to New Testament exegesis and, therewith, his christology. The key "problem areas" raised by critics deserve some attention here.

The first has already been noted: Schillebeeckx's definition of christology as reflection upon the Jesus-experience of the earliest communities. His hope is to lead his reader through the primitive Christian journey toward recognition of Jesus as the Christ. An understanding of how the New Testament was formed out of this early human experience of Jesus will, ideally, enable contemporary people, in a parallel context, to arrive at their own experience of faith. Toward this end, he reconstructs the plurality of early, still-forming christologies as a kind of assurance that we are not alone in the pluralism of our age. Since Nicea, the Church has held to one orthodox christology, based on the Johannine gospel. Schillebeeckx accepts this development of the historical experience of the Church, in spite of his own focus upon the synoptic gospels in the *Jesus* book. The structure of this work is weighted heavily by analysis of early christologies until it poses the christological question in the contemporary church. While Schillebeeckx is criticized for ignoring the historical development of the intervening centuries, it seems clear that this gap is not to be perceived as a dismissal of ecclesial developments. To the contrary, he accepts these christological developments in a manner consistent with his own assertion of the authority of historical experiences. He is only balancing those intervening developments with an emphasis on the New Testament origins in a manner that was new to believers, not to mention desperately needed in the Church.

Finally, perhaps the most significant area of controversy in Schillebeeckx's christology is his interpretation of the paschal event and, especially, the resurrection accounts. I will deal at length with these issues in chapter three, focusing on Schillebeeckx's christology, mysticism of the cross, and negative contrast experience. For now, it is enough to say that the concentration of exegetical/christological criticism around Schillebeeckx's handling of the resurrection accounts highlights, by negative contrast, the precise way in which the human experience of suffering is a privileged locus of revelation. That is, Schillebeeckx's own, intuitive analyses of the resurrection accounts model in unique and compelling fashion how particular experiences of suffering give rise to the graced knowing that is faith's ultimate authority.

CONCLUSION

This first chapter has considered Edward Schillebeeckx's methodological development as it has been increasingly shaped by the reality of human suffering. It has shown Schillebeeckx's life in its unique configuration of family background, Dominican spirituality, cultural particularities, and historical milieu. This personal focus has illuminated the importance of an individual theologian's particular, lived experience in the development of a theological method. The unique historical subject both shapes and is shaped by multiple, interwoven events in an ongoing, reciprocal process. Beyond this, the theologian—Edward Schillebeeckx—is rooted in a prior mystery, the divine ground of being. This is the matrix of the hermeneutical spiral through which we have imaged the growth and development of his theology. This matrix functions as the sifter of his new learnings from the disciplines of hermeneutics, critical theory, and biblical exegesis. As the emphases of these disciplines and the tenor of the world converge in the increasing pull of the future, Schillebeeckx comes to identify this matrix, this ground-already-there, as the horizon of the eschatological promise. Simply put, he gives priority to the proclamation of the "God-who-comes" in negative resistance to injustice and the positive nurturing of conditions that foster life and freedom. Schillebeeckx appropriates from these three pivotal disciplines the elements and techniques that he finds evangelically fruitful. And the criterion for gospel truth is the criterion of human flourishing manifest through the life of the Incarnate One: the blind see, the deaf hear, the lame walk, the hungry are fed, and where there was sadness and sorrow, joy abounds. And this is the manner in which the reality of suffering forms the development of Schillebeeckx's theology in substance and in method: The eschatological promise of abundant life functions as ground, goal, and critical standard. Worldly structures and communities find their positive impetus in this promise, however they envision or articulate it. This promise becomes the measure of the humanity of our societal structures and practices and thereby the impetus for resistance and ongoing reform. And the reality of suffering—both that which issues from human agency and that over which no one has control—magnifies the promise when, for the present, the promise goes unfulfilled. When the inexplicable horror of reality flies in the face of a loving God, the nature of the promise *as promise* crystallizes. The need for faith is heightened at the place where it is most in danger of being destroyed. It is in precisely this place that Schillebeeckx insistently proclaims the gospel message. In doing so, he discovers that in the midst of suffering life takes on deeper meaning and human beings enter further into mystery. He doesn't pretend to know why or how. Hermeneutics, critical theory, and modern biblical exegesis interacted with his own experiences and growing consciousness of suffering on the way to this place. The elements he absorbed will continue to serve his task. But before all these—and after them—there is the promise, known to Christians through the paschal mystery.

For Christians, the paschal mystery holds together the future and the foundations of the world. For people who suffer, it raises the question of the origin of suffering, sin, and evil. Schillebeeckx, in his later theology, waves away such speculation as a waste of time when the concrete immediacy of suffering demands attention. But his early work grew out of a profound, if nuanced, rootedness in Thomas Aquinas. Aquinas does deal with the origin of suffering, and he deals with it in relationship to the traditional doctrine of original sin. Schillebeeckx's early works give evidence of Aquinas's influence in this regard, in ways that have implications for his later development, especially in the area of political mysticism. And so, despite that dismissive wave of Schillebeeckx's own hand, I will turn in chapter two to Thomas Aquinas and his influence on Schillebeeckx's engagement with suffering.

NOTES

1. See Edith Wyschogrod, *Saints and Postmodernism: Revisioning Moral Philosophy* (Chicago: University of Chicago, 1990), xiii. For explicit Christian applications, see Ann W. Astell, "Postmodern Spirituality: A *Coincidentia Oppositorum?*" and Philip Sheldrake, "The Crisis of Postmodernity," *Christian Spirituality Bulletin* (summer 1996):2–9.

2. Schillebeeckx, *God Is New Each Moment* (Edinburgh: T&T Clark, 1983).

3. "DePetter set Schillebeeckx the task of inquiring into the best ways of surmounting conceptualism. Towards that end Schillebeeckx made an analysis of the interplay between question and answer and speculated about the possibility of a nonconceptual component of

reason." Philip Kennedy, *Deus Humanissimus: The Knowability of God in the Theology of Edward Schillebeeckx* (Fribourg, Switzerland: University Press, 1993), 47.

4. Schillebeeckx cautions that Kennedy, Erik Borgman, and Ted Schoof give too much emphasis to DePetter's influence upon him. While acknowledging DePetter as his "beloved master," Schillebeeckx is anxious to point out the roots of his formation in the work of Merleau-Ponty. His ongoing study of Merleau-Ponty evolved naturally into a study of Ricoeur, whose works continue to be of the greatest importance for him. Even as he cites these two as the *most* significant influences upon his thought, he cautions against making too much of a study of influences. By his own admission, he has absorbed fragments from countless thinkers over the years, has incorporated what has been helpful— sometimes gripped more by a brief article or a single phrase than by an entire study. Edward Schillebeeckx in personal interview with author at the Albertinum, Nijmegen, the Netherlands, July 28, 1995.

5. *New Catholic Encyclopedia* (Washington, D.C.: Catholic University of America, 1967), 256–57.

6. Diane Enns, "'We-Flesh' Re-Membering the Body Beloved," *Philosophy Today* (Fall 1995), 263–79, 264.

7. Enns, "'We-Flesh' Re-Membering ," 264.

8. Erik Borgman, "Van cultuurtheologie naar theologie als onderdeel van de cultuur: De toekomst van het theologisch project van Edward Schillebeeckx" ("From Culture-theology to Theology as a Part of Culture: The Future of Schillebeeckx's Theological Project") *Tijdschrift voor Theologie* 34 (1994): 335–60, 335.

9. Kennedy, *Deus Humanissimus,* 48.

10. Borgman, "Van cultuurtheologie naar theologie als onderdeel van de culture," 337.

11. Borgman, "Van cultuurtheologie naar theologie als onderdeel van de culture," 338.

12. Edward Schillebeeckx, *I Am a Happy Theologian: Conversations with Francesco Strazzari,* trans. John Bowden (New York: Crossroad, 1994), 89.

13. English translation, London: Sheed & Ward, 1963; Dutch, 1958. In the foreword to the English edition, Cornelius Ernst notes that *De sacramentele Heilseconomie* was published as "Part 1 of a projected book in two parts, though it now appears that the author intends to publish in a single volume a revised version of the matter of Part 1 together with the matter originally intended for a separate publication. The work here presented . . . may be regarded as a non-technical summary of the projected single volume of *De sacramentele Heilseconomie.*" Ernst further observes that "the detailed and creative examination of biblical, patristic, and liturgical sources" embodied in the earlier work may only be glimpsed in *Christ: The Sacrament.* At this time it must be noted that the projected volume Ernst spoke of was never published; however, Schillebeeckx has recently completed work on an as yet unpublished, contemporary sacramental theology, which would seem to bring to full circle his life-long theological project.

14. English translation, New York: Crossroad, 1979. Literal translation of the original Dutch title offers a clearer illustration of Schillebeeckx's intentionality: *Jesus: The Story of a Living One* (1974).

15. Schillebeeckx, *Christ: The Sacrament,* 6.

16. Schillebeeckx, *Christ: The Sacrament,* 6

17. Schillebeeckx, *Christ: The Sacrament*, 29.

18. Schillebeeckx, *Christ: The Sacrament*, 76.

19. Schillebeeckx, *Christ: The Sacrament*, 76.

20. See introduction, n. 10.

21. Schillebeeckx, *I Am a Happy Theologian*, 42.

22. Schillebeeckx, "Toward a Catholic Use of Hermeneutics," in *God the Future of Man* (New York: Sheed & Ward, 1968), 7–8.

23. This is the heart of Philip Kennedy's thesis in *Deus Humanissimus*.

24. See Mark Schoof, "Dutch Catholic Theology: A New Approach to Christology," *Cross Currents* 22 (winter 1973): 415–27; also, William Portier discusses the Dutch Catholic experience in "Interpretation and Method," in *The Praxis of Christian Experience: An Introduction to the Theology of Edward Schillebeeckx*, ed. Robert Schreiter and Mary Catherine Hilkert (San Francisco: Harper & Row, 1989), 18–34. Portier relies upon John A. Coleman, *The Evolution of Dutch Catholicism, 1958–1974* (Berkeley: University of California Press, 1978).

25. Schillebeeckx, *I Am a Happy Theologian*, 15.

26. Schillebeeckx, *I Am a Happy Theologian*, 17.

27. Mark Schoof, "Masters in Israel: VII. The Later Theology of Edward Schillebeeckx." *Clergy Review* 55 (1970): 949.

28. Mary Catherine Hilkert, "Hermeneutics of History in the Theology of Edward Schillebeeckx," *The Thomist* 51 (1987): 97–145.

29. Summarizing DePetter's conceptualism and Schillebeeckx's changing relationship to it, Schoof indicates that metaphysics retains its importance for Schillebeeckx, but only as a *conclusion.* "Masters in Israel," 952.

30. In *God the Future of Man* (New York: Sheed & Ward, 1968), M.C. Hilkert marks 1967 as the date of Schillebeeckx's hermeneutical shift ("Hermeneutics of History"). Kennedy puts it at 1966 (*Deus Humanissimus,* 307). Probably both are correct: the latter marking Schillebeeckx's deliberate engagement, the former the first publication explicitly dealing with hermeneutics.

31. Schillebeeckx, *God the Future of Man,* 11.

32. Schillebeeckx, *The Eucharist* (London: Sheed & Ward, 1968), 16.

33. Schillebeeckx, *The Eucharist,* 82.

34. Schillebeeckx, "Towards a Catholic Use of Hermeneutics," 10.

35. Werner G. Jeanrond, *Text and Interpretation as Categories of Theological Thinking,* trans. Thomas J. Wilson (New York: Crossroad, 1988), 35.

36. Schillebeeckx, *The Understanding of Faith: Interpretation and Criticism* (London: Sheed & Ward, 1974), 22.

37. Schillebeeckx, *The Understanding of Faith,* 14.

38. Schoof, "Masters in Israel," 953.

39. First published as *Jezus, het verhaal van een levende* (Bloementhal: H. Nelissen/ Baarn, 1974).

40. Schillebeeckx, "Towards a Catholic Use of Hermeneutics," 34.

41. Schillebeeckx, "Towards a Catholic Use of Hermeneutics," 36.

42. Schillebeeckx, *The Understanding of Faith,* 39.

43. Schillebeeckx, *The Understanding of Faith,* 40.

44. Schillebeeckx, *The Understanding of Faith,* 40.

45. Schillebeeckx makes this point in his discussion of language and hermeneutics in *The Understanding of Faith;* later, he develops and illustrates the point in his discussion of manifold experiences of God and approaches to suffering across the spectrum of world religions, in *Christ,* 670–723.

46. Schillebeeckx, *The Understanding of Faith,* 40.

47. Schillebeeckx discusses at length the unity of the two aspects of divine speaking in the course of salvation history in the chapter entitled "Revelation-in-Reality and Revelation-in-Word," in *Revelation and Theology,* vol.1, trans. N.D. Smith (New York: Sheed & Ward, 1967).

48. Schillebeeckx, *The Understanding of Faith,* 40.

49. Schillebeeckx, *The Understanding of Faith,* 13.

50. Schillebeeckx, *The Understanding of Faith,* 41.

51. Robert Schreiter, "Edward Schillebeeckx: An Orientation to His Thought," in *The Schillebeeckx Reader,* ed. R. Schreiter (New York: Crossroad, 1984), 22.

52. Schillebeeckx, "The New Image of God: Secularization and Man's Future on Earth," in *God the Future of Man,* 189.

53. Schillebeeckx, "The New Image of God," 189.

54. Schillebeeckx, *The Understanding of Faith,* 57.

55. Schillebeeckx, *The Understanding of Faith,* 59.

56. Schillebeeckx, *The Understanding of Faith,* 60.

57. Schillebeeckx, *The Understanding of Faith,* 62. Schillebeeckx goes on here to emphasize that "the relationship must also remain the same in different referential frameworks. This means, therefore, that the truth that was expressed in the definition of Chalcedon must remain sound in every other referential framework which structurizes the datum of faith. The criterion for orthodox faith is therefore not an unchangeable formula and not even a homogeneous one, just as, on the other hand, any new character is no indication as such of a wrong development in faith. The criterion consists of a certain proportion in which subsequent expressions (in their different contexts) find themselves with regard to the intentionality of faith as inwardly determined by the mystery of Christ."

58. Schillebeeckx, *The Understanding of Faith,* 70.

59. Schillebeeckx, "The New Image of God," in *God the Future of Man,* 170. (This is Schillebeeckx's oft-repeated motive for doing theology.)

60. Schillebeeckx, "The New Image of God," 171.

61. Schillebeeckx, "The New Image of God," 177.

62. Schillebeeckx, "The New Image of God," 178.

63. Schillebeeckx, "The New Image of God," 179.

64. Schillebeeckx, "The New Image of God," 183.

65. Schillebeeckx, "The New Image of God," 184.

66. Schillebeeckx, "The New Image of God," 185.

67. William Portier, "Interpretation and Method," in *The Praxis of Christian Experience* ed. R. J. Schreiter and M. C. Hilkert (New York: Harper & Row, 1989), 29. Portier calls it a "prolonged flirtation" in "Edward Schillebeeckx as Critical Theorist: The Impact of Neo-Marxist Social Thought on His Recent Theology," *The Thomist* 48 (1984): 341–67; 353. Portier provides in this article an excellent and thorough rendering of Schillebeeckx's dialogue with the young theologians of contestation who critiqued secularization theology as torn between the extremes of capitulation to the modern world or total rejection of it—either of which would leave the world exactly as it was, untouched by the Gospel (351).

44 Chapter One

68. Schillebeeckx, *The Understanding of Faith*, 130.
69. Professors Ted Schoof, O.P., and Erik Borgman, interview by author, Katholiek Universiteit van Nijmegen, July 26, 1995; Borgman develops his analysis in "Van cultuurtheologie naar theologie als onderdeel van de cultuur: De toekomst van het theologisch project van Edward Schillebeeckx," *Tijdschrift voor Theologie* 34 (1994), 335–60.
70. See, for instance, Schillebeeckx, *The Understanding of Faith*, 65, 95.
71. Borgman, "Van cultuurtheologie naar theologie als onderdeel van de cultuur," 350.
72. Kennedy, *Deus Humanissimus*, 143ff. Kennedy's project explores God's knowability in Schillebeeckx's theology. The terminological shift noted also indicates a shift in Schillebeeckx's audience from this time on: "The addressee of Schillebeeckx's later theology is now no longer, in the main, religiously troubled European Roman Catholics, but, by a deliberate preference, *anyone* who is economically poor or politically downtrodden" (150). I would suggest, more realistically, that the suffering plight of the poor and oppressed becomes formative of Schillebeeckx's theology, and that this theology, ideally addressed to any sufferer, is practically addressed to those in solidarity with the economically or politically oppressed and all who experience the suffering of alienation.
73. The Institute for Social Research in Frankfurt was formed in the early 1920s to address the decay of the social system in post–World War I Germany. Frustrated by the failure of Marxist theory and praxis, and overwhelmed by the degree of human suffering inflicted by the very system hailed as a liberating force, the members of this institute undertook a sweeping social critique. Preeminent members of the institute included Theodor Adorno, Max Horkheimer, Herbert Marcuse, Walter Benjamin, and Erich Fromm. In 1934, endangered by the boldness of their critique in the face of the National Socialist regime, these thinkers transplanted the institute to Columbia University in New York City. From there they (all except Benjamin, who committed suicide before the move) continued their development of a critical theory of society—all society and all culture emanating from the traditions of the West. Rooted in Marxist theory, they rejected its expression as inadequate and parallel to capitalism in its systematization of oppression and domination. Children of the Enlightenment, they turned the lens of Enlightenment upon itself and what it had spawned in the Western world. The movement's seminal work, Horkheimer and Adorno's *Dialectic of Enlightenment*, was a critical negation of the rational, idealist, progressive view of history: a critique undertaken for the sake of the Enlightenment itself. See Theodor Adorno and Max Horkheimer, *Dialectic of Enlightenment* trans. John Cumming (New York: Continuum, 1993; original edition: *Dialektik der Aufklärung*, New York: Social Studies Association, 1944); for a thorough analysis of the principles of the Frankfurt School, see Susan Buck-Morss, *The Origin of Negative Dialectics* (New York: The Free Press, 1977.)
74. Buck-Morss, *Origin of Negative Dialectics*, 61.
75. Buck-Morss, *Origin of Negative Dialectics*, xiii; Bloch influenced the thought of the theologians of hope, i.e., Moltmann, et al., who in turn influenced Schillebeeckx. Schillebeeckx himself directly takes over Bloch's notion of "the *threatened humanum*," which is the positive hope expressed through the negative dialectic. See *The Understanding of Faith*, 65.
76. Buck-Morss, *Origin of Negative Dialectics*, 4.
77. Buck-Morss, *Origin of Negative Dialectics*, 47.
78. Matthew Lamb, *Solidarity with Victims*, (New York: Crossroad, 1982), 29.

79. See Adorno and Horkheimer, *Dialectic of Enlightenment,* 12.
80. Adorno and Horkheimer, *Dialectic of Enlightenment,* 15.
81. Adorno and Horkheimer, *Dialectic of Enlightenment,* 16.
82. Buck-Morss, *Origin of Negative Dialectics,* 76.
83. James Wiseman acknowledges Schillebeeckx's dependence upon Adorno's development of negative dialectics but notes Schillebeeckx's own admission that, in a different perspective, perhaps closer to his own, the expression had already been indirectly suggested to him by Paul Ricoeur in his statement of an "ethic of conviction." Wiseman provides the quote: "[I]f we take this ethic at its highest point, as it is expressed in the Sermon on the Mount, it becomes clear that the problem is not to bring this ethic to immediate realization, but to express it indirectly by the whole range of pressures it exerts upon the *ethic of responsibility.*" Wiseman, "Schillebeeckx and the Ecclesial Function of Critical Negativity," *The Thomist* 35 (1971): 207–46, 220.
84. Adorno and Horkheimer, *Dialectic of Enlightenment,* 41.
85. Adorno and Horkheimer, *Dialectic of Enlightenment,* 25.
86. Adorno and Horkheimer, *Dialectic of Enlightenment,* 24.
87. In other words, suffering is *ingredient* to cognitivity in the same way that mysticism is. More accurately, it is part and parcel of the implicit intuition that characterizes faith-knowing. We will develop this point when we deal with mysticism and negative contrast experience in chapter three of this dissertation.
88. Adorno and Horkheimer, *Dialectic of Enlightenment,* 19.
89. Buck-Morss, *Origin of Negative Dialectics,* 88.
90. Lamb, 32; also, for an analysis of Marx's relationship to religion in the light of the seemingly implicit contradiction of Lamb's statement, see Schillebeeckx's *Christ: The Experience of Jesus as Lord,* 706–15, and especially 714: "[F]or Marx himself, the real and direct object of his ideological criticism is not the criticism of religion but the criticism of society."
91. Buck-Morss, *Origin of Negative Dialectics,* 90.
92. Buck-Morss, *Origin of Negative Dialectics,* 85.
93. Jürgen Habermas, "The Entwinement of Myth and Enlightenment," in *The Philosophical Discourse of Modernity* (Cambridge: MIT Press, 1990), 127.
94. Habermas, "Entwinement of Myth and Enlightenment," 128.
95. Habermas, "Entwinement of Myth and Enlightenment," 129.
96. Schillebeeckx, *Church,* trans. John Bowden (New York: Crossroad, 1990), 50.
97. For instance, Schillebeeckx carelessly includes Habermas as a member of the Frankfurt School when briefly summarizing elements of critical theory. *See* his "Critical Theories and Christian Political Commitment," in *The Language of Faith: Essays on Jesus, Theology, and the Church* (Nijmegen: Concilium, 1995), 72. As we have indicated here, Habermas is a divergent "son" of the Frankfurt School—at times identified as "second generation," but self-proclaimed critic, nonetheless.
98. Schillebeeckx, *The Understanding of Faith,* 125.
99. Schillebeeckx, *The Understanding of Faith,* 124–25.
100. Philip Kennedy notes that "the main works of Habermas to which Schillebeeckx deferred were *Theory and Practice* and *Knowledge and Human Interests.* In those books Habermas began the first stage of his explanation of a relation between knowledge and human activity." See *Deus Humanissimus,* 280–81.

101. Schillebeeckx, "The New Critical Theory," in *The Understanding of Faith,* 108.

102. Schillebeeckx, "The New Critical Theory," 108.

103. Portier, "Schillebeeckx as Critical Theorist," 348.

104. Marsha Hewitt challenges Habermas's notion of communicative reason on the basis that it lacks a historical subject or "addressee." Thus, he leaves out the concrete conditions of the truly alienated and oppressed. Further, the operations of communicative reason presuppose an "ideal speech" situation enacted by competent speakers. Hewitt questions the basis of the criteria for such competency, noting this as one more concrete factor that Habermas fails to address. In a theory with no addressee, she queries, "to whom do the voices belong, and of what do they speak?" See Marsha Hewitt, "The Politics of Empowerment: Ethical Paradigms in a Feminist Critique of Social Theory," in *The Annual of the Society of Christian Ethics* (November 1991), 185–86.

105. Portier chronicles Schillebeeckx's engagement with "the theologians of contestation" in counterpoint to his ongoing dialogue with critical theory in "Edward Schillebeeckx as Critical Theorist"; see especially 350–54.

106. Portier, "Edward Schillebeeckx as Critical Theorist," 353. (Portier here is quoting Schillebeeckx from *The Understanding of Faith,* 132.)

107. Portier, "Edward Schillebeeckx as Critical Theorist," 354.

108. Portier, "Edward Schillebeeckx as Critical Theorist," 355.

109. Portier, "Edward Schillebeeckx as Critical Theorist," 356.

110. Schillebeeckx, *Jesus: An Experiment in Christology,* Dutch, 1974; trans. Hubert Hoskins (New York: Crossroad, 1979), 33.

111. Schillebeeckx, *Jesus,* 32.

112. Schillebeeckx, *Christ: The Experience of Jesus as Lord,* Dutch, 1977; trans. John Bowden (New York: Crossroad, 1980; British Title: *The Christian Experience in the Modern World,* SCM Press, 1980). Schillebeeckx says of this study: "Here we are directly concerned with the question how *New Testament Christianity* experienced and analysed salvation in and through Jesus, and with the question of the historical circumstances (then and now) through which this New Testament witness finds a normative orientation for our experience and interpretation of salvation in Jesus." As for the nature of christology, Schillebeeckx says: "I am convinced by the Christian eschatological vision that any christology which is relevant to life is possible only in the form of a *pro-logomenon:* a word before the last word, a search for the right "legomenon" or word." *Christ,* 24–25.

113. Schillebeeckx, *Christ,* 35.

114. Schillebeeckx, *Christ,* 32.

115. Schillebeeckx, *Jesus,* 19.

116. Schillebeeckx, *Jesus,* 58.

117. Schillebeeckx, *Jesus,* 17.

118. Schillebeeckx, *Jesus,* 20.

119. John Nijenhuis cites this preoccupation as one of the main motifs of the *Jesus* book; see his "Christology without Jesus of Nazareth Is Ideology: A Monumental Work by Schillebeeckx on Jesus," *Journal of Ecumenical Studies* 17 (1980):125–40, 126.

120. Schillebeeckx, *Jesus,* 21.

121. Schillebeeckx, *Jesus,* 103.

122. George MacRae, Review of *Jesus: An Experiment in Christology,* in *Religious Studies Review* 5 (1979):270–73.

Chapter Two

Roots of Developing Contrast

THOMAS AQUINAS ON
HUMAN SUFFERING

Thomas's reflections upon human suffering always involve the relationship of suffering to evil and to the sin of the world. And, for Thomas, the question of evil is raised only against the background of God's existence. In fact, in the *Summa Theologiae,* it is precisely the question of God's existence that gives rise to the question of evil.[1] The challenge that evil and suffering poses to the existence of God is the heart of the age-old theodicy problem. Thomas's contextualizing of the challenge is instructive in considering how to perceive the roots of Schillebeeckx's developing notion of negative contrast experience.

For Thomas, the reality of human suffering, sin, and evil can only be discussed from the perspective of faith in the God whose essence is love. Immediately Thomas anticipates the question that humans always put to the postulation of an all-powerful God of love and mercy: "How can this loving creator permit creatures to suffer and evil to reign?" The question arises from the all-too-constant experience of suffering and evil in the world. Indeed, for Thomas, as for Schillebeeckx, experience is the ground of human knowing. Human beings "know" through their being-in-the world, a world mediated through the senses. If this is true, then the presence of extreme suffering shapes and filters all other knowing. Understandably, the goodness, mercy, and power of God are, by turns, thrown into question.[2] Thomas (and so, too, Schillebeeckx) challenges the starting point of the question. The immediate starting point is, of course, the concrete experience of the present moment in which suffering and evil may be overwhelming. But the *ultimate* starting point is in the ground of the one doing the questioning. That is, the ground of being, the ultimate horizon, of the experiencing human subject.

This is, of course, late twentieth-century theological language. It is the language of Schillebeeckx; but it is what Thomas means when he situates the question of suffering and evil in the context of the greater reality of God's love and mercy. Admittedly, this places the discussion of suffering and evil in the realm of faith and therefore, for some, in the realm of subjectivity. For Thomas, that is precisely the point. To place the discussion of suffering and evil outside the question of God is to alter the nature of the discussion. So, too, to pit the reality of evil against the reality of God is to alter the nature of God by postulating a dualistic creation. Thomas holds that God's nature is love, and in the utter freedom of love God poured forth God's own being in creation. And that creation is good: The world and all it contains, especially human beings, are good. How do we know this, when we live amidst so much evidence to the contrary? Again we must have reference to the ground of faith. Standing on this ground, the evidence to the contrary becomes the occasion of yearning for the once and future goodness of creation and of human existence.

EVIL AS "EVIDENCE TO THE CONTRARY"

The image of a good creator who unconditionally wills the happiness of human beings seems contradicted by the harsh reality of evil and suffering. Evil, indeed, presents glaring evidence to the contrary of any proclamation of a divine desire for human flourishing upon the earth. And the very concrete reality of evil bears itself out in countless scenarios of human suffering at every level of life in every part of our globe. How, then, does the image of a good, loving, and all-powerful God maintain credibility? And how can the Promise of such a God sustain human beings?

In every age, there have been those who postulate a first principle of evil as a power separate from but parallel to God.[3] For Thomas, there is no such first principle of evil. There is only one eternal first principle of creation, and it is the principle of good: God. There is no equal and opposing force of evil, because God is One, and God is the source of all that exists. Further, there is no way in which evil has its source in God. There can be no potentiality for evil in the One who is the living essence of goodness and of love. All of this leads to the assertion that evil has no being, no substance of its own. According to Thomas Aquinas, evil is a privation of good; it is an absence of something that *should* be there. Any substance or being that evil seems to have derives from the good that is its subject.[4] Evil, in other words, is parasitic upon the good. Inquiring into evil and its cause under the query "Whether evil is a nature?" Thomas answers:

> One opposite is known through the other, as darkness is known through light. Hence also what evil is must be known from the nature of good. Now . . . since every nature desires its own being and its own perfection, it must be said also that the being and the perfection of any nature is good. Hence it cannot be that evil signifies being, or any form or nature. Therefore it must be that by the name of evil is signified the

absence of good. And this is what is meant by saying that *evil is neither a being nor a good*. For since being, as such, is good, the absence of one implies the absence of the other.[5]

The classical assertion that evil has no being of its own has always had its opponents. It is particularly problematic, however, in our complex age in which the scope of evil and its incumbent suffering exceeds the reach of human imagination. How can we argue for the insubstantiality of evil and at the same time take seriously the ravages of poverty, violence, and oppression in our world? Knowledge and technological potential continually increase to transcend previously conceived boundaries. Yet, starvation remains a condition of life for two-thirds of the world's population. Historical hatreds fuel destruction in disparate parts of the globe as cultures ceaselessly destroy each other for little reason beyond their "otherness." Perhaps worst of all, our affluent Western cities breed pockets of poverty and violence that rival the worst scenarios that the "Third World" has to offer. How can proclaimers of the God of justice and of love acquiesce in a doctrine purporting that evil has no substance of its own? How can preachers of the *truth* look upon the suffering of brothers and sisters and maintain that evil is not an overwhelmingly concrete and present reality?

We can't. Nor does Thomas suggest that we should. Thomas is only concerned to emphasize the absolute goodness of a nevertheless mysterious God and to insist that we speculate about evil from this base. Thomas does, indeed, take evil seriously. He may not have been conscious of the vast scope of social evil and suffering known to us today; but then, his thirteenth-century world was small by comparison to ours, and the means of communication within it primitive. Thomas is very aware of physical evil in the natural world of creation, and he attributes this to God's *permissive* will.[6] That is, God never *wills* evil, but evil results from the evolutionary processes of the universe that have good as their source and end. Moral evil has its source in human freedom, also an intended good of the Creator. This brings up the dimensions of grace and sin, to be considered next under the rubrics of "original justice" and "original sin." First, however, it is useful to examine how Thomas's definition of evil as privation bears itself out in his own analysis of pain and sorrow. Though many other avenues of Thomas's thought could be pursued in this regard, I chose this one because its accessibility provides the substantial base from which the more abstract realities of original justice and original sin may be approached.

In three consecutive questions, Thomas discusses "pain or sorrow, in itself," its causes, and its remedies. The concrete reality of suffering that is our overriding concern is manifest here in very personal and, by today's standards, even holistic terms.[7] In his arguments, Thomas reveals the elements of contrast and contingency most pertinent in relation to Schillebeeckx's development of negative contrast experience vis-à-vis suffering.

THE PERSONAL SUFFERING
OF PAIN OR SORROW

Thomas draws upon the authority of Augustine to identify pain as a passion of the soul. For Thomas, "passions" have to do with the "appetite." He speaks about pain in contrast to pleasure because the two are passions toward opposite ends and are therefore contingent upon these ends. The two things requisite for pleasure are conjunction with the good and perception of this conjunction; the two things requisite for pain are conjunction with evil and perception of this conjunction. In the case of bodily pain, Thomas explains that the cause of pain is in the body, but the movement of pain is always in the soul.[8] Reflecting on whether the pain of sorrow is always an evil, Thomas concludes that all sorrow is not evil; sorrow is good insofar as it denotes the perception and rejection of evil. Thomas emphasizes that the human inability to feel and to respond appropriately are themselves "manifest evils."[9]

From this sense of the integrity of body and soul in the experience of bodily pain, Thomas moves to distinguish pain and sorrow, concluding that sorrow is a species of pain, as joy is a species of pleasure. Pain and pleasure arise from the apprehension of an external sense, while sorrow and joy arise from the apprehension of an interior sense. "External sense perceives only what is present; but the interior cognitive power can perceive present, past, and future. Consequently, sorrow can regard present, past, and future, whereas bodily pain . . . can only regard something present."[10] Speaking of the contrariety of pain and pleasure, Thomas notes that, even though opposite, one contrary can be the accidental cause of the other. That is, from sorrow at the absence of something good or loved, one seeks it more eagerly. Here is an important root of what Schillebeeckx will come to speak of as negative contrast experience. Thomas states that "the sorrows of the present life lead us to the comfort of the future life." Schillebeeckx would not accept the connotation that suffering should be accepted passively on earth as we wait for the consolation of heaven. He does, however, assert that we cannot know the essence of the salvation we long for except through the negative experience of contrast in suffering. As human beings, we begin to identify what salvation might be for us in terms of those conditions from which we desire liberation. This much can be addressed concretely, over against the concrete experience of salvation's opposite. It seems to be characteristic of the human condition throughout all of human history to begin here, with the concretely *negative* experience of present suffering. As suggested earlier, Thomas, in whose tradition Schillebeeckx stands, suggests another starting point.

Original Justice

The starting point for the question about suffering, which becomes a question about good and evil, must be located in the ground of faith in the goodness of

God and creation. From this ground, the evidence to the contrary becomes the occasion of yearning for the once and future goodness of creation and of human existence. Now the task is to explore what this means.

Thomas's starting point is, quite simply, God. Out of the perfection of divine goodness and love, God brought forth the universe, the earth, and all living things. Finally, the relational essence of the Triune God overflowed in the creation of men and women able to participate in divine being and relationship. Thomas's vision of creation before the fall, rendered as paradise, is founded on the texts from Genesis and augmented by the church fathers, especially Augustine. When he speaks of Adam, Thomas quite literally means the first individual human person whose initial condition is described as the state of original justice. "Original justice" is first and foremost purely God's gift. That is, it refers to a condition over and above even the perfection of created human nature. "The nature in its perfections *gave support* to the gifts of original justice."[11] And original justice consisted in a triple rectitude whereby Adam's mind was subjected to God, his inferior to his superior powers, and his body to his soul. [12] That is, it consisted in an ordered balance that was both the cause and the effect of Adam's right relationship to God. Everything was divinely ordained to facilitate humanity's achievement of the end for which it was created: the perfect union with God that is the essence of human happiness.

The state of original justice entailed happiness, but with qualification. Thomas describes Adam's knowledge and experience of God as midway between earthly knowledge and that perfect knowledge we humans shall have in heaven, when God is seen in God's own essence.[13] Thus, human happiness in paradise was not yet the final happiness to which humanity is destined, but it was characterized by natural integrity and perfection within creaturely limits. And here some important distinctions must be made regarding the natural and the supernatural. Original justice was a supernatural gift given by God at creation. It perfected human nature which, though created good, was subject to its own inherent defects. Original justice preserved nature from the defects of its own composition; in addition to protecting it from its possible ills, it fulfilled all of its natural potentials and capacities. Beyond these natural perfections, original justice entailed the endowment of "preternatural gifts," including freedom from all suffering and sorrow.[14] Finally, original justice bestowed the supernatural grace by which the first humans could live fully in the presence of God. Original justice includes a divine infusion into natural creation. In this sense, it is grace fulfilling human nature from within and lifting it to participation in divine life. While the distinctions between nature and grace are important, they are not to be imagined in any dualistic sense. That is, nature is itself graced, created by God and existing in God. Yet, God remains "other," distinct from creation, and it is in this sense that Thomas employs the language of grace. Grace is the supernatural gift that admits human beings into that which is proper to God alone: It is a sharing in the divine life.

Original justice, then, is a gift involving both supernatural and preternatural elements, a gift that constitutes nature in a state of integrity. Its deepest meaning is in the loving submission of the human person to God. There is a profoundly reciprocal relation between this submission and every other subordination of nature, in that the balance of creation is both "produced and sustained by this relationship."[15] Grace, the root of this relationship, sustains the whole complex that Thomas refers to as original justice. In sum,

> original justice includes sanctifying grace in the substance of the soul, charity in the will together with the other infused virtues stemming from grace in their appropriate psychological powers, the strengthening of the will's natural orientation towards moral good, tranquility of the sense appetites, the body's immunity from suffering and death. With grace the root, the final, efficient and specifying cause, this gift is a single gratuitous, supernatural endowment of human nature. When grace was lost, all was lost.[16]

Everything in Thomas's depiction of Adam in the state of original justice affirms the premise that God wills humankind's flourishing on earth as integral to the journey to total fulfillment in heaven. It is this primordial and intended reality to which evil poses "evidence to the contrary." And this, finally, is what is most important for our consideration of suffering in the theology of Edward Schillebeeckx. Original justice is not the final fulfillment of heaven. But it entails the perfection of earthly existence that most closely images what is meant by the salvation human beings long for. It lives in the caverns of human memory as loss, as absence darkly felt but nevertheless real. It is a positive reality that is revealed by contrast through its opposite: the all-too-present negative evidence of suffering and evil. It is precisely as a powerful root of the dynamic Schillebeeckx will later call "negative contrast experience" that we examine original justice and its counterpart, original sin. Schillebeeckx does not draw these parallels himself. Rather, they reveal traces of his early Thomistic formation, subtly reemerging in new and nuanced patterns.

For theologians today, and for Schillebeeckx's thought in particular, what Thomas understood literally retains its deep, mythic truth. It has long been accepted that the creation story is more truly a story of our end than of our beginning.[17] While Thomas finds this image in the past, Schillebeeckx finds it in the promised future. Yet, the integral state in which the gift of original justice constituted created nature has a historical verity measurable only by our loss. The positive memory evoked is as real as the ache of loss. The positive memory becomes for Schillebeeckx an eschatological vision, a harbinger of hope, an emblem of the salvation historically experienced in fragmentary ways. From the methodological perspective of Schillebeeckx's dynamic of negative contrast experience, this positive eschatological ground becomes the context of any consideration of suffering, sin, and evil. Moreover, there is a profound connection between this ground and what Thomas depicts as the state of original justice. Thomas insists that evil is "nothing," that it is an absence of the good that should be present. The primordial loss at the origins of humanity is the loss of original justice. This absence of original justice is precisely what is meant by original sin. What this means for theodicy is simply that God did not create the world the way it is. God did not create death or will evil and suffering. God created human beings in the divine image, capable of flourishing in justice and love. Original justice was the gift— really, a full complex of gifts—given to enable this flourishing. And somehow, through a free human act at the origins of the race, this very particular gift of grace that sustained human nature in its integral state was lost. This absence of original justice is precisely what is meant by original sin.

We cannot fathom what the free human act was that forfeited original justice. Thomas expresses it as disobedience, and we will see how, in his own way, Schillebeeckx picks up this thread. What is important is that the reality of suffering attests to the fact that something has been lost, and the loss has wrought irreparable damage. Both Thomas and Schillebeeckx perceive suffering as something gone awry in God's good and just creation. Thomas is clear about human responsibility for the loss that has become substantial in suffering. Schillebeeckx perceives the major role of human agency, but he also acknowledges that the excess of innocent suffering is unexplainable, a surd in God's creation. What is important for this discussion is that neither Thomas Aquinas nor Schillebeeckx attributes the evil and suffering of the world to God. Both begin from the starting point of God's unconditional love and overflowing graciousness. In Thomas's construct, human receptivity to and dependence upon this divine love, manifest in the particular grace of original justice, is essential to happiness and the harmonious ordering of creation. The loss of this grace through a free act leaves humanity bereft of the power to maintain this integral order. In other words, human nature is stripped of what it most deeply needs to be itself in harmony and peace. "With the loss of grace, all was lost."

Original Sin

The loss of the grace of original justice left humanity in the state in which we know it, the state marked by original sin. The key to the meaning of original sin is *loss*. More precisely, the key is *what was lost*. Schillebeeckx always would focus on God's pure positivity and the goodness of creation. God wills the happiness of men and women and the flourishing of creation. Thomas's construct of original justice supports this focus. In the face of the concrete, often overwhelming reality of suffering and evil, only faith can continually return humankind to this positive, primordial ground. In fact, though as humans we are much more familiar with original sin than original justice, the meaning of original sin depends upon the meaning of original justice. With the loss of original justice, human nature is simply left to itself. "Left to itself" does not imply some degraded condition. Grace, and particularly the grace of original justice, was proper to human nature. "So the wounds of nature relate to its historical constitution that has been lost; . . . it stays itself, but forlorn."[18]

The state of original justice was, for Thomas, a state within human history. That is, it depicts a reality within the limits of creation. While the human experience of God in the state of original justice was not yet the experience of eternal beatitude, it entailed a vision of truth through which all of life was perceived, understood, and accepted. All passions were ordered toward the good, and these consisted only of joy and love, because fear and sorrow pertain to evil, which was neither present nor imminent.[19] Despite the reality of limits, it seems there was an equanimity in the initial state of our first parents, a gratitude that colored their seeing and receiving and was somehow mirrored in a harmonious balance throughout creation. Finitude was not a source of pain or anxiety. This finitude included an experience of death in the sense of passing over from creation to eternity; but this death is foreign to humanity's understanding, in that it would not be characterized by suffering or anguish. Of course, Thomas (and the church fathers before him) could only imagine the properties of this original condition of grace by reasoning backward from the effects of original sin. And these effects are unleashed by that free human act through which original justice was lost.

Thomas argues for our creation in grace by quoting Augustine's description of the forfeiture of divine grace through the first disobedience:

> Hence Augustine says *(De Civ. Dei xiii. 13)* that, *as soon as they disobeyed the Divine command, and forfeited Divine grace, they were ashamed of their nakedness, for they felt the impulse of disobedience in the flesh, as though it were a punishment corresponding to their own disobedience.* Hence if the loss of grace dissolved the obedience of the flesh to the soul, we may gather that the inferior powers were subjected to the soul through the grace existing therein.[20]

The divisions of body and soul, reason and emotion, humanity and nature that issue in the fragmented web of the world's suffering somehow have their origin in this central act of disobedience. It is reflection upon this present condition that yields "an inkling of an earlier condition of happiness destroyed by some mysterious disaster."[21] The medieval logic by which Thomas attributes suffering to the evil of punishment that follows upon sin may sound harsh to modern ears. Similarly, the dualistic terms of "lower powers" either subjected to or at war with "higher powers" are problematic. Increasingly, today's theological thinking recognizes that the dichotomizing of body and soul, reason and emotion, humanity and nature is itself a manifestation of sin that continues to propagate multiple dimensions of suffering.[22] Thomas presented a whole and integrated vision of creation sustained by the spirit of God who is its source and end. Human beings, especially, participate in divine being. Yet, his language bears the marks of his culture as well as the cosmic hierarchical structuring bequeathed to him by the Greek philosophical tradition. It is important to acknowledge the difficulties

Thomas's language and constructs can evoke in the present milieu. My concern, however, is with the deeper existential significance of original sin which, through Thomas, influences the roots of Schillebeeckx's development vis-à-vis suffering. The deeper existential significance of original sin is, essentially, disobedience. It is not so much the disobeying of a command as a turning away from God. In Thomas's profoundly Augustinian understanding, original sin as a condition of human nature is the loss of original justice through the free act of our first parents. The key element in original sin is the sense of a negative conversion: That is, the soul turns away from God, its fitting end, thus incurring loss. The complex damage to the human condition arising from the initial loss continues to bear itself out in the actual sin of particular human beings turning away from their highest good and toward a lesser perceived good.[23] Actual sin involves an active substitution of created goods for the ultimate, divine good. Very importantly, Thomas notes that actual sin does not destroy human nature's inclination to good but diminishes it by establishing negative patterns of action that make the actualization of grace increasingly difficult.[24] This is how original sin entails the weakened and wounded condition of human nature that makes it so difficult for human beings to act according to their best instincts and desires. Moreover, this is how the character of loss, which is the essence of original sin, can skew the direction of human desires. And, finally, against this backdrop, it is clear that the actual sins of humanity both contribute to evil and suffering and engender and perpetuate the complex and murky environment in which evil thrives.

The concrete reality of sin, evil, and suffering in our own day or in the chronicles of human history is indisputable. But it is rare to consider suffering's ultimate root, original sin, as a concrete part of that history. Even less often is the state of original justice regarded as "a historical constitution that has been lost."[25] Thomas certainly regarded it as such. It is safe to say that what Thomas taught literally retains its metaphorical significance for us today. But this may simply indicate a characteristic but erroneous modern identification of the terms "historical" and "literal," together with an insufficient appreciation of metaphor.

Schillebeeckx, in his earlier writings, gives evidence of an early formation that could not help but be touched by literalist interpretations. Even here, however, he is conditioned by the historical perspective engendered in him by Chenu, in particular. Schillebeeckx's later hermeneutical development will gradually nuance his treatment of the roots of suffering in original sin while illuminating the deepest meaning of the historical truth of human experience. Yet, the core of his earliest, traditional understanding will remain the animating spirit of even his most sophisticated critical appropriations of anthropology, myth, and symbol where evil, suffering, and original sin are concerned. This is because that essential core relates to the ground that must be the starting point of the question about suffering: the ground of being, the horizon of faith of the experiencing human subject. However vast the cosmic scope of suffering, the essential drama takes place on this very personal ground. The core of that drama is the core of Schille-

56   Chapter Two

beeckx's understanding of original sin: the nature of disobedience and, by contrast, obedience. The deepest meaning of obedience is communion, manifest in
freedom and wholeness; by contrast, disobedience issues in unfreedom and fragmentation.

Schillebeeckx's early works address this dimension of suffering and sin in very
personal, even privatized terms. While his later works deal increasingly with the
complex social dimensions of suffering, sin, and evil, obedience remains their
discernible core. No longer overtly concerned with doctrines of original justice
and original sin, Schillebeeckx's thought continues to be informed by the tension
of these contrasting paradigms, which sustains his roots. Before explicitly examining these developments, I will look at Thomas's influence on two particular
works of Schillebeeckx's early period.

EVIDENCE OF SCHILLEBEECKX'S
THOMISTIC APPROACH TO SUFFERING

The "turning away" that constitutes the disobedience at the heart of original sin
is the other side of the "turning toward" that recalls the state of original justice.
The internal movement that leads us actively to create this remembered and
longed-for state is the dynamic of metanoia. Central to the experience of metanoia is Schillebeeckx's notion of negative contrast experience. The language of
negative contrast belongs to Schillebeeckx's later theology, where it emerges in
his appropriation of critical theory. There his emphasis will be upon political
protest and transformative social action. But, as indicated in the introduction to
this volume, if the imperative to social action dominates Schillebeeckx's later
work, it is because the imperative to personal conversion in his early work intensifies and develops in the face of global suffering. The solidarity that both gives
rise to and is increased by ethical praxis is the other side of our human solidarity
in the legacy of original sin. Both are concerned with the mystical dimension of
negative contrast that is the dynamic, moral root of metanoia. This root is the key
to understanding how suffering operates as a formative factor in Schillebeeckx's
theology. And this key to continuity lies precisely in the realm of mysticism. The
lingering contrasts of original justice and original sin give evidence of the Thomistic cast of Schillebeeckx's approach to suffering in two illustrative early
works: *Mary, Mother of the Redemption* and "The Death of a Christian."

Mary, Mother of the Redemption

The story of Mary's role in salvation history that Schillebeeckx presents in *Mary,
Mother of the Redemption* was, in 1954, a progressive and humanized account.
The theology here strongly manifests Schillebeeckx's training in personalist phe-
nomenology, historical theology, and his own scripture-based spirituality.

Mary's humanity is at the forefront: She is preeminent among the redeemed, but it is Christ himself who is the redemption.[26] Over and over again, in the 1950s as in the 1990s, Schillebeeckx labors to make us realize the meaning of Thomas's central assertion that humanity is God's chosen manner of being in the world. Here he states: "At the very heart of this history of man's [sic] salvation is the *man* Jesus, who is the living God himself, acting in a truly human, historical form."[27] It is in this context that Mary has her role: "Mariology is concerned with the mother of one definite person—Jesus of Nazareth."[28] Here Schillebeeckx's ongoing emphasis upon the universal and transcendent significance of the particular and the concrete comes to the fore. Mary's historical but decisive human acts become "the poles between which God's redemptive act breaks into human history."[29]

The concrete particularity of Mary's life has further import when looked at in the light of certain scriptural parallels. Schillebeeckx perceives in Mary a personal summing-up of Israel:

> The Yahweh who comes as Saviour "in the midst of" or even "inside" Israel (Zephaniah) is . . . parallel to Jesus, that is, Yahweh the Saviour, whom Mary conceives in her womb (Luke). Mary, living in the stream of Old Testament messianism, had a *presentiment* of the profundity of this tremendous reality, the Son of God.[30]

Mary's natural discernment of God's action therefore occurred in a manner which, though unique and special, is recognizable in terms of our own contemporary theological reflection. Mary's experience of the particular events of her life was conditioned by the Jewish traditions that had formed her and by the expectations of the concrete community in which she lived. "Mary's religious life did not, therefore, develop from a state of positive not-knowing or ignorance towards a state of positive recognition and knowledge, but rather from an *implicit* but *real* awareness to an *explicit consciousness*."[31] There are strains in the history of Israel that are particularly evident in the person of Mary; these both prepare her for and enable her to receive the word entrusted to her. Among these, the spirituality of the *anawim* marking the post-exilic books of the Old Testament becomes paramount for Schillebeeckx.

The anawim [32] are the "backbone of the Jewish people"—poor and lowly servants who trust in God and remain faithful despite suffering and humiliation in this life. In contrast to the anawim are those who trust in themselves instead: "the 'arrogant,' the 'proud,' the 'wicked' . . . the self-centered people who do not understand the meaning of religious humility."[33] In her own historical moment, Mary embodies the spirituality of the anawim of Israel's past and points to its future enfleshment in Christianity. Schillebeeckx draws attention to the ways the New Testament continues to promote the spirituality of the anawim: the story of the publican and the Pharisee, the Magnificat's exaltation of the lowly and displacement of the proud, the sustained contrasts of the Beatitudes. Here, especially, Schillebeeckx cites the concrete future impact of Mary's persona, itself shaped by Israel's past. He suggests that the vision of the anawim pervading the Beatitudes gains its vibrancy from Jesus' human memory. Jesus knew how to speak of enfleshed humility because "he had already experienced the concrete realization of this ideal in the house in Nazareth, in the persons of Mary and Joseph."[34] And this humility had nothing to do with passivity, but everything to do with the wise and active trust that is the essence of loving obedience.

This loving obedience achieved its fulfillment in Christ, who was, in his person, the antidote to Adam's disobedience. Schillebeeckx speaks of "objective redemption" as the reality already established in Christ. Christ *is* redemption, he *is* grace. Objective redemption is the "counterpart to the objective fact that *in* Adam the stain of original sin clings to mankind [*sic*]. In Jesus, as our head, the redemption . . . is an established fact."[35] "Subjective redemption," then, is the process whereby what is already an accomplished reality in Christ is actually realized in Christian lives: It overflows into Christendom as "our actual vital union with Christ." In actual human experience, therefore, the objective and subjective aspects of redemption are inseparable. For the actual human experience of redemption, personal cooperation is absolutely necessary. At the same time, the already established nature of redemption has preeminence in the state of being redeemed.

This "state of being redeemed" has a quality of universal participation that corresponds to the lost state of original justice.[36] It is the reality to which the universality of original sin stands in contrast.[37] In the book under discussion, Schillebeeckx presents the universality of original sin as a reality from which Mary is excluded, implicitly because of her already-redeemed status. The point of this is to highlight, by contrast, just what original sin *is* in the human condition. It is a negative manifestation of solidarity—the "universal solidarity of humankind in sin."[38] And this solidarity is much more than a matter of biological descent. The human being is formally a spiritual being; the body is integral to the personal existence of a human being. Thus, the unity of the human community is founded on the spiritual level, though it absolutely requires the physical level. Unity consists in a society of persons for which the biological community merely forms the substructure. Schillebeeckx acknowledges that this can only be understood with reference to its supernatural perspective. The mystery of original sin can be understood only if viewed in the context of Adam's representative function within the perspective of the call to all men and women that unites them to each other.

In justice, Adam was established as the mediator of grace. "It is exactly in this task, as mediator of grace, that Adam failed culpably."[39] The violation at the heart of original sin is the violation of relationship. The vision of original justice was a vision of creation's harmony and humanity's solidarity in nature and in grace. The vocation to mediate grace is the *human* vocation; it is the vocation to mediate life, the divine life to which Adam had access at its source. Adam's failure resulted in a negative solidarity, solidarity in sin. This is a solidarity manifest in division, distrust, hatred, and violence. It is our union in what we derisively call "the human condition," identifying ourselves by the very source of all the world's suffering and ills. That source is the violation of the primary relationship, the failure to trust, which has leaked its damage into the relational framework of the race. It is that failure to trust, that breaking of communion, that is called disobedience. And it is, by contrast, complete trust and unbroken communion that is the essence of obedience. Writing in 1954, Schillebeeckx states that "the human community in personal intimacy with God, or sanctifying grace, is possible since original sin only as redeeming grace." The implication is that intimacy with God and human relationship in community are two sides of the same reality, the substance of which is sanctifying grace. Grace is the gift of divine life humanly received and freely, spontaneously shared. Relationship is the means by which grace is communicated; therefore, it is not too much to say that grace is, of its nature, relational.

The "human community in personal intimacy with God" evokes the state of original justice lost by original sin. It is the state that human beings continue to seek; its absence is the essence of every deprivation human beings continue to suffer. And that deprivation gives rise to the complex machinations by which evil gains a foothold in the world, wreaking great havoc and untold suffering, even unto the suffering of the innocent. The doctrine of original sin is, after all, an insight into the human condition that the church fathers read back into the Genesis story of creation.[40] That insight was already present in the inspiration of the Genesis account. That first loss, in which we all share, was irrevocable. And yet, Schillebeeckx emphasizes that God does not begrudge God's gifts; God still calls us to grace.[41]

God's unremitting offer of love, despite human sin, takes new form in the possibility of redemption in Christ. Drawing explicitly on Thomas, Schillebeeckx describes the manner in which Christ, though not subject to original sin, entered into the human condition of sin. Christ's full humanity entailed the full experiencing of the human limitations and sufferings that are the consequences of original sin in our race. Only in this full human experiencing could Christ attain for us the fullness of redemption. It is strange to think of Christ being redeemed; yet Schillebeeckx takes pains to emphasize that, though he had no need of redemption, Christ took on "fallenness" in becoming human and was himself truly redeemed in the resurrection.[42] "It is important to grasp this fact—in the representative sense, Christ *is* humanity, fallen and redeemed. He is the 'representatively redeemed.' This is precisely what is meant by 'objective redemption.'"[43]

It is the reality of this "objective redemption" that makes it possible for human beings to make the personal choices involved in "subjective redemption" in spite of the real and painful ongoing effects of original sin. Questions will always abound as to why God permitted humanity's original misuse of freedom in the first place. Ultimately, Schillebeeckx admits, this is a mystery that eludes us.

More fundamental is the greater and prior reality of God's unconditional love. It is in the tension of this paradox that redemption takes place. That redemption is, in the true sense, a restoration. Ideally, it is a restoration of human beings to that grace whereby they once again have a choice vis-à-vis that obedience which is communion. Though faith attests that God is both ground and horizon, the concrete immediacy of sin and evil controverts this. It is here, in the ambiguous space of contrast, that grace operates and meaning emerges. It is possible to recognize the meaning and discern the grace only in experience. Schillebeeckx will say as much in his later theology, where he holds up the life story of Jesus of Nazareth as the criterion for meaning. At this still early point on the trajectory, he speaks of the contrasts in terms of disobedience and obedience. Jesus' death was "the expression of his total obedience to and constant union with the Father." His fulfillment of his vocation to the ultimate limit makes the fulfillment of humanity's life-destiny "an indestructible possibility for every human being."[44]

How do we discern "humanity's life-destiny" in our own concrete circumstances? How do we recognize the direction of its fulfillment? How do we meet this possibility? And how does this relate to the reality of suffering that is the ongoing effect of sin in our world despite the "objective" fact of redemption? In a very personal way, Schillebeeckx addresses these questions in another work of his "early" period, "The Death of a Christian."

"The Death of a Christian"[45]

Writing in 1955, Schillebeeckx analyses the meaning of death as a "phase" in the context of eschatology. He examines the objective reality of death, first naturally, then in terms of the history of salvation, culminating in a reflection upon the meaning of Christ's death. It is against this background that Schillebeeckx reflects at length upon the meaning of death in the personal experience of the individual Christian. The parallels to "objective" and "subjective" redemption are clear.

Schillebeeckx begins his discussion by pointing out the Church's age-old attitude of "serene eschatological optimism" in the face of death.[46] Indeed, this corresponds to what he will later refer to as God's promised future, the positive ground of being on which all of his theology rests. It is from this place, more traditionally named, that Schillebeeckx engages the subject of death. He looks at death first as a natural, biological event that proves humanity's participation in nature and the transitoriness of the material world. At this level, death is the clearest manifestation of the limitedness of the human condition. From here, he moves to the initial stage of revelation in the time of the Old Testament Patriarchs, a stage marked by an unquestioning acceptance of death without explicit thought of a hereafter. A peaceful passing at the end of a long life seemed an ideal blessing. However, the increasing political complexity and overwhelming misery experienced by the Jews prompted a new level of reflection upon the great events of life: birth, labor, suffering, and death. In this light, the calm acceptance of death as a mere fact of human limitation no longer sufficed. Schillebeeckx notes that the implicit philosophical consideration within the developing religious reflection of Israel was what made it possible to "bridge the gap between a purely natural notion of death and death seen immediately as punishment for sin."[47]

Varying philosophical strains within the development of the Scriptures account for conflicting approaches to suffering and death even up to the present day.[48] The absurdity of death gave rise to a literature of protest presenting death either as a constructional error in creation or as absolute end, which is in turn contradicted by strong indications regarding a continued life of the soul.

The incarnational nature of the human person is dramatically evident in the "full-stop" that death puts to worldly existence. The inextricable relationship of body and soul is never more evident than here, at life's limit. With the physical cessation of life, the soul is left in isolation. Contrary to all Platonic notions of the soul being set free, Schillebeeckx asserts that, in death, the soul "loses its situation." The sense of a promise in the soul is contradicted by the fact of death and the prospect of oblivion. It is here, at this crisis point of contradiction, that the purely philosophical perspective leads into absurdity. The very fact of this absurdity is somehow indicative of the "manner in which the history of the Fall and of salvation has an intimate effect on philosophy itself."[49] And, however inadequate in isolation, the philosophical perspective is essential on the way to the second phase of revelation.

The light cast by revelation upon the philosophical turn in the spiral within the development of the Hebrew scriptures leads to the knowledge that a religious tragedy lay at the origin of death:

> Revelation here teaches that God would fulfill the promise of immortality . . . if man [*sic*] would remain "walking with God in the Garden," as Genesis puts it; that is, if man would truly allow God to be the living God in his life. It was in some way by religious reflection on the absurdity of death that the Jews, who believed in the intelligibility of all the works of Yahweh, came to compose the Genesis story of the fall into sin.[50]

Schillebeeckx notes that this is what Paul summarizes (Romans 5:12) and the Church defines. (The Council of Trent determined that the punishment aspect of death is a dogmatic truth.) But it is not acceptable *merely* to say that death (and, by extension, all suffering) is a punishment for sin.[51] Somehow, in the transmission of humanity's earliest insight into its own nature, God frequently became identified along the way as the punisher. Schillebeeckx prefers to emphasize the pole of revelation whereby humanity becomes known to itself in relationship to a consistently loving and faithful God. The anthropological touchstone is the truest one that we have. And so, the developing self-understanding of Israel in its second stage of revelation is to be taken seriously. Death *is* absurd. And that absurdity does not originate in God, but in human beings. The symbolic and mythological fall construct clearly manifests this truth of human self-understanding: Humanity, through sin, made its own situation of promise into an absurdity. The promise of immortality in the soul originates in God; whatever thwarts that promise originates in us. Death is not a punishment for sin that is meted out; rather, sin *is* death. The turning away from the reality of the promise toward something illusory bears within it its own loss, suffering, and death. Physical death is the outward manifestation of this. Yet even this, Schillebeeckx asserts, does not fully explain death. The further revelation in Christ shows how God transformed humanity's "guilty and absurd" experience into a "saving mystery."[52]

Christ's death burst the limits of death's scandal and absurdity and "brought life back to humanity, because whatever the living God touches becomes itself alive, even though it be very death."[53] It is important to note here that the emphasis is on *life*. Something that only becomes explicit in Schillebeeckx's later christology is already implicit here: It is not Christ's death, but Christ's life fully given, that saves. Life is God's, divinely and humanly given in Christ. Death is what humankind has brought into existence—the one thing God did not possess.[54] Schillebeeckx says that we "knew the bitterness of presenting death to God on the cross." And, it was the overpowering, outrageous nature of God's love to become truly *one* with us so as to accept that painful gift. It is precisely in this, Schillebeeckx suggests, that the miracle occurs.[55] If our death is sin's visible manifestation, Christ's death is the visible expression, the moment of realization, of perfected love.

The title of the article under discussion is "The Death of a Christian," and everything Schillebeeckx has said to this point is now brought to bear on the very personal event of death in the life of the believer. Objectively, dying is not an act, but something that happens to us. But now, in the light of revelation, "the attitude of mind in which we accept death can give it the value of an act." Schillebeeckx delineates three facets of that attitude of mind: First, dying is a deed of obedient love, a *fiat,* a humble acceptance of God's intervention. Second, "death must be an act of perfect contrition." That is, like Christ, who felt the contrast between the evil of the world and the all-holiness of God (that contrast which was the cause of death), we experience sorrow not only for our own sins, but for all the sin and evil of the world. In this we know deeply the justice of what is happening in death—" for I, however holy I may be, see myself in solidarity with all humankind."[56] And third, "the adoration of God and loving contrition must grow into a genuine, salutary penance, into the experience of death as the uttermost self-denial for love of God."[57]

These are three facets of an attitude, a whole and integrated attitude that does not merely have to do with the moment of death, but with all of life. Even as Schillebeeckx speaks of "daily practice in acquiring the attitude of mind in which we must die," his emphasis is on the quality of a life lived in love. It is the balance of life's choices in respect of good and evil that is stabilized in the moment of death. "Our entire life is given us by God to test our love. . . ."[58] In very traditional, almost pious terms, Schillebeeckx speaks of the need for self-detachment in order to see God face-to-face when finally we have accepted death. Death itself, and the misery and suffering that are so often the experiences of death-in-life, are in themselves undesirable. Yet, they become the means of cultivating the disinterested, self-forgetful love of God that renders dying a positive act. Because on our own strength we are incapable, quite simply, to love enough truly to see God, "the divine finesse comes to our aid with the help of suffering and death." Schillebeeckx continues:

> God converts the very consequences of evil itself into the certain means of salvation, so that we, who would not have the courage to take the initiative in the necessary purifying of our lives can get the purification we need by free acceptance of what in any case it is not possible to avoid.[59]

All of this talk of self-denial and purification seems to contradict the assertion of the fundamental goodness of the human person and of all creation. It is not, however, a contradiction; rather, it reflects the deep Thomistic understanding of original justice and original sin conditioning Schillebeeckx's thought. Original justice *is* fundamental goodness, and human beings are still rooted in it, as surely as we are rooted in God. And yet, just as surely, original sin has tangled our roots and disoriented our vital connection to the ground of our being. It is not the true self we reject in self-denial, but the false self constituted by misguided desires for illusory goods. The purification is the weeding and untangling—indeed, the painful pruning that allows healthy life to spring forth. The "self-detachment" and "purification" required to spontaneously accept death and see God face-to-face have to do with the removal of obstacles that hinder us from claiming our lives and becoming our authentic selves. Whatever the language, there is no claiming of one's authentic self outside the depths of God.

Schillebeeckx suggests that it is the bearing of death in our hearts that makes of life a loving sacrifice. This is not morbid if "sacrifice" is understood to mean making something holy by giving it away in love. And, of course, it is also true that we must possess our lives in order to give them away. Only then is sacrifice active freedom and not self-immolation or drudgery.[60] The way of possession is the way of dispossession; we claim our lives, Schillebeeckx says, by letting go a little more each day. Personal sufferings gradually loosen our grasp in preparation for the final letting go in death. The act of dying is beyond the power of mere humanity; thus, Schillebeeckx says, "to die is an act of grace." Of course, to speak of our own dying in this way is one thing. To witness the suffering and death of loved ones is another thing entirely. It is another kind of letting go. It brings the realization that here someone "passes through the most bitter suffering he can bear, but at the same time his belonging to God's grace can be experienced most vividly." With humble simplicity, Schillebeeckx notes the "powerful surge of divine grace" that a Christian family often experiences after the death of a loved one; "in spite of the blow they experience more intimately than ever that they are in the hands of God."[61]

For all of this, Schillebeeckx acknowledges the "crippling disintegration" of death within the limits of human experience. Only resurrection faith changes death's meaning. That is, God's acceptance of Christ's sacrifice of love is now an intrinsic factor of death for believers. "The Christian idea of death as a sacrifice is therefore no damper on life, but an enlightenment that places everything, even the smallest detail, in its true perspective. 'Death is precious,' not only to the dying but to the living too."[62]

Though Schillebeeckx's emphasis here is upon the experience of death in the life of the individual Christian, his analysis makes clear that the personal mystery both affects and is affected by the communal experience, immediate and universal. And the community in question clearly cuts across the world and time to the very origins of humanity. The experience of death involves our solidarity with humanity both sinful and redeemed; it returns us to the depths of the past in order to face us with the future. It confronts us with irrevocable loss within the context of a promise broader and surer than anything we can imagine. In this, death holds within it the seeds of contrast that are the dynamism of metanoia. But death's meaning, ultimately, resides in the life it evokes. Contemplation of death deepens our consciousness of life, of goodness, and of truth. Living in the face of death intensifies the meaning of the present, illuminates every choice, and increases our regard for each other and the whole of creation. At the end of the twentieth century, in Schillebeeckx's later theology, this has implications that were not imagined in the middle of the century, in his earlier theology. And yet, the seeds are there—seeds that Schillebeeckx himself might name "implicit intuition."

"WHAT THE ANSWER OF OUR
LIFE TO DEATH WILL BE"

Schillebeeckx introduces his article, "The Death of a Christian," as an attempt to examine "what the answer of our life to death will be." In a way, that single formulation encapsulates the manner in which suffering is a formative factor in the development of his theology. Schillebeeckx emphasizes that, in itself, death is not something that we do, but something that happens to us. It is the eschatological attitude of mind with which we approach death that, by the grace of God, can transform it into an act in the deep human sense. That eschatological attitude essentially means living not only *toward,* but *from* the promise. This is what it means to ask the question about suffering from the ground of one's being, the ground which is one and the same with the horizon of God's promise. Within the concrete limits of human finitude, the immanence of death is commonly more real to us than the promise of life. Analogously, sin seems more real than grace, suffering more evident than well-being, and evil more dominant than good. And it is the peculiar effect of original sin that the negatives should seem to predominate, that our consciousness should allow them to hold sway. Even as we hold death "precious," it is not precious in and of itself; it is never to be glorified. Only life is to be glorified. Death acquires its meaning from life; it takes any substance it has from the life that embraces and integrates it and makes of it something that it has no power to become on its own. Here again is the essence of contrast, which does not yet have a language at this stage of Schillebeeckx's theology but which is clearly present in his reflections upon death and its relationship to original sin and original justice.

The encounter with death holds within it all the elements of suffering and the essence of the agonizing contrast between sin and grace in our world. Schillebeeckx's early reflections upon death hold insights which, in the light of his later theology, reveal themselves as turning points and constants of suffering's formative role. The "turning points" are those things such as original justice, original sin, and the notion of sacrifice, which are not major themes *as such* in his later theology but are recognizable beneath the concepts and language wrought by the spiraling influences of hermeneutics, critical theory, and the new biblical exegesis. "Constants" are those persistent threads that gather both vividness and nuance through repeated emergences in the maturing texture of Schillebeeckx's work. Most significant among these are the notion of contrast, the sense of the promise, the reign of God, redemption, human freedom, grace, and solidarity.

It is not our intent laboriously to trace these "turning points and constants" but rather to be attentive to them as they signal the formative effects of suffering in Schillebeeckx's emerging theology. In every case, whatever contributes to or hinges upon the dynamic of metanoia is of utmost significance. Increasingly, contrast becomes both the revelatory place and the invisible seed of metanoia. In "The Death of a Christian," suffering emerges as the contrast in this world between God's life and love and human sin. Schillebeeckx's discussion of death as sacrifice takes on the positive cast of self-abandonment in freedom, wherein we trust God to be our all. The positivity of God and of life is paramount; it is the essence of the sustaining promise. Though the sense of a promise in the soul is documented in the Hebrew scriptures, Schillebeeckx points to Christ as the definitive embodiment of the promise, and therefore the Christian model for facing death. All of his references to self-detachment are expressions of the authentic attachment that is freedom. Schillebeeckx does not point to Christ as the sole attachment; rather, he points to him as embodying the ultimate freedom. Christ's freedom lies in the trust through which he attaches himself to God alone, and it is in this that Christians are called to follow him. In his reflections upon what is required for the final letting go in death, Schillebeeckx's consistent focus is upon loving God with all one's mind, heart, soul, and strength—and one's neighbor as oneself. This is the meaning and purpose of everything. The essence of this primary and defining attachment is its witness to God as "superior"—superior to any other thing that one might cling to as life. God is life. The notion of "superiority" applied to God rings strange in contemporary ears. Yet, in a nuanced way, Schillebeeckx uses this term again, and to profound effect, in his later theology. In *Church: The Human Story of God* he speaks of the "defenceless superior power of God,"[63] gathering into one phrase the force of contrast already implicit in "The Death of a Christian." That the supreme moment of clinging to God alone is the moment of death or its near approach—the limits of vulnerability—is already eminently clear in this early article. It is in the depths of vulnerability that Christ surrenders himself into the hands of God, trusting God to continue to be life for him, trusting that the attachment that sustained him in life will sustain him in and through death.[64]

It is precisely in this act of defenseless vulnerability that we see the redeeming reversal of Adam's failure. Adam's failure to "remain walking with God in the garden," his free refusal to let God be the living God in his life, is the refusal of vulnerability in trusting relationship to God. This is the essence of the original sin by which humanity "made its own situation of promise into an absurdity. . . . Sin affects us to the very root of what we are; it is the letting go of the living God and therefore the germ of the collapse in man."[65] By contrast, redemption lies in Christ's reversal, in his choice to trust God's promise precisely in his darkest hour, even though faithfulness itself had brought him thus to the nadir of his existence. If the "letting go of the living God" brought death into the world, Christ's choice to remain "holding God's hand" brought life back to humanity and vindicated the promise. In the depths of vulnerability, God's "defenceless superior power" is revealed. Schillebeeckx describes what this means for the ordinary Christian: "Death in this spirit becomes a journey to an encounter with Christ: serene acceptance, even though in the midst of bodily torment, of this disclosure of self through which we give our life into God's hands, and hope for salvation from him alone. The Christian experiences the gratuity of redemption most strongly in death: *non ex operibus, sed ex gratia.*" [66]

What Schillebeeckx speaks of in personal religious terms in this early work takes on an increasingly social, communal cast in his developing theology. Yet, what he accomplishes here remains the vital core of his later christology and political theology. The process of metanoia exemplified in the individual's approach to death is at the heart of Schillebeeckx's ongoing articulation of faith and justice amidst increasingly complex manifestations of world suffering. In a human way , despite the personalized religious terms of his early work, he nevertheless makes the pain and ugliness of death and, by extension, all suffering, abundantly clear. Death has no meaning at all apart from the positive context of God's promise, which is life itself. The clinging to God and letting go of all that is not God which is necessary for the acceptance of death is precisely what is necessary for the full living of life. The solitary human encounter with death evokes the full extent of negative contrast experience: The depths of solitude open out into the extremes of solidarity. Solidarity will constitute the persistent thread throughout Schillebeeckx's work, holding contrasts in tension and establishing itself as the constant amidst the variables that circumscribe suffering in its many aspects. Genuine solidarity is inseparable from the process of metanoia in the individual soul. The attitude of fundamental trust that is the heart of metanoia is also the heart of human solidarity in relationship and community. Schillebeeckx's language for what this means and how it looks in the world will develop with his increasing engagement of hermeneutics, critical theory, biblical exegesis, and the world itself. But it will always have the meaning of Mary's *fiat*: that love which goes to the ultimate limit.[67] Later, Schillebeeckx will say the same thing this way: "Acceptance of God is the ultimate, precise name which must be given to the deepest meaning of commitment to this world."[68] Here, Schillebeeckx's theology begins to be boldly political precisely by being faithful to his earliest understanding of obedience vis-à-vis original justice and original sin.

The development of his theology from this point on corresponds to the inevitable trajectory of the movement of the most profoundly personal metanoia. And, increasingly, that movement is a reciprocal, spiraling relationship of the personal with the communal in all its complex local, global, and religious manifestations. The obedience at the heart of metanoia is obedience to truth, and the relational underpinnings of Schillebeeckx's theology become evident in his reflections upon truth in the period of his political awakening, which was clearly aided by his hermeneutical development: "Truth is brought to light only within human intersubjectivity. . . . Assent to truth is accomplished in dialogue with people of both the present and the past."[69] The human and Christian failure to realize this has resulted in what is being experienced in the twentieth century as "the bankruptcy of all systems, including Christianity as a monological system. The truth is not to be found in a system, but in a dialogue."[70] Elaborating, Schillebeeckx suggests that truth is to be found in the polyphonic chorus of all humankind.[71]

Solidarity in this human, communal discernment of and assent to truth is the other side of solidarity in sin manifest in the human experience of evil and suffering. But human solidarity in original justice is prior to human solidarity in original sin. Creation is prior to freedom; grace is prior to sin; God's initiative is prior to human response, and God's continuing initiative is ever calling us back to a promise that remains unbroken despite all human failure. This is an affair profoundly personal, and at the same time overwhelmingly universal. It is continually challenged by the reality of suffering that stems from the evil that is beyond the scope of any personal human choice. And yet, it is vindicated by this: It is only from within the realm of personal human choice that evil and suffering can be adequately addressed—one by one, and in solidarity with each other. "To refuse to give a place to evil in one's own life and in that of society and to combat it wherever it occurs is to give expression to one's trust that good must have the last word."[72] This is the fundamental human "no" to evil that is based in the more fundamental human "yes"—the authentic *fiat* living both from and towards original justice.[73]

CONCLUSION

This chapter has sought to understand the ways in which Schillebeeckx's roots in the thought of Thomas Aquinas have influenced his approach to suffering. Respectfully recognizing Schillebeeckx's own refusal to enter the maze of theodicy, the writer has nevertheless examined representative elements of Thomas's thought on human suffering and its connection to the origins of good and evil. One discovery is that the understanding of original justice and original sin in Thomas's theology of creation clearly supports Schillebeeckx's own understanding of the fundamental goodness and positivity of God expressed in creation. Schillebeeckx's anthropology, likewise, bears out the implications of the classical model of original justice and original sin. Examination of two of Schillebeeckx's early works, *Mary, Mother of the Redemption* and "The Death of a Christian" brought to light early manifestations of the personal process of metanoia that provides the element of continuity throughout his theology. "The Death of a Christian," particularly, enfleshes the classical symbols of original justice and original sin while, in the same movement, it evokes the suffering-related themes that only become explicit in Schillebeeckx's later work. Central among these, and inseparable from each other, are the notions of negative contrast and solidarity.

Chapter two has illuminated those elements of Schillebeeckx's theology that both deepen the personal dimension of suffering as mystery and heighten the communal and political dimensions of suffering as challenge. Common to both of these dimensions is the significance of solidarity, both personal and cosmic.

But this illumination only raises more questions of an increasingly troubling nature. Symbols of solidarity provide a context of relationship; the symbol of the promise nurtures hope for salvation; but the harsh suffering and fragmentation of our contemporary world serve to reduce the credibility of these symbols at an alarming rate. For all of the insight of these "constructs," how is one to take seriously Schillebeeckx's most fundamental insight from Thomas Aquinas about the meaning of God's incarnation in Jesus Christ: "The basis of faith in God is the belief that the fact of human existence is a promise of salvation. . . ."?[74] The next chapter, which addresses Schillebeeckx's christology, explores what this means for human beings whose existence is overwhelmed by the experience of suffering.

NOTES

1. *Summa Theologiae,* Blackfriars edition, 3 vols. (New York: Benziger, 1947) I, q. 2, a. 3.
2. The classic theodicy question struggles from all angles with the fact of evil and suffering as evidence that God is either not omnipotent, or else less than loving and merci-

ful (therefore not good). At different stages throughout Christian history, there have been those who have sought to solve the problem by attributing suffering to the divinity. In contemporary theologies influenced by process philosophy, for instance, this is evident in arguments constructed over against the specifically Thomistic doctrine of God's immutability (*Summa Theologiae* I, q. 9). John Hick critically surveys the historical levels of conflict in *Evil and the God of Love* (London: Macmillan, 1985; originally published in 1966). More recent approaches to the question abound; for an excellent representation of the diversity of current thought, see David Tracy, "Evil, Suffering, and Hope: The Search for New Forms of Contemporary Theodicy," *Proceedings of the Catholic Theological Society of America* 50 (1995):15–36. For interpretations of Thomas Aquinas's thought on the relation of God to human suffering that support the insights basic to our arguments in this chapter, see Michael J. Dodds, *The Unchanging God of Love: A Study of the Teaching of St. Thomas Aquinas on Divine Immutability in View of Certain Contemporary Criticisms of This Doctrine* (Fribourg: Ed. Universitaires, 1986); see Dodds, "Thomas Aquinas, Human Suffering, and the Unchanging God of Love," *Theological Studies* 52 (1991):330–44 for a more pastorally oriented abstract of the longer work. Also helpful are Herbert McCabe, "The Involvement of God," in *God Matters* (London: Geoffrey Chapman, 1987) 39–51, and William Hill, "Two Gods of Love: Aquinas and Whitehead," and "Does Divine Love Entail Suffering in God?" in *Search for the Absent God*, ed. Mary Catherine Hilkert (New York: Crossroad, 1992), chapters 9 and 11, respectively.

3. For instance, the opposing gods of such ancient mythologies as those found in Mesopotamia, Babylonia, Greece, and Rome; these found their way into the Christian tradition via various forms of gnosticism; see Mircea Eliade, *Myth and Reality* (New York: Harper & Row, 1963) 29–30, 54–67; also, for an explanation of Plato's dualism and some of its later manifestations, see John Hick, *Evil and the God of Love,* 27ff.

4. Thomas Aquinas, *De Malo,* q. 1, a. 2.

5. *Summa Theologiae* I, q. 48, a. 1.

6. *Summa Theologiae,* I, q. 1, a. 3; and I, q. 49, a. 2.

7. Speaking of the remedies of sorrow or pain, Thomas asserts that "every good disposition of the body reacts somewhat on the heart, which is the beginning and end of bodily movements." And, to the remedies for sorrow that include pleasure, tears, the sympathy of friends, and the contemplation of truth, he adds the benefits of sleep and baths to "bring nature back to its normal state." *Summa Theologiae* I–II, q. 38, a. 1–5.

8. "Pain at the loss of good proves the goodness of the nature, not because pain is an act of the natural appetite, but because nature desires something as good, the removal of which being perceived, there results the passion of pain in the sensitive appetite." *Summa Theologiae,* I–II, q. 35, a. 1, ad 3.

9. *Summa Theologiae,* I–II, q. 39, a. 1, a. 2, a. 3.

10. *Summa Theologiae,* I–II, q. 35, a. 2.

11. Edmund J. Fitzpatrick, *The Sin of Adam in the Writings of Saint Thomas Aquinas* (Mundelein: St. Mary of the Lake, 1950), 12.

12. *Summa Theologiae,* I, q. 95, a. 1.

13. *Summa Theologiae,* I, q. 94, a.1, ad 1.

14. Discussing "whether or not death and similar evils are natural to man," Thomas employs the example of the material chosen to make a knife. The smith selects iron because of its qualities of being both hard and malleable, able to be sharpened. Iron also

has the qualities of being breakable and tending to rust. These are defects that are not selected but are nevertheless part of the composition of the knife. So, too, the corruptibility of the body is a defect that is not selected by nature but is a part of the composition of human nature. God made up for this defect at the time of creation with the gift of original justice. God did not will death, but human beings incurred it by sin, through which the gifts of original justice were lost (*Summa Theologiae*, I–II, q. 85, a. 6). Similarly, regarding other evils suffered, such as the evil of blindness, Thomas says "when man was first created God had given to him the help of original justice by virtue of which he was preserved from all ills of this kind. Of which help all human nature was deprived on account of the sin of our first parent . . . ; from the privation of which help diverse evils follow, which are found to be of diverse kinds in diverse persons, although they share equally the fault of original sin" (*De Malo*, q. 5, a. 4, ad 1).

15. T. C. O'Brien, "Original Justice," appendix to *Summa Theologiae* (New York: McGraw-Hill, 1965), 26 no. 8: 145.

16. O'Brien, "Original Justice," 149–50.

17. Mircea Eliade documents the ambiguous interweaving of cosmogony and eschatology in ancient myths of diverse cultures; see *Myth and Reality,* especially 54–67; also *Myths, Dreams, and Mysteries: The Encounter Between Contemporary Faiths and Archaic Reality,* (London: Collins, 1968), especially 43ff, and 66–80; for an analysis of the deep mythological underpinnings of the emerging Judeo-Christian understanding of sin and evil, see especially Paul Ricoeur, *The Symbolism of Evil,* trans. Emerson Buchanan (Boston: Beacon, 1967), 171–74 and 232–78.

18. T. C. O'Brien, "Fallen Nature," in appendix to *Summa Theologiae* (Blackfriars, New York: McGraw-Hill, 1965), 26:158.

19. *Summa Theologiae,* I, q. 95, a. 2.

20. *Summa Theologiae,* I, q. 95, a. 2.

21. Charles Journet, *The Meaning of Evil,* trans. Michael Barry (London: Geoffrey Chapman, 1963). 220.

22. For example, Kathleen Sands critiques Western Christian thought for the ways that its inherent dualism justifies divisions and hierarchies, thereby exacerbating suffering in many instances. She locates the most pervasive roots of Christian dualism in the myth of the fall itself, right within the construct of paradise. As an alternative vision, she calls for a positive integration of the realities of evil and tragedy in the depths of the human struggle which is itself sacred; see *Escape from Paradise: Evil and Tragedy in Feminist Theology* (Minneapolis: Fortress, 1994). In a more nuanced approach, Elizabeth Johnson critiques dualistic elements in the tradition, distinguishing genuine doctrine from damaging distortions. She succeeds in illuminating underemphasized areas that can contribute to a more integrated, relational, and experience-centered approach to God and human suffering; see *She Who Is: The Mystery of God in Feminist Theological Discourse* (New York: Crossroad, 1992), chapter 12.

23. "The absence of original justice is the quasi-formal element in original sin, and concupiscence is the quasi-material element; just as also in actual sin, turning away from an immutable good is the quasi-formal element, and turning to a mutable good is the quasi-material element so that in like manner in original sin the soul may be understood as turned from, i.e., averted and turned to, i.e., converted, just as in actual sin the act is as it were averted and converted" (*De Malo*, q. 4, a. 2).

24. *Summa Theologiae,* I–II, q. 85, a. 2.

25. T. C. O'Brien, 158.

26. Schillebeeckx uses the term "redemption" here in the same sense in which he uses it in the title; that is, to denote Christ as not only the redeemer, or agent of redemption, but also as existentially embodying the fullness of redemption. On a related note, today there are voices in the Church pressing for a new Marian dogma naming Mary "Co-Redemptrix." We would do well to attend to Schillebeeckx's assertion in the introduction of this early book: "We are redeemed by God alone, but in and through the human form in which he manifested himself to us—we are redeemed through Jesus Christ. . . . But, by virtue of our free consent, which is necessarily implied in the Redemption, all of us—and, in a very special and profound way, Mary—share, as human beings, in the Redemption. We are 'co-redeemers,' even though this takes the form of an 'active receptiveness' towards the God-man, Christ, who is the only Redeemer." Thus Schillebeeckx prepares the way for this stringent, cautionary observation: "This is one of the main reasons why the Church tends to avoid the Marian title of 'co-redemptrix' in her official documents, and generally has recourse to less over-charged formulations, such as 'partner in the Redemption.' The Church is so profoundly aware of the fact that 'Jesus' means 'Yahweh has saved' that she feels that the term 'co-redemption' might imply that Mary, though subordinate to Christ, was nonetheless complementary to him in the bringing about of the Redemption. The Church is absolutely convinced of the fact that there is one and only one Mediator between the Father and us, his children . . . 'the man Christ Jesus' (1Tim. 2:5–6)." *Mary, Mother of the Redemption,* xiii–xiv.

27. Schillebeeckx, *Mary, Mother of the Redemption,* , 4.

28. Schillebeeckx, *Mary, Mother of the Redemption,* 4.

29. Schillebeeckx, *Mary, Mother of the Redemption,* 5.

30. Schillebeeckx, *Mary, Mother of the Redemption,* 18.

31. Schillebeeckx, *Mary, Mother of the Redemption,* 19.

32. Schillebeeckx is writing in the context of the growing popularity in the Church of an *anawim* spirituality based on a stream of biblical scholarship that had begun at the end of the nineteenth century, represented in works such as A. Causse, *Les Pauvres d'Israël* (Strasbourg, 1922), and A. Gelin, *Les Pauvres de Yahvé* (Paris: Les Éditions du Cerf, 1953). The writer of the foreword to the 1964 English translation of Gelin's work acknowledges the critical claims of opposing scholars who maintained that there is no proportionate scriptural basis for the notion of the *anawim* as typifying Israel's response to God. He resolves the problem by suggesting that Gelin's position arose from a more integrated pastoral sense of Israel, the Old Testament, and the Church than that of his technically correct critics. He further notes the timeliness of the work in light of the Church's recent Vatican II emphasis upon being the church of the poor. The writer of the foreword adds his own insight, of interest to us, connecting obedience to the spirit of the *anawim*: "Speaking of Christ, St. Paul writes 'He learned obedience through the things which he suffered' (Heb. 5:8). The Greek word used here for 'obedience' (*hypakoue*) is often used in the Septuagint translation of the Old Testament to render the Hebrew word for 'poverty' ('*anawah*). Like ourselves, therefore, the Son of God too had to learn 'poverty of spirit.'" Albert Gelin, *The Poor of Yahweh,* trans. Kathryn Sullivan (Collegeville: Liturgical Press, 1964), foreword by Barnabas M. Ahern.

33. Schillebeeckx, *Mary, Mother of the Redemption,* 28.

34. Schillebeeckx, *Mary, Mother of the Redemption,* 31.

35. Schillebeeckx, *Mary, Mother of the Redemption*, 36.

36. This quality of universal participation is evoked by certain feminist eschatologies informed by contemporary science's assertion of a common creation story. For an explanation, and for implications for our understanding of sin and salvation, see Sallie McFague, *The Body of God: An Ecological Theology* (Minneapolis: Fortress, 1993), 197–212; for an overview of emerging ecofeminist eschatology in light of traditional Christian eschatology, see Peter Phan, "Woman and the Last Things," in Ann O'Hara Graff, ed., *The Embrace of God: Feminist Approaches to Theological Anthropology* (Maryknoll, N.Y.: Orbis, 1995), 206–28.

37. Regarding the innocence-before-the-fall, Ricoeur notes that "to say that it is lost is still to say something about it; . . . it is to attest that sin is not our original reality, does not constitute our first ontological status; sin does not define what it is to be a man [*sic*]; beyond his becoming a sinner there is his being created. That is the radical intuition which the future editor of the second creation story will sanction. . . . The *imago Dei*—there we have both our being created and our innocence; for the 'goodness' of the creation is no other than its status as 'creature.'" *The Symbolism of Evil*, 250–51.

38. Schillebeeckx, *Mary, Mother of the Redemption*, 40.

39. Schillebeeckx, *Mary, Mother of the Redemption*, 42.

40. Ricoeur distinguishes three hermeneutical levels: 1) the primordial symbols of sin, 2) the Adamic myth, and 3) the speculative cipher of original sin (*The Symbolism of Evil*, 237); for the development of the doctrine in the early church, see Henri Rondet, *Original Sin: The Patristic and Theological Background*, trans. Cajetan Finnegan (New York: Alba House, 1972).

41. Schillebeeckx, *Mary, Mother of the Redemption*, 46.

42. Schillebeeckx highlights the significance of Christ's solidarity with *fallen* humanity, having "taken to himself precisely the *sarx*, a human existence which is branded with the sign of sin, condemned to suffering and death" (*Christ: The Sacrament of the Encounter with God* [New York: Sheed & Ward, 1963], 31). From the point of view of his later theology, it seems a case might be made for the reality of solidarity in grace as the axis upon which his theology turns. The explicit notion of solidarity and the approach to suffering actually develop in relation to Schillebeeckx's increasing emphasis upon human experience and, especially, the *threatened humanum*. Yet, the very "threatenedness" of the *humanum* is based in the reality of original sin—and this remains a constant in Schillebeeckx.

43. Schillebeeckx, *Mary, Mother of the Redemption*, 47.

44. Schillebeeckx, *Mary, Mother of the Redemption*, 47.

45. "The Death of a Christian," in Edward Schillebeeckx, *Vatican II: The Struggle of Minds* (Dublin: Gill and Son, 1963); Dutch, 1955.

46. Schillebeeckx, "The Death of a Christian," 61.

47. Schillebeeckx, "The Death of a Christian," 63.

48. Gustavo Gutiérrez illuminates the conflicting schools of thought within the Wisdom tradition itself in his study of the book of Job from the perspective of today's poor: *On Job: God-Talk and the Suffering of the Innocent*, trans. Matthew J. O'Connell (Maryknoll: Orbis, 1987).

49. Schillebeeckx, "The Death of a Christian," 65.

50. Schillebeeckx, "The Death of a Christian," 67.

51. In a certain way, there is truth in this traditional connection of death and suffering

with sin; however, to common understanding the notion is abhorrent, and it renders God abhorrent. It is a common pastoral problem that people anguish over what they have done, what sin they have committed, to bring down God's wrath in some particular suffering or in the death of a loved one. It is often impossible to convince them that this suffering or death is not due to their sin but to the human condition as marked by original sin. Thomas emphasizes that death is punishment for original sin, and it is the result of sin through accidental cause, as when a stone falls because one accidentally removes the pillar that sustained it. Just so, the sin of the first parents is the cause of death and all such like defects in human nature, for the sin of the first parents removed original justice. Original justice had held together the whole body, in subjection to the soul, without any defect. The withdrawal of original justice, like the withdrawal of grace, is a punishment or penalty. "Consequently, death and all consequent bodily defects are punishments of original sin" (*Summa Theologiae*, I-II, q. 85, a. 5).

52. Schillebeeckx, "The Death of a Christian," 69.

53. Schillebeeckx, "The Death of a Christian," 70.

54. Death was no part of the divine being, nor did God make death. Thomas explains that human beings die because original sin leaves us without the aid which prevented the body's own tendency to corruption. Corruptibility is a defect of matter not chosen by nature. The loss of original justice left humans without a whole complex of preventive aids of which incorruptibility is the most emblematic. "God, to whom every nature is subject, in forming man supplied the defect of nature, and by the gift of original justice, gave the body a certain incorruptibility. . . . It is in this sense that it is said that *God made not death*, and that death is the punishment of sin" (*Summa Theologiae*, I-II, q. 85, a. 6; cf. n. 14 above); see also the discussion of finitude and death, above.

55. Schillebeeckx, "The Death of a Christian," 72.

56. Schillebeeckx, "The Death of a Christian," 76.

57. Schillebeeckx, "The Death of a Christian," 76.

58. Schillebeeckx, "The Death of a Christian," 82.

59. Schillebeeckx, "The Death of a Christian," 82–83.

60. "We are redeemed by Christ's death as a loving sacrifice, not by Christ's death as a welter of pain and suffering" ("The Death of a Christian," 72).

61. Schillebeeckx, "The Death of a Christian," 84.

62. Schillebeeckx, "The Death of a Christian," 86

63. Schillebeeckx, *Church: The Human Story of God,* trans. John Bowden (New York: Crossroad, 1990), 85; for a more extensive elaboration of this phrase as a central focus, see "Doubt in God's Omnipotence: 'When Bad Things Happen to Good People,'" in Schillebeeckx, *For the Sake of the Gospel*, trans. John Bowden (New York: Crossroad, 1990), 92–102.

64. In "The Death of a Christian," Schillebeeckx's emphasis is upon Christ's acceptance of death in the transforming context of trust in God: "That which before was the outward visibility of inward sinfulness, death, now in Christ becomes the visible manifestation of the highest possible awareness of God, the proof of God's superiority in the deed that was a total forsaking of self. Christ's death . . . is giving self over into the hands of God in the full awareness that in the supreme crisis of human life salvation can be expected only from him," 73.

65. Schillebeeckx, "The Death of a Christian," 67.

66. Schillebeeckx, "The Death of a Christian," 77.

67. What Schillebeeckx says about devotion to Mary expresses the substance of what will organically grow into a political theology: "Our devotion to Mary, then, must go right to the heart of the living Christian faith. It must be a *fiat* which goes, in sacrificial love, to the ultimate limit. Life is only good if it is offered as a gift. Life is love, a love which gives" (*Mary, Mother of the Redemption,* 174).

68. Schillebeeckx, "Secularization and Christian Belief in God," in *God the Future of Man,* 76.

69. Schillebeeckx, "Towards a Catholic Use of Hermeneutics," in *God the Future of Man,*" 28.

70. Schillebeeckx, "Secularization and Christian Belief in God," in *God the Future of Man,* 66.

71. Schillebeeckx, "Secularization and Christian Belief in God," 66.

72. Schillebeeckx, "Secularization and Christian Belief in God," 76.

73. For an example of Schillebeeckx's later development of this foundational theme, see *Church: The Human Story of God,* 6.

74. Schillebeeckx, *Church,* 75.

Chapter Three

Schillebeeckx's Christology

The hidden mentorship of Thomas Aquinas reveals itself at the point in Schille-beeckx's theology where suffering meets christology. The profound ambiguity of the human experience of suffering and evil is not resolved by Thomas's eluci-dation of the fall from original grace, and Schillebeeckx knows this. Yet, implic-itly he lifts up this still-relevant point of the classical fall construct: Obedience to God, properly understood, is the only thing that saves us from—or, rather, *through*—suffering, sin, and evil. And the proper understanding of obedience is to be gleaned from the life, death, and resurrection of Jesus. As stated before, "obedience" here has the relational connotation of committed trust and unbroken communion. Christians cannot think away suffering or the surd of evil damaging God's good creation. We can only look to Jesus, in whom God has the last word over the very real and destructive experience of suffering. Ultimately, it is the Jesus of the Gospels who focuses Schillebeeckx's engagement with suffering.

The Jesus of the Gospels does not speculate about the origins of suffering and evil in sin, but concerns himself with the concrete suffering in front of him.[1] Schillebeeckx takes his cue from Jesus' characteristic manner of relating to peo-ple in immediate situations of suffering: "Jesus was evidently little interested in whether this suffering was the consequence of sin or was innocent suffering. He identified himself with the sufferer—*saddiq* or not: neither piety nor lack of piety set any limits to his approach. . . . In his ministry, Jesus sees the alleviation of the suffering of others as his own task."[2]

Jesus' mode of relating to particular men and women who suffer is the best indication we have of God's relationship to human suffering. It is also the best indicator of who Jesus is. Most importantly here, it provides parameters for reflection about what suffering might mean.

Suffering is, for Schillebeeckx, a quintessential *human* experience. He makes this observation out of the place of convergence of two no less contrasting think-ers than Augustine and Irenaeus. Augustine, of course, is the architect of the dominant Western paradigm of original sin as the root of suffering and evil. From

the east, Irenaeus sees suffering as a sign that good and evil are mixed in humanity on the way to salvation. Schillebeeckx himself believes that the fruits of the
two traditions can be brought up to date in a way that is complementary. At the
very least, the views of Augustine and Irenaeus converge in the fundamental conviction that it is better to have known *human existence* than not. Augustine's own
experience of grief over the death of a beloved friend leads him to conclude that
human beings are the first who have a right to speak where suffering is concerned; and yet, in the depths of suffering he realizes that, if indeed we are created for happiness, then only God can bring salvation.[3] If this observation is true,
then it may be that the place of suffering is where humanity's deepest meaning
can be revealed. The emphasis on "can be" respects the reality that, all too often,
the place of suffering is the place of human degradation and despair. The harsh-
ness of this reality makes it imperative to remember the degradation and despair
of Jesus upon the cross. The scandal of this particular degradation has no salvific
meaning, and, in fact, no meaning at all apart from the context of Jesus' lived
human history. Thus, before it is possible to consider the meaning of the cross
for human suffering, one must consider the humanity of Jesus as vehicle of God's
salvation.

JESUS' HUMANITY AS SALVATION
COMING FROM GOD

How is one to understand the assertion that "the fact of human existence is a
promise of salvation"? In our pluralistic world, how is one to understand Jesus
as revealer of God and paradigm of humanity? These questions immediately pose
counterquestions. However, Schillebeeckx's own forthright statements about the
nature of christology open the inquiry.

Addressing the question, "Can Christology be an experiment?"[4] Schillebeeckx
provides a brief analysis of the underlying principles of the major christological
project represented by his *Jesus* and *Christ* books. His introductions to both
works qualify these writings as merely "prolegomena" to a christology. He now
clarifies what this means by distinguishing the cognitive order from the order of
reality. Thus he sums up the aim of the two books: "Soteriology . . . precedes
christology in the order of the genesis of christological knowledge."[5] In the order
of reality, however, it is the person of Jesus that is foundational; christology precedes soteriology. The simultaneity of these two truths crystallizes the central
dynamic of Schillebeeckx's theology and contextualizes the reality of suffering.
The cognitive order coincides with the contingency of human experience. That
is, Christians come to know who God is in Christ in and through their human
experience. In the order of reality, however, Christ, through whom God created
all that exists, precedes all being and knowing. These are, of course, metaphysical distinctions. The real emphasis of the two Jesus books taken together is, quite

simply, that human salvation lies in the living God, and God's honor lies in human salvation. "In the man Jesus the revelation of the divine and the disclosure of the nature of true, good, and really happy humanity—as ultimately the supreme possibility of human life—completely coincide in one and the same person."[6] And this raises the counterquestions set aside earlier. Even Schillebeeckx's own clarifications of his christological intent only serve to multiply those questions.

The core of Schillebeeckx's theological project is summed up in the two-part assertion that humanity is a promise of salvation, and that Jesus' humanity constitutes salvation coming from God. Today, more than ever, these claims evoke questions and counterclaims arising from ordinary human experience and from the critical speculations of theological pluralists.[7]

The most important of these questions emerged at the conclusion of the previous chapter: How is it possible to assert that the fact of human existence is a promise of salvation in the face of the reality that, for much of humanity, existence is overwhelmed by suffering? This, of course, is more than a primary question. It constitutes the central matter of my thesis and the compelling challenge of Schillebeeckx's project. Every human life is touched by suffering in some form; however, the dramatic and violent nature of the economic, social, and physical suffering afflicting so much of the world's population constitutes the overwhelming evidence against the proclamation that God wills the happiness and well-being of men and women. Human existence as experienced by masses of humanity does not measure up as a "promise of salvation."

Secondly, by what authority can one single out the humanity of Jesus as salvation-coming-from God? This poses the central christological question with which I am concerned in this chapter. The counterclaims from an increasing number of theological voices question not only traditional identifications of Jesus as unique and universal saviour, but traditional assumptions about what it means to be human. This proposes an entire study unto itself; here, the discussion will be confined to Schillebeeckx's christology as he has elaborated and defended it in the context of contemporary pluralism.

Human existence as promise of salvation and Jesus' humanity as salvation-coming-from-God constitute, for Schillebeeckx, two different articulations of the same fundamental truth. The work of this chapter lies in elucidating what this means. Because human experience is the starting point for all reflection, and because, as Schillebeeckx both states and illustrates, soteriology precedes christology in the cognitive order, the first consideration is what it means to be human and what it means to expect salvation. But even so, it is acutely clear that such considerations operate in time against the horizon of a prior reality. To "start with experience" is to engage history, to reflect upon human movement through time variously recalled and diversely interpreted. Above all, it is to operate in linear fashion—with a starting point which, however far collective memory is cast, is always "after the fact." "After the fact" in terms of the order of reality in which christology is prior to soteriology. After the fact of Creation. After the fact of the Fall. After the fact of the Incarnation.

It is plainly evident at this point that, for Schillebeeckx, the contemplation of humanity, even before the focus turns to Jesus, is undertaken in a context of creation-centered faith. That is, humanity is embedded in the tapestry of creation that comes from God, exists in God, and is returning to God. This is the foundational paradigm of Thomas Aquinas.[8] It is a stance of faith, which Schillebeeckx shares and for which he makes no apologies. At the same time, however, he upholds humanity, the *humanum*, as valuable in its essence—worthy of Christians' highest commitment and calling forth their most profound efforts.[9] In commitment to the authentic flourishing of the *humanum*, men and women, whether believers or not, have to do with that One believers name God. This divine horizon is at one and the same time indispensable ground and totally beside the point. For Schillebeeckx's operations it is indispensable ground. In relation to nonbelievers it is beside the point. The point is that human life is precious; it is sacred within the sacredness of the created order—whatever "sacred" is understood to be. From a purely anthropological perspective, Schillebeeckx has delineated "coordinates" for a universal valuing of our shared humanity. In every society, in every culture, the flourishing of the *humanum* is to be the criterion against which every political and religious system is to be measured and evaluated. However, from the time of his earliest appropriation of hermeneutics and critical theory until the present, Schillebeeckx has been adamant in cautioning against any attempt to positively define the *humanum*. This is not merely because "it is impossible to formulate the positive content of the *humanum* without reverting to many different, fragmentary and mutually contradictory views."[10] It is also to guard against "modern theories claiming to protect the *humanum* which have in fact resulted in a degradation of humanity."[11] Speaking from a Christian perspective on the deep, universal human desire for freedom, happiness, and well-being, Schillebeeckx says:

> Christian faith resists any premature identification of the *humanum*. In its resistance and in its protest, which is joined to the universally human protest, christianity remains critical and insists that it cannot accept any uniform positive definition of the *humanum*. The power to realize this *humanum* and to bring about an individual and collective peace is reserved for God, the power of love. This is the "eschatological reservation."[12]

Thus, it is only via the "hope which expresses itself negatively in resistance to every threat to the *humanum*" that it is possible to speak about human meaning.[13] On the basis of hope and resistance rooted in the promised future, Schillebeeckx attempts to articulate what all human communities might agree upon as the "common denominator" of human well-being through his well-known "anthropological constants."

TOWARD A VISION OF THE *HUMANUM*: ANTHROPOLOGICAL CONSTANTS

In the absence of a concrete definition of what a true and good—a fulfilled—humanity would look like, Schillebeeckx proposes a set of seven constants that "point to *enduring* human impulses and orientations, values and spheres of value, but at the same time do not provide us with *directly* specific norms or ethical imperatives" for true and livable humanity.[14] In actual fact, he sets forth six coordinates, with "the irreducible synthesis" of these six constituting the seventh constant. This chapter will examine each of these coordinates with particular attention to its implications for human suffering in relation to Schillebeeckx's christology.

Relationship to Human Corporeality, Nature, and the Ecological Environment

The first anthropological constant asserts the corporeality of the human person as the means of relationship to nature and the ecological environment. This coordinate raises the moral significance of the integrity of human embodiment vis-à-vis technological science. It is from the perspective of the vulnerable, enfleshed individual that we approach the "boundaries which we have to respect if we are to live a truly human life."[15] With this coordinate, Schillebeeckx asserts the humanizing potential of technology used in appropriate relationship to human persons and the natural environment. He notes our human responsibility to establish the norms of relationship to our corporeality and to the natural environment within the context of our particular, concrete situations. This raises, by contrast, the dehumanizing potential of technology when humans do not respect limits/boundaries within a given situation.

Writing in 1978, Schillebeeckx astutely warns that manipulation of the most elemental dimensions of human life will result in a kind of oppression that will give rise to spontaneous resistance and protest.[16] Twenty years later, we see all too clearly in our world the evil potential of technological capabilities originally designed for human advancement and well-being. Bioethical issues, especially in the most vulnerable areas of the beginning and end of human life, come immediately to mind. The human right to liberation and a wholeness that presumes a sound ecology, while often given the benefit of political and corporate rhetoric, does not drive the forces of scientific technology; to the contrary, the globalization made possible by such technology has been called the overwhelming evil of our time.[17] In the extremes of globalization, the concrete particularity of the relationship of the human person to his/her corporeality is pivotal: it safeguards the human reference in all of our actions.

Being Human Involves Being-in-Relation with Others[18]

Schillebeeckx's second anthropological constant asserts that human beings are inherently beings-for-others, made for encounter.[19] He draws on Levinas's image of the face as an image of ourselves for others, illustrating that it is in and through intersubjectivity that humans transcend the bounds of their own particularity.[20] Here differences are affirmed and each person is enabled to flourish in his/her uniqueness. "This also implies that well-being and wholeness, complete and undamaged humanity must be universal."[21] Such wholeness is meant for everyone, which leads us beyond the interpersonal level to the presence of a "third," that is, the dimension of society.

Relation to Social and Institutional Structures

In society the human person is necessarily related to social and institutional structures, and this constitutes Schillebeeckx's third anthropological constant. The hermeneutical spiral everywhere and always operative makes itself visible here in Schillebeeckx's important observation about the nature of the relationship of human persons to institutions. Humans create structures in the course of history. Gradually, these structures "become independent and then develop into an objective form of society in which we live our particular lives and which again also deeply influence our inwardness, our personhood. The social dimension is not something additional to our personal identity; it is a *dimension* of this identity itself."[22]

Schillebeeckx is critical of the tendency to treat institutions almost as unchangeable metaphysical realities. While institutions are necessary for human freedom and the concrete realization of values, they do not have general validity. To continue to support and realize authentic human life they must be subject to human critique and reform in every age. "This gives rise to the specific ethical demand to change them where, as a result of changed circumstances, they enslave and debase men and women rather than liberate them and give them protection."[23] Changing them requires an understanding of the original truth of institutions, which often were called to life in the first place precisely as instruments of liberation and protection. This raises the importance of solidarity with our past as crucial to our identity, leading us into the fourth anthropological constant.[24]

The Space-Time Structure of Person and Culture

People and cultures are conditioned by time and space. Historical and geographic situatedness form an anthropological constant that is humanly inescapable. Schillebeeckx reminds us that no social structure can remove the dialectical tension between nature and history, which combine uniquely to shape the particular substance of every culture. The givenness of this dialectic reaches its extreme limit in the final boundary situation of death. Beyond all the forms of suffering that our human technology and social intervention can alleviate, there are sufferings and threats to human existence over which we remain powerless. And it is precisely here that the question of human meaning arises. Human historicity, dramatized in the finality of death, faces us with the ultimate limit situation. The most poignant human suffering occurs at the place of powerlessness where meaning is sought.[25] Schillebeeckx tells us that it is at this point that we recognize that humanity itself is a hermeneutical undertaking, a task of understanding. It is impossible to escape history, impossible to escape our particular, concrete situatedness. It is in full, painful consciousness of contingency that human beings are able to unmask the meaninglessness of existence, and thus uncover a way forward in meaning.

Schillebeeckx notes the assistance to be gained from the empirical, analytical, and theoretical sciences in distinguishing truth from falsehood in the human project of understanding. Yet, he emphasizes that "truth . . . is only possible as *remembered* truth which at the same time is to be *realized.*"[26] Schillebeeckx's sense of *understanding* here is essential to what he means by both *experience* and *history.* As we have noted before, history is a history of experience, and for Schillebeeckx understanding is fundamental to the way in which human beings experience. That is, understanding is constitutive of experience. Another way Schillebeeckx expresses this is by saying (repeatedly) that all experience is *interpreted* experience.[27] Put this way, it is self-evident that any "presumption of adopting a standpoint outside of *historical* action and thought is a danger to true humanity."[28]

As understanding is constitutive of experience, and experience constitutive of history, so *particular* history is constitutive of particular yet binding norms in particular cultures. Schillebeeckx illustrates what he means by suggesting that the privileged culture that conditions life in the West imposes upon Western men and women a concrete ethical responsibility toward less privileged cultures. This norm is not universal, but neither is it random or arbitrary. It pertains with a "here and now" urgency to those who have benefited from the general prosperity of the West. Schillebeeckx refers to this as an extension, really, of the presuppositions of the second and third constants. It may be added that this kind of integral, historical consciousness and situated responsibility emerges also from the first anthropological constant.

Focusing on the implications for international solidarity on behalf of the poor, Schillebeeckx acknowledges the reality of exploitation of underdeveloped nations by the West. He is not avoiding the issue of culpability, but rather making the point that, quite apart from casting or accepting blame for the past, there is a situated immediacy in which we must act justly *now.* Right-acting in the present will necessarily entail examination of behavior in the past and transformed processes of communication and decision-making in the present, resulting, ideally, in greater reflection and altered motives for acting in the future.[29] Here are the communal elements of what Christians traditionally call "conversion." What is important is that there is a universally recognizable *human* constant by which such transformed action in the world is effected. In the call to international solidarity on behalf of the poor, there is a universal meaning with very particular ramifications for the West, and very particular—though *other*—ramifications for struggling, and perhaps victimized nations.

The question is raised (Schillebeeckx himself raises it) as to where to look for the *norms* of ethical action in such situations. Here Schillebeeckx warns that we cannot trust our culturally bounded understanding in the present. Our imaginations are limited by the situatedness of our experience; thus, we are compelled to draw upon the treasury of a reality larger than our own circumscribed one. It is here that the critical remembrance of suffering humanity demands a critical remembrance of the great human traditions, including the great religious traditions. All of this is integral to the hermeneutical praxis that is part and parcel of the process of history.

The Relation between Theory and Praxis

The essence of hermeneutical praxis is the mutual relationship of theory and practice, which comprises the fifth anthropological constant. The necessity of permanence and stability for truly viable humanity requires, paradoxically, continuous change in response to changing conditions.[30] This is the dynamism required for the hermeneutical task of creating the kind of enduring culture worthy of the *humanum* and capable of bringing *salvation*.[31]

Human Religious and "Para-Religious" Consciousness

It is noteworthy that Schillebeeckx's discussion of universal anthropological constants introduces the vocabulary of *salvation* immediately prior to the claim of a human religious and "para"-religious consciousness, also called the utopian element. Schillebeeckx's use of the word always encompasses its full etymological meaning of "whole-making." Salvation is a fundamentally *human* concept. And yet, the true human meaning of salvation necessarily includes a religious or "para-religious" dimension. This sixth anthropological constant is concerned expressly with the human future. Human beings in every society seek ways to make sense of "contingency or finitude, impermanence and the problems of suffering, fiasco, failure and death which it represents, or to overcome them."[32] This human search is the basis of every political, social, or religious system. Men and women in every culture struggle to construct visions of meaning, to give expression to what truly inspires worthwhile, sustainable humanity. There is a profound and universal human desire to live toward a principle of life as a meaningful whole—a "utopia," as it were.

Though this desire comes to expression in many forms, both religious and non-religious, in its purest state it is commonly characterized by compassion. In its most corrupt state, this desire gives birth to societies that are "utopias" only for an elite few for whose sake the suffering of the "less-than-human" masses is offered up. The Nazi regime comes immediately to mind, but the Jewish Holocaust is in fact an overwhelming symbol of the less-defined ethnic cleansings that continue throughout the globe in this very hour. This dark, painful stream of human misery flows from the twisted perversion of an originally life-giving desire for full, human living. At the very least, it flows from the unconsciously exclusive grasping of the right to full humanity by a privileged few. Worse, and far too frequently, it stems from the conscious will to control events and manipulate human lives in the interest of massive agendas shaped by greed for wealth and power. This is the face of evil that tells against all desire for the good and truly human. Schillebeeckx maintains that this is, in fact, the dark reversal of the authentic yearning at the heart of enduring human traditions. That is why, wherever such perversions prevail, there have always been voices of protest rising up, often in the name of time-honored religions and cultures. And most of these traditions voicing a desire for the authentic *humanum,* apart from a few controlled by a principle of fate, involve a sense of humanity as active subject of the world's transformation. For religious men and women, the principle of goodness and truth, the essence of "totalizing" reality, is the living God, the Lord of history. Schillebeeckx argues, however, that whatever this desire or its principle object is called, it is always a form of faith. He unabashedly maintains that " 'faith,' the ground for hope, is an anthropological constant throughout human history, a constant without which human life and action worthy of men [*sic*] and capable of realization becomes impossible."[33]

Certainly, there are and have always been those persons and movements that eschew any form of faith, those who espouse nihilism and declare life absurd. Schillebeeckx suggests that this not only falls far short of the *humanum,* it represents its dark opposite; indeed, this sixth constant functions as a term of negative contrast. That is, nihilism's denial of the possibility of livable humanity actually strengthens faith and hope and demonstrates that they are part of the health and integrity of our humanity.[34]

Irreducible Synthesis of These Six Dimensions

The seventh anthropological constant is really the synthesis of the six that have been elaborated. "The reality which heals men and women and brings them salvation lies in this synthesis."[35] At this point Schillebeeckx emphatically warns against the danger of submitting any of these constants to some higher spiritual priority. The prioritizing of the "spiritual" over the "merely human" is profoundly damaging. In the context of Schillebeeckx's overall schema, it would be fair to say that it is damaging both to the *humanum* and to the *imago dei*. And such damage is an all too common occurrence.

The other danger Schillebeeckx warns against is the temptation to prioritize or, worse, to focus exclusively on any one of the six constants. These constants are not norms, but rather coordinates within which norms must be established. They do not stand alone but stand in interrelationship as a framework for human wholeness: that is, salvation. These coordinates, taken together, help us to achieve a realistic awareness of the current human situation in light of the ideal. It is, Schillebeeckx argues, the analysis of the gulf between reality and the hoped-for ideal that provides the direction for transformative action. Such analysis, discernment, and action require honest dialogue with respect for diverse and often conflicting views. Schillebeeckx's recommendations in this regard matter-of-factly echo the principles of Habermas's communicative action theory. At this point, the criticism frequently directed at Habermas's project might be turned upon Schillebeeckx. Is it realistic to expect that in all cases the "community" of dialogue participants around a table will fulfill the requirements of equality, mutuality, and unbiased openness to diverse and opposing views? Is it realistic to presume even a fundamental equality of education and articulateness on all sides of the table?

These questions, directed at Habermas, are valid. The very generality with which Schillebeeckx glides through the recommendations for a communicative process exempts him, however, from the critique. That is, he views this as one dimension of a much larger, and necessarily messy, picture. He moves from the requirements of dialogue to recognition of the "necessary pain of pluralism." He never loses sight of the concrete situatedness of humanity manifested richly in culture and problematically in politics. With all of this in clear view, he proclaims that politics "is the difficult art of making possible what is necessary for human salvation."[36] Inherent in this statement is the simultaneous understanding of the supreme importance of sociopolitical praxis and its limits vis-à-vis the true scope of human salvation. And this brings the inquiry, at last, to the fundamental question of salvation itself.

THE HUMAN QUESTION OF SALVATION

Salvation is, fundamentally, a human question. It is a question—in the very deepest sense, a "quest." And it is human—in that this questing, this searching, is the creative dynamism that defines the core of humanity. The longing for wholeness is always conditioned, never fulfilled, and continually pointing beyond what is achievable in the present. And yet it fuels and sustains all activity for genuine transformation, personal, communal, and political. The system of anthropological coordinates, even in the ideal of a perfect synthesis, simply establishes the conditions for the flourishing of the *humanum*. It neither delivers it nor defines it. Yet, it is indispensable in sketching the limits of human possibility even as it remains subject to human failure.

The anthropological constants, as minimum common denominator of what is required for truly *human* existence, arise out of the pervasive experience of what is not-human, not-livable, not-salvation. Images of whole and healthy humanity, that is, salvation, arise out of experience of anti-humanity, or salvation's opposite. Images of the flourishing *humanum* arise out of knowledge of suffering ineluctably illumined by fragmentary experiences of joy. Thus, it is no surprise that Schillebeeckx's delineation of the anthropological coordinates follows upon a lengthy treatment of the *threatened humanum* in a "critical remembrance of suffering humanity."

Schillebeeckx undertakes this "critical remembrance" as an analysis of humanity's search for a way of life that will overcome suffering. The search, like the problem that gives rise to it, is quintessentially *human*: "Even against the background of meaningful, joyful and satisfying experiences and hoped-for salvation, the history of suffering among people, and indeed in the animal world and throughout the universe, is the constant theme of every account of life, every philosophy and every religion; and today even of science and technology."[37]

In this sense, the historically human experience of suffering has necessarily both conditioned and been conditioned by religious experience, beginning with ancient mythologies. Schillebeeckx observes that all religions, in contrast to "critical rationality," take suffering seriously and register a protest against it. "Religions do not have their origin *in* suffering, but suffering becomes a problem only for the person who believes in God. This is already a lesson from human history of which we should take critical note."[38]

This lesson from history implies that, for all our contemporary secular concern with freeing human values from religious bias, the deepest and highest human values have always been shaped and articulated by religions. The supreme catalyst for such formulation has always been the reality of suffering. And, in Western culture, effectively extending well beyond the "Western world," the most pervasive religious force shaping the vision of the *humanum* has been Christianity. Schillebeeckx points out, however, that it is a mistake to say that the "humanizing values" have been so absorbed by our culture that Christianity itself is no longer needed. Indeed, to say so is to absorb the "great Christian tradition" into the mechanistic functionalism that defines our society. It is utterly to miss the deep meaning at the core of humanity's search, and thus deny what the human spirit has always implicitly grasped: The fullness of the *humanum* is an eschatological reality, possible only as promise. Only when we have said this can we say, and rightly, that there is no distinction between "human salvation" and "Christian salvation." The anthropological constants themselves have an eschatological cast; they reveal that there is something absolute at the core of the human search for salvation. This "absolute" reality is what believers call God, the One Christians have met in Jesus.

Nothing brings human beings face-to-face with absolute reality as powerfully as the experience of contingency—the felt knowledge of finitude. Even the theoretical (let alone practical) realization of humanist ideals is thwarted by the factual reality of suffering, global and personal. The paralysis of the developed world vis-à-vis recurring waves of genocide in Rwanda or Algiers reflects but two representative cases. On a smaller scale, every instance of communal or personal failure reveals the impotence of knowledge and technology to alleviate the most fundamental human suffering. Whether we find ourselves at the limits of positive accomplishment or at the limits imposed by failure, as a society or as individuals, we are pushed back to the horizon of a prior reality. Our deepest commitment to life and the *humanum* is grounded in this prior reality; and we come to know this most definitively when we have to do with the *threatened humanum*.

The horizon of which Schillebeeckx speaks is the absolute reality that believers recognize as God. Christians are those who have come to identify this reality through the concrete and definitive contours of the human life of Jesus. Speech about Jesus ordinarily falls into categories of soteriology and christology. As noted at the beginning of this chapter, Schillebeeckx's classification of soteriology as prior to christology in the cognitive order, and christology as prior to soteriology in the order of reality. The liberative, whole-making goals of soteriology in the system of anthropological coordinates must be recognized, even though they can only point to the fullness of salvation. Christology must be recognized as the prior order of reality in which soteriology (and anthropology) is grounded. Christology thus corresponds to the absolute reality denoted by the horizon that will be considered next.

Following Schillebeeckx, we are always moving within the hermeneutical spiral. And thus, we find ourselves back where we started, though on richer ground, contemplating from a new vantage point this ultimate horizon: the order of reality in which christology is prior to soteriology. Absolute reality precedes our human experience of reality. "In the beginning was the Word and the Word was in God's presence and the Word was God." To assert the prior order of christology is to assert the prior order of the Word who was present to God in the beginning and through whom all things came into being. Here the issue is the language of universality, on which hinges so much current christological debate, not only between religions but among Christian theologians as well.[39] It is beyond the scope of this work to sketch the complicated terrain of this dialogue; it will, instead, limit the discussion to Schillebeeckx's quite recent handling of this debate.

The ground of Schillebeeckx's christological position lies in the approach to the mystery of the *humanum* as described. At the heart of everything Schillebeeckx writes is the conviction of Thomas Aquinas that, in Jesus, humanity is itself a manner of being of the Son of God.[40] It is not simply that God becomes human in Jesus Christ; it is that humanity becomes divine in Jesus Christ. In this lies the promise of salvation in which we all have a share by virtue of our flesh-and-blood existence. Universally. And this is true only as the heart of the more fundamental reality of creation: The one in whom all that exists came to be is the one who takes our flesh, so that through our fleshly existence, in relationship with each other and all that has been created, we might participate in divinity. It is in this sense that Schillebeeckx speaks of the flourishing of the *humanum* as the essence of the salvation that God wills universally.

A humanist might question by what right we Christians speak of this hoped-for flourishing as "God's will." Members of many of the world's religions might question our preoccupation with "salvation."[41] And many Christian thinkers challenge anything approaching a claim to universality. Schillebeeckx operates from a standpoint of utter respect for the pluralism of beliefs, including the position of nonbelief. In fact, he has proclaimed that the primary dialogue partner of the Western theologian is the nonbeliever. Thus, as we have already seen, he labors seriously to establish the *humanum* as not merely the starting point, but as the very substance of theological reflection. But, theological reflection by definition penetrates beyond what is observable in human experience and functions at the level of faith. The starting point of theological reflection, then, is the "experience with experiences" that is known as the experience of faith. Schillebeeckx's foundational premise in any discussion of christology is the foundational nature of the experience of faith.

Standing on this ground of experienced faith, Schillebeeckx deals with the controversial questions of the identity, uniqueness, and universality of Jesus Christ.[42] The issue here is the particular significance of Jesus for salvation in a world overwhelmed by suffering. What may help in understanding Jesus' humanity as salvation-coming-from-God is a discussion of these questions and the terms they entail.

"ABSOLUTE REALITY" AND THE HISTORICAL JESUS

"Absolute reality" has been described here as the horizon beyond all our experiences, that horizon that believers name "God." For Christians, this corresponds to the order of reality wherein christology has priority over soteriology. But, in current christological discourse, "absolute reality" evokes the language of universality and uniqueness—language which, in relation to Jesus as Saviour, has caused much conflict and division. For Schillebeeckx, the claim of such language is a human claim; it comes from the profound experience of the mystery of the *humanum*.

Schillebeeckx has established that what it means to be human is, for Christians, not the same as the functional understanding of the world—a world still too much in the grip of instrumental reason. In fact, the contrast between common assumptions of human meaning and what Schillebeeckx is getting at is, indirectly, often a potent source of suffering. This is a manifestation of society's sinfulness in which all humans share. By the same token, in inchoately trying to express the real meaning of the *humanum* through hope-for-salvation, the definition approaches a humanity that we cannot touch—except in the life of Jesus. Then, in faith, we as Christians know that we are dealing with the one who embodies and realizes the universal meaning of being human. This stance of faith necessarily entails the historical point of view of the Christian tradition.

The affirmation of faith in the universal liberating significance of a finite being, historically situated and conditioned, is both foundation and stumbling block; it has ever been thus. It is not merely a point of controversy in interreligious dialogue or in the dialogue with nonbelievers. It has become the major material of christological debate among Christian theologians. As Schillebeeckx notes, this is where even a number of Catholic theologians are in opposition. Tolerance is carried to the extreme when theologians, in effect, erase all differences among religions in the name of equality. Schillebeeckx decries this "religious indifferentism" as an oversimplification that is not acceptable. He vehemently maintains that it is "impossible to ignore the historical point of view of the great Christian tradition in its fundamental dogma": the existential conviction that in Jesus God is eschatologically, definitively revealed in an irreversible manner within Christian history. Silence about this aspect of definitive irreversibility is a renouncing of the heart of Christianity and a reduction of christology to a Jesuology, rendering Jesus merely one incarnation among many other incarnations. The modern fear of appearing to be intolerant has, in fact, led to just such a damaging silence. And the reality of suffering, which is our overriding concern, is neither alleviated, understood, nor rendered meaningful by this silence.

Carefully, Schillebeeckx goes about the delicate task of upholding the mystery of the *humanum* at the heart of every religious expression while articulating the unique identity of Christian faith without absolutism, relativism, or superiority. And, in fact, the critical remembrance of *suffering* humanity is pivotal for an understanding of Jesus' humanity as salvation-coming-from God. In a recent article of urgent tone, Schillebeeckx develops eight theses concerning the identity and universality of Jesus.[43] What is important here is his steadfast commitment to history as the place of God's self-revelation and humanity's response in faith. It is, in fact, this historical rootedness that enables Schillebeeckx to pierce through the contemporary christological controversy. If the historical tradition of experiences of faith are taken seriously, then Christian doctrine will be accorded a proper reverence.[44] In this spirit of historical understanding, Schillebeeckx asserts that, since Chalcedon, the Christian cannot forget that neither Christianity nor Jesus Christ is absolute or absolutely unique. Only the God of Jesus, the creator, is the very God of all humanity. What is absolute in Jesus, according to the Christian faith, is God and God alone. God is thus reflected in the relativity of history in unique historical form. In other words, Jesus is according to Christians a particular manifestation in history of a nevertheless absolute meaning.[45] It is God who is the absolute reality of which we have spoken. It is God who is the universal meaning that the *humanum* points to in its yearning.

How do we as Christians know that this divine, universal meaning is what the *humanum* strains toward, and that it is embodied in Jesus Christ? When all is said and done, Schillebeeckx acknowledges that even the force of history is not enough on which to base a proclamation of Jesus as universal saviour. It is not merely history, nor the historical-critical method of biblical exegesis, that can account for such a proclamation, but only the centrality *in* historical Christianity of the confession of faith. "That Jesus Christ is a confessional name indicates the basic structure of all christology: this confession is the foundation and origin of the New Testament."[46] And it is only from the confessional stance of faith that we can speak of Jesus as the answer to the general human question of the universal meaning of history.[47] Schillebeeckx's hermeneutics of history is here capsulized.

AN APPROACH TO UNIVERSAL MEANING

Human beings, as Schillebeeckx has illustrated through his anthropological constants, have always sought meaning. Over time, and through the concrete development of culture, the immediate search for a meaning to human life has developed into the question of the universal meaning of human history. The broadening of the question corresponds to the broadening of the human horizon of experience and knowledge, leading to the concern for the "other" in its postmodern connotation of diversity and difference. More than ever, we are aware that the question of meaning is not a question of logical development. Meaning cannot be constructed idealistically or posited theoretically without denying the all-too-concrete reality of meaninglessness. The surplus of human suffering and disaster in our history is more than real; for many people, it is overwhelming. If meaning cannot be discerned in the very midst of this meaninglessness, then human history is doomed to failure, and life itself truly is absurd. The realities of famine and plague, the violence of persecution and injustice, and the atrocities of war that burdened the peoples of antiquity in the pages of the Old Testament continue to reign in our world. The advances of civilization increase both their scope and our guilt. And the specter of death cannot be vanquished by all our technology; human beings suffer the exigencies of their finitude and the loss of loved ones regardless of what degree of technological and cultural sophistication they happen to enjoy.

Thus, the question: In the midst of so much meaninglessness, how do we approach universal meaning? Schillebeeckx believes that the ultimate meaningfulness of history can be approached (We can do no more than approach it!) through the dialectic of theory and praxis embodied in the Christian experiential tradition. The Christian praxis of prayer and liberation can, in fact, give inspiration and orientation to practical reason.[48] The meaninglessness of history embodied in human suffering can be transformed only piece by piece, through concrete action within particular circumstances. As fragments of salvation emerge through the human response to pain and injustice, suffering is not only rendered meaningful, it renders negative history meaningful. That is, suffering dialectically contributes to the ultimate meaning of history. To put it another way: Through the dynamic of negative contrast, suffering spurs human beings to the transformative praxis that is creative of the meaning God desires for creation. God, the Lord of history, can thus give a future to the fragments of liberation wrought by the praxis of men and women.

> In the Christian religious experiential tradition, that which is sought, hoped-for and still unexpected—expressed in the New Testament by powerful pictures like the kingdom of God, universal brotherhood and sisterhood, a heavenly banquet, the freedom of the children of God, the universal kingdom of justice and peace—is not a vague utopia which is completely in the future, nor a theoretical anticipation of a total meaning of history. What is hoped for is, rather, vividly anticipated in a career and praxis: that of Jesus, whose person, message and praxis, despite historical failure on the cross, is confirmed by his resurrection from the dead by God as in fact a praxis of the kingdom of God: salvation for all men and women. In this life-story, being a historical victim, i.e., suffering, takes on its own cognitive significance and power (though this cannot be given a place in theory) for all humankind on its long way in search of truth and goodness, justice and meaning.[49]

Schillebeeckx is concerned with the human response Jesus evoked in history.[50] That response was typically a concrete acceptance or rejection of Jesus' own humanity and what it pointed to. And the relationship of Jesus' unique life and praxis to the question of universal human meaning has its roots in something prior to the specifically Christian experiential tradition: Schillebeeckx reminds us of the uniqueness of Jesus' situation within the line of election in Israel. The Jews themselves were "unique," awaiting in Jesus' time a universal intention of humanity. The election of the prophets traditionally concerned the well-being of Israel: A prophet was one who would serve the people. And so, the common election from the descendants of Abraham became concentrated in Jesus, the man in service of humans. Prior to the tradition of the New Testament, there was simply Jesus: a particular, concretely situated Jew at a unique moment in the history of his people. And there was Israel, seeking history's meaning, seeking a universal portent. For Jews, as Schillebeeckx points out, according to the horizon of their faith, this Jesus was a "scandal."[51]

Jesus' life, unprepossessing as it was, aroused a passionate response in those who encountered him, and even in those who merely heard about him. The seeds of opposition among his own people were symbolized early on in the story of Herod's dramatic reaction to his birth. The news of Jesus' coming, whatever that coming might mean, aroused a fear in one evil man that sparked the slaughter of the innocents.[52] And so, from the very beginning, the coming of God in human flesh surfaced the hidden powers of darkness even as it freed people for goodness and love.

"In Jesus something extraordinary has made its appearance within history, something which his opponents traced back to 'demonic sources,' but his followers to an inexpressible closeness to the deepest core of all reality: God."[53] In his human career, Jesus became known for his works of healing as well as for his preaching and teaching. It was, indeed, the stories of his "miracles" that often drew the crowds to listen to his words. Then, it was the authority with which he spoke that held them spellbound. That authority emanated from the same "inexpressible closeness to the deepest core of all reality" which empowered his healing ministry. Schillebeeckx's analysis of what was at work in the miracle stories reveals something more of what it means to say that Jesus' humanity is itself salvation-coming-from-God.

"THE MIRACLES OF JESUS"

Wherever people suffer, miracles are hoped for. People of simple and genuine faith actively pray for miracles of liberation, of release from illness, of the restoration of loved ones or of peace. Others, when in situations of pain and despair, secretly hope for something like a miracle, even when they scorn its possibility. "Miracles" are fragments of salvation. Even in the most sophisticated of contemporary circumstances, people describe as "miracles" those experiences wherein a burden is inexplicably lifted, darkness penetrated, pain alleviated, the way forward cleared. Miracles are experiences of grace: felt knowledge of reality's deepest meaning.

These experiences of grace are, ultimately, evidence of God's action in the world. Schillebeeckx is most concerned with such evidence as it surfaces in the joy and relief expressed by people in the New Testament in relation to Jesus. He notes that the profane Greek word for miracle, *thauma,* never occurs in the Gospels. "They say only that certain sayings and actions of Jesus aroused a *thaumadzein* among the people, that is, made them feel surprise and amazement."[54] The people who felt this amazement stood within the history of God's covenant with Israel. It was in the context of this historical relationship that they recognized in Jesus of Nazareth the saving acts of God, like those accomplished of old. The signs and mighty acts of God on behalf of those who suffered in their history were visible now, in a new way, in this Jesus. "Jesus as it were underwrites God's help to people in distress."[55] For those who understood the message of the ancient prophets, Jesus was not a scandal, but the one in whom God's rule was already present, the one in whom the "time of salvation" was now dawning. "This is 'realized' eschatology."[56]

Indeed, Schillebeeckx's most important designation for Jesus is that of "escha-tological prophet." Jesus is the one in and through whom God's promised future begins to come to light even now. Certainly, this recognition, which Schille-beeckx attributes to the Q community, is a hermeneutical interpretation. On the basis of history, certain acts are remembered and now expected of the one who is to come. In the healing of lepers and the raising of the dead, Jesus performs the miracles expected of the eschatological prophet, and he is validly identified as such. This is the meaning that Schillebeeckx attributes to Jesus' reply in the Q logion: "'The blind see, the lame walk, and to the poor the good news is pro-claimed. Blessed is he who is not scandalized by me.'"[57]

These images, Schillebeeckx points out, have profound metaphorical signifi-cance. To be blind is a sign of separation from God; to see is to have access to salvation; and the "eschatological prophet" is the "light of the world." And yet, to assert this metaphorical significance is not to deny that Jesus restored physical sight and mobility to real people. It is simply to point out that the deepest mean-ing of these acts is that "Jesus is enlightening and liberating for those who come to meet him."[58] The interwoven threads of what is kerygmatic and what is histori-cal in the Gospels are difficult to tease apart. But it is of the very essence of hermeneutics that the deepest truths inhere precisely in the inextricable inter-weaving of literal and metaphorical realities remembered, interpreted, forever re-imagined.[59] The "miracles" of Jesus are perhaps the supreme example of this hermeneutical fact. Their true import lies in the intentionality with which Jesus performs or doesn't perform them. For an example of the latter, Schillebeeckx points to the temptation narratives:

> Jesus refuses to perform "legitimizing" miracles, without use or benefit to others but to his own advantage. Jesus does the miracles of the charismatic eschatological prophet, and no others. Through his miracles he brings a joyful message to the poor, not just in words but in actual fact. He is the eschatological prophet who brings the tidings of joy: "Your God reigns" (Isa 52:7; 61:1).[60]

It was on the basis of Jesus' concrete acts on behalf of others that he was histori-cally recognized as "eschatological prophet." With this recognition, the miracles of the eschatological prophet in scriptural memory were attributed to him, in addition to the historically verifiable ones, which exegetes increasingly believe he actually performed. There is, Schillebeeckx explains, an "epic concentration" by which the universal import of Jesus' unique particularity is recognized. The primacy of history in the hermeneutical circle is affirmed in this: The marked, concretely historical acts of Jesus are always the ground and criterion of every hermeneutical meaning and interpretation.

What is important, for Schillebeeckx and for us as Christians, is the meaning of Jesus' miracles in light of his humanity as salvation-coming-from God. Jesus' miracles are always and only performed in response to the concrete needs of people in the moment, people who are suffering; they are never self-legitimizing. In this, Jesus is most clearly and simply himself, revealing his real personality and essential nature: "Jesus does not seek self-legitimation. He is not worried about his own identity but is himself in all that he does; his identity is to identify himself with people in distress and fear in order to release them from their self-estrangement and restore them to themselves, so that they are made free again for others and for God."[61]

It is, in fact, precisely in being himself in this way that Jesus simultaneously reveals God's will for human flourishing and all that militates against it.[62] He is God's being-as-human, and as such illuminates the world's insufficiency, which comes to expression in all forms of evil, sin, and suffering. And so Schillebeeckx says that miracles must be viewed within this field of good and evil, "'the power of the evil one' as over against 'the power of God.' That is why it is 'expulsions of evil spirits' and healings of the sick (for the Jews illness, in the broadest sense of the word, means 'being in the power of the evil one') that play so central a role in the accounts of Jesus' miraculous acts."[63] Note that Schillebeeckx says here "the power of evil *as* over against the power of God." The subtle emphasis reminds us of Schillebeeckx's impatience with theodicy, and of his reliance upon Thomas Aquinas' understanding of evil as nothingness in the sense of "not-being." There is no dualism implied here; evil is not a substantive force competing with goodness. In the very substantive cases, however, of human illness and tangible suffering, evil's nothingness takes shape as visible diminishment of life: human life and life in all its created forms. Over against this visible diminishment, God's desire for abundant human flourishing is manifest in the miracles of Jesus:

> The gospels make it clear that a salvation which does not manifest itself here and now, with respect to concrete, individual human beings, can have nothing in the way of "glad tidings" about it. The dawning of God's rule becomes visible on this earth, within our history, through victory over the "powers of evil." This it is that the miracles of Jesus exemplify. In the struggle with evil Jesus is totally on the side of God.[64]

Schillebeeckx points out that in the gospel of Mark, in particular, it is Jesus' human presence that is experienced as saving good by distressed people who come to him in trust. "Here salvation is given to people who in their sense of its opposite, of misery and evil, fulfill the only proper condition for ever being able to receive the gospel as *glad* tidings." Here is concretely represented "the long course of accumulated human suffering, on the look-out for Jesus, who brings deliverance."[65] This immediate deliverance personally experienced through encounter with Jesus is not the whole story, however. It is the visible dimension of a salvation whose deeper realities surface only through questions about its source. Initially, in Mark's account, the divine mystery at the source of Jesus' miracles stirs the voices of the evil spirits who cry out their recognition of "the Holy One of God." Thus begins the unfolding that will lead to the cross.

Thus far, it has been clear that the miracles of Jesus are never self-legitimizing, always disclose mercy, and require trust on the part of the persons in need of healing. In Schillebeeckx's reading of the gospel of Mark, it is enough, initially, that Jesus brings people saving health and makes them glad. It is enough that people trust Jesus' human presence. If those healed and delivered do not yet perceive that in Jesus God's rule is at hand and Satan, or evil, retreats, that is not cause to criticize them. The whole story will only become clear in the experience of the Church.⁶⁶

The necessity of trust reaches a new level in what becomes known, throughout the New Testament, as the "faith formula": that is, the oft-repeated affirmation in one form or another that "your faith has saved you." The new level of trust has to do with movement beyond the external dimension to the source of salvation and its implications for living. Drawing now upon Luke, Schillebeeckx emphasizes that Jesus' intent in working cures is to invite men and women into saving relationship with God. This saving relationship both effects and requires a personal change of heart, which is the point of all the miracles illustrated in the healing stories. Schillebeeckx notes that this purpose is illuminated in the story of the ten lepers. All ten were made well, but another form of trust is operative here in the prospect of relationship with God in Jesus. Only one of the ten got the point. "In going back to Jesus he acknowledged that it was Jesus who afforded him God's help."⁶⁷

There is a subtle reversal at work here, it seems. While all along we have been leading up to the point of recognizing that it is *God* who acts in Jesus, Schillebeeckx seems now to be saying that, as true as this is, there is also something crucial about recognizing *Jesus*. It is not only a question of trust in God, the absolute, merciful reality to which Jesus points. It is a question of trust in Jesus as God's unique manner of being-among-us: the human being of God. There is something compelling and definitive about Jesus' humanity. What it is can only be experienced in personal encounter, but the New Testament provides images pointing to the experience that gives rise to the confession of faith.

Schillebeeckx presents Mark's image of the woman with the hemorrhage straining to touch the hem of Jesus' garment. This is not an image of magical power going out from Jesus but, rather, "a desperate gesture on the part of an ordinary woman full of trust. And 'she was healed.'"⁶⁸ Schillebeeckx points out that what is decisive here is the personal act of resorting to Jesus; the density of this image is increased by the miracle story of Jairus' daughter into which this narrative is woven. Schillebeeckx observes that, after the interruption and ensuing fatal development, "the faith with which you came to me, carry on with, is the eventual reply. The point is: to go on hoping against hope and clinging to Jesus and expecting from him the help of God. To 'persist in having faith' here is not having an overall trust directly in God, but turning here and now to the person of Jesus, who provides assurance of God's help."⁶⁹

As we follow Schillebeeckx in this focus on the importance of Jesus' own person, we might find his next observation almost contradictory. He notes that the problem in Nazareth was not that people didn't believe Jesus had power to work miracles, but that they didn't attribute this power to God. What he really means is that it is essential to hold both Jesus' humanity and the divine power at work in him together. The point of Jesus' ministry is to be the one who brings God's help, who proffers salvation. The problem in Nazareth is that "they were asking for miracles which would make no demand for metanoia or imply a call to fellowship with God."[70] Jesus' miracles can only be understood as works of the kingdom and can only reach people through faith. "Jesus' mission to Israel is a summons to faith."[71]

It is the Syro-Phoenician woman, Schillebeeckx suggests, who exemplifies the kind of faith that *should* be found in Israel (Mt 15:23ff). Jesus' reluctance to fulfill the request of a sufferer in this instance throws his earthly mission into relief against the backdrop of his post-resurrection identity, and differentiates pre-Easter and post-Easter faith. "Jesus' earthly mission is that of 'Son of David' to Israel, while only with the resurrection is he revealed as 'the universal Christ.'" We find ourselves here on the dividing line between the concrete particularity of the historical Jesus and his identity as universal saviour. It is a densely ambiguous line, the crossing of which entails the paschal journey.

THE MYSTICISM OF THE CROSS AND NEGATIVE CONTRAST EXPERIENCE

The meaning of the paschal journey in Christian history has too often been concentrated in the symbol of the cross taken out of context and raised up in an isolation that glorified suffering and death for their own sake. Schillebeeckx's interpretation of the meaning of the cross in Jesus' life must be understood in conjunction with the centrality of what he has called Jesus' "Abba experience."[72] Jesus' relationship with God is the defining experience of his life, the ground of his being and the source of his mission.[73] That mission is the proclamation of the reign of justice and love, the fulfillment of the eschatological promise. It is precisely here that Jesus' concrete, historical particularity finds its force and meaning. And it is here that Schillebeeckx's insistence upon God as the *positive* ground and horizon of all negative experiences of suffering becomes evident. If Schillebeeckx has a manifesto, it is that in Jesus we as Christians discover a God whose cause is the cause of human beings, a God "bent on humanity." God's self-gift took definitive form in Jesus of Nazareth. And Jesus' life exemplified God's own "non-alienating self-emptying in favor of the other"[74] to the point of death. Schillebeeckx emphasizes Jesus' life and mission not to diminish the role of his suffering and death, but to preserve the crucifixion's critical and productive force. Jesus' manner of living and relating made tangible the message he proclaimed. Schillebeeckx's strongest identification of Jesus as eschatological prophet reflects the ways Jesus concretized God's promised future in his human presence and the living response it evoked.

The most powerful image of that enfleshment, as Schillebeeckx presents it, is that of Jesus' table-fellowship. Jesus at table with all classes of people in diverse situations becomes the paradigm for the kingdom, an image of the fulfillment of Gospel praxis. Some of Schillebeeckx's section headings in the *Jesus* book might be viewed as "cameos" of who Jesus is as eschatological prophet and bringer-of-salvation from God:

> *Jesus' caring and abiding presence among people, experienced as salvation coming from God.*
> *Being sad in Jesus' presence an existential impossibility: his disciples "do not fast."*
> *Jesus' eating and drinking in fellowship with his own and with "outcasts," tax-gatherers and sinners, brings freedom and salvation.*
> *The eschatological messenger of God's openness toward sinners.*
> *Jesus as host: a copious gift of God.*[75]

The relationality of these images of Jesus accurately reflects the relational ground of his being in, with, and for God—a God who is *for* humanity. Jesus' unique relationship with the God whom he addressed as "Abba" can be gleaned only from his consistent message and concrete manner of life. Schillebeeckx notes that "apart from a few cases . . . , Abba (a secular term, taken from family life) does not occur in Jesus' time in the language of prayer addressed to God." Yet, unusual as it is, the use of the term and the simple, unaffected relationship it implies is characteristic of Jesus.[76] There is no possible ground in the human history of disaster for the assurance of salvation that Jesus imparts; there is no basis for the hope of a future opened up by God that he proclaims—except in the experience of contrast which Jesus knows in the depths of his own being-in-relationship with God. Jesus thus "identifies himself in person with the cause of God as that also of humanity, and with the cause of humanity as God's cause."[77]

Thus, the rejection of Jesus' message and ministry effects the decisive turning point in his life. The unutterable depth of his experience of the world's resistance lay in the union of his life and purpose with God. In an incomparable way, Jesus knew the extremes of "negative contrast experience," the "refractory nature of a reality that resists all human plans."[78] His deepest core was shaken by reality's defeat, not of his human plans, but of God's plan, a plan for humanity's wholeness and well-being. Jesus had shared fully God's "risky trust" in humanity, he had surrendered himself in his own irrevocable trust in God. This experience of the defeat of God's plan in him was the beginning of his experience of death, and his sustained trust in God in the face of all resistance was the beginning of his experience of resurrection and the vindication of God's plan. Though Schillebeeckx does not say it in quite this way, he seems to mean that experiences of negative contrast mysteriously bring us to the heart of God's purposes for us.[79] It is in the face of the world's negativity that we see and experience the power of Jesus' unbroken trust in God. *This* inviolable thread of communion with God standing in resistance to the evil of the world is the heart of Christian faith. This, for Schillebeeckx, is what resurrection faith proclaims.

The Cross: Obedience unto Life

But what of the cross? This dominant and powerful symbol of Christian faith must have some meaning of its own. This is attested to wherever human beings come up against their own impotence in the face of suffering. Schillebeeckx maintains that Jesus' suffering and death must be contemplated precisely in light of his life of positive trust in God. Jesus' lived manifestation of God's "pure positivity" not only remained intact, but achieved its greatest intensity during the crucifixion experience. In the obedience he lived, Jesus knew a double suffering. In sharing the lot of the poor and outcast who were his chosen companions, he opened himself to the suffering he sought to alleviate. And, perhaps more profoundly, he suffered the ongoing pain of rejection as those most in need of God's saving truth turned away from his preaching. "Like God, Jesus preferred to identify himself with the outcast and the rejected, the 'unholy,' so that he himself ultimately became the Rejected, the Outcast."[80] But this double suffering was inseparable from his positive mission to stand unceasingly against evil and the sin of the world while proclaiming with his life God's all-embracing love. And, when evil threatened to consume him, it was Jesus' "Abba experience" that sustained him in his life praxis. Jesus' unbroken communion with God empowered the preaching that challenged structures of evil and oppression and thus brought him to the cross. Yet, negative contrast entered even into Jesus' Abba experience. For this communion was not always experienced as presence. In the experience of failure and abandonment, God's presence—even to Jesus—was experienced only darkly as absence. And, in this dark absence, Jesus' trust attained its truest form. Jesus' utter surrender to the mercy of God throughout his life brought him not only to, but through, death. It is Jesus' love to the point of death, rather than death itself, which is salvific. This is what Schillebeeckx means when he says that "we are not redeemed thanks to the death of Jesus, but despite it."[81]

The New Testament reveals that the struggle to make sense of the historical fact of the crucifixion gave rise to three complexes of tradition, existing side by side.[82] The three emerging traditions were all based on the Gospels' unanimous understanding that Jesus had embraced death on the cross freely. They include a) the contrast-scheme of Jesus as eschatological prophet-martyr; b) Jesus' death as part of God's plan of salvation in history; and c) Jesus' death as redemptive atonement, not only willed but required by God as sacrifice.[83] The first of these interprets Jesus' death as the destiny of a metanoia prophet, in line with Israel's history and with the message of John the Baptist. Jesus' call for repentance and obedience to God's law arouses the wrath of his opponents, who are undermined by his authenticity. The age-old Jewish contrast between God's law and human laws comes into focus here, and Jesus' "martyrdom" comes to be seen as divine endorsement. "One might say that no intrinsic significance is attributed to Jesus' death 'in itself,' but that it gives expression to the fact that Jesus' person and ministry and prophetic career is itself the 'light of the world.'"[84]

The second complex of tradition sees Jesus' death as part of the divine economy of salvation. The cross was a scandal, understood in the Hebrew scriptures as a terrible curse, an anathema, and experienced by early Jewish-Christians as an embarrassment. This led believers to develop a kind of apologetics for this occurrence in the life of the one they now called Lord. Here the legacy of the "suffering righteous one," variously developed in the Hebrew testament, figures heavily. This translates into the "divine must" of the suffering of the Son of Man in Mark's gospel as an essential prerequisite for "being glorified." Even here, there is no soteriological significance attributed to Jesus' death *per se*. In line with the Jewish tradition, it is the righteousness of the suffering one that is exalted and glorified; neither the suffering nor the death are salvific, but rather the righteousness and fidelity that lead to it. At this point, the salvation-economy scheme overlaps with the eschatological prophet-martyr scheme.

The third complex of tradition, the soteriological scheme, does not rest upon any supportable base in Jewish scripture and spirituality. The idea of Jesus' death as a redemptive, atoning sacrifice for human sin has no reliable antecedents. Schillebeeckx explains that this is not contradicted by 1 Cor. 15:3–5, which begins "For I handed on to you as of first importance what I also received: Christ died for our sins in accordance with the Scriptures." The strands of tradition in this passage "are themselves the product of a longer process of reflection and merging together of traditions."[85] Moreover, attempts to read into Isaiah 53 the theme of the suffering messiah also prove baseless.

> As it turns out, therefore, the soteriological formulae form a very old and self-contained complex of tradition, the emergence of which cannot be accounted for either by secondary deduction from other interpretations of Jesus' death or by referring it to Jewish theologies of the martyr's vicarious suffering. All such interpretations come up against difficulties presented by the history of tradition, as well as the absence from the oldest stratum of the *hyper* formulae of any reference to Isa. 53, in spite of the material affinities.[86]

The last possible basis for the soteriological interpretation of Jesus' death must be sought, Schillebeeckx suggests, in clues left by Jesus in his dealings with his intimate friends at the end of his life. Clearly, Jesus was conscious that he faced death at the hands of his opponents, and he tried to prepare his friends for the shock of it. The Last Supper accounts depict an intentional farewell meal in which Jesus effectually integrates his approaching death into his life and mission. Schillebeeckx maintains that even elements that seem to lend soteriological significance to Jesus' death ultimately point to his life. "Jesus' whole life is the hermeneusis of his death. The very substance of salvation is sufficiently present in it."[87] The institutionalized remembrances of the Last Supper which depict Jesus' death as "ransom for the many" must be interpreted within the context of this meal as symbolic of Jesus' entire life of service. It is Jesus' life freely given in service throughout his days that "ransoms" or saves us. Schillebeeckx urges us to see the Last Supper in relation to all the meals of Jesus. It is in the sharing and fellowship signified by the meals that God's offer of salvation resides. "But such fellowship 'in face of approaching death' assumes within this total context a very pregnant significance."[88] That significance lies in a twofold fidelity. First, Jesus maintains radical confidence in God's faithfulness to him and to the promise of salvation, despite all impending evidence to the contrary. Jesus will not countenance the possibility that his coming death has the power to thwart God's plan. Second, his final sharing of a meal in the face of death confirms the bonds he has established with and among his friends and disciples as the very substance of God's rule. Even imminent suffering and death cannot wipe out this reality. *This* reality of communion is the essence of salvation vindicated by the resurrection.

Herein lies the clue to the meaning of the cross vis-à-vis the negative contrast experience of human suffering in our world. Jesus' death on the cross gains its meaning from his own integration of it into the whole of his life of fidelity to God and God's cause (the cause of humanity). Unwavering faithfulness to God and solidarity with men and women both lead to the cross *and* define its meaning.[89] Jesus' words and gestures in his farewell meal both prepare his followers for the cataclysm to come and point them to the ultimate meaning of the crucifixion. The intimacy of bread-breaking, the humility of foot-washing, the hope of the cup shared now as pledge of the future: These define the cross by sustaining, transcending, and thus contextualizing it. Life frames death.

Death on a cross was not what Jesus expected as the outcome of his life's mission when he was baptized in the Jordan; nor did he imagine such an end during the earliest days of his public ministry. Along the way, however, the prospect of death became increasingly inevitable. While the cross signaled the historical failure of Jesus' life project, it was foreshadowed by earlier failures as Jesus soberly came to grips with the rejection of his message and work. Schillebeeckx makes it very clear that Jesus' mission in Galilee was a failure, and he knew it. It was in this grim knowledge that Jesus moved away from Galilee and toward Jerusalem, despite the protective warnings of his companions. He was still seeking with a more concentrated, focused strategy to succeed in promoting the mission entrusted to him. He himself could not know that his very failure would become integral to God's plan. Indeed, it is only in full realization of the ambivalence of Jesus' experience that we can even speak of the cross as part of the divine economy of salvation. Dimensions of Jesus' mission were hidden even from him in his humanity. Just as Jesus integrated his approaching death into his life's mission, so God incorporated the fiasco of the cross into the plan of salvation. Jesus' earthly career came to such an end because of human inability to receive and believe the very substance of salvation in ordinary life, but God chose to use even that refusal to further the divine/human project. In a real way, God uses what human beings supply to accomplish our salvation in ways beyond our imagining.

Here, in what is, humanly speaking, the fiasco and failure of the cross, we enter upon the core of mysticism.[90] We have referred variously to the peculiar cognitive force of suffering, the epistemological priority of suffering, and the privileged locus of revelation in suffering.[91] This kind of knowing, issuing from what Schillebeeckx pervasively refers to as "negative contrast experience," is the truest form of mysticism. It is, in fact, the closest we can come to a contemporary understanding of the mysticism of the cross.

> Contrast experience, . . . especially in recollection of man's [*sic*] actual history of accumulated suffering, has a critical cognitive value and force of its own, which are not reducible to a purposive *Herrschaftwissen* (the form of knowledge proper to science and technology) or to the diverse forms of contemplative, aesthetic and ludic "goal-less" knowledge.[92]

Negative contrast experience exercises a critical function with regard to both forms of knowledge and is, Schillebeeckx maintains, the only genuine dialectical link between the two. "The particular cognitive value of the passive contrast experience is a knowledge which demands a future and opens it up."[93]

The cross itself depicts the utter extreme of passive contrast experience, revealing its meaning *only* through contrast, only via the pathway to a still unseen future that opens up purely through anguished longing and unquenched hope. Indeed, the passion of Jesus is, for Schillebeeckx, the part of the christological narrative where Jesus himself truly is passive. In the first of what Schillebeeckx discerns as three phases in Jesus' process of identification, Jesus is the active subject of the narrative, his identity clarified by his own words and actions. "However, a violent contrast appears with the passion narrative . . . now the centre of the stage is taken by . . . a suffering man whose claims have evidently proved to be a failure."[94] Here, Jesus' identity is clarified by what others do to him. He becomes defenseless and vulnerable, confronted with the threat of failure as he is delivered into the hands of his enemies. At this point, the connection between Jesus of Nazareth and the Christ becomes ambiguous. The disciples do not understand, nor can they connect this humiliated figure to the coming kingdom of God. "At this point of the account there is uncertainty about the identity of Jesus, and the failure of Jesus, which takes place before [the disciples'] very eyes, has a decisive role to play here."[95] Only the fullness of the story, including the crucifixion and resurrection, will ultimately reveal what that role is.[96] In the meantime, as Schillebeeckx describes the heart of the struggle at Gethsemane,

Jesus "entrusted to God what from a human point of view seemed to be the failure of his message."[97] Faithfulness does not "save" Jesus from his earthly fate. Disarmed and disarming, yet resisting all that would break his communion in trust, Jesus still endures the cross.

In the passion, what had been Jesus' active preaching and praxis of God's reign becomes the trusting surrender to the God of the promise that is itself a passive resistance to evil. And precisely there, in Jesus' existential experience of helplessness, "God brings about in the one who had been faithful to him the divine success."[98] And God accomplishes this without power or compulsion. That our salvation should be accomplished at precisely this meeting point of God's vulnerability and our human freedom is paradoxically fitting. How this is so is revealed nowhere more than in the human experience of incomprehensible suffering. "Human suffering and the problem of evil go hand in hand with our history as a permanently thriving 'epiphenomenon' of our localized freedom."[99] Salvation, which has to do with suffering, has also to do with the sin that is original in us. And that is, essentially, the disease infecting our personal and collective freedom, a suffering in its own right. More original in us, however, is the graced justice in which we were created, our positive ground and horizon. If salvation is the utter restoration of our alienated being, then it must occur at the point of our utter freedom (or potential for freedom). In actual human experience at its best, freedom is limited; in the all-too-common experiences of damage and disaster marked by both suffering and evil, freedom is often profoundly crippled, distorted beyond recognition. It is precisely here, in the contrast experiences wrought by un-freedom, that God reverences the gift of freedom at our core—*especially* when it is marred beyond recognition. Into this nadir of negative humanity God comes, drawing absolutely near, in defenseless vulnerability. This is the reality that Jesus experienced upon the cross; this is the reality of every scene of human suffering that we can imagine. It is an unseen reality, experienced only in faith.

But what of all the instances of suffering in which persons of faith *do not* experience this unseen reality of God's saving nearness? Indeed, what of Jesus' own cry of abandonment? Jesus' being was sundered, severed from the meaning that sustained his life, stripped of the promise and every vestige of hope. The final agony of the cross plunged him into a darkness more painful than the nails that pierced his flesh. His sense of abandonment by God was real; it was existentially excruciating. And the words of the psalmist that Mark and Matthew place in his mouth accurately evoke Jesus' felt experience. Schillebeeckx points us, however, to the whole psalm as the context in which we must hear Jesus' cry. The development of the twenty-second psalm reveals the power of both remembrance and future hope. Excruciating images of present suffering are thrown into contrastive relief by vivid memories of God's acts of deliverance and mercy in the past; these memories enable the psalmist to praise God in the midst of trial, and to proclaim a future full of hope.[100] Ultimately, the psalmist recognizes that, unseen and unfelt by him, God was more than near; God was his sustaining presence amidst dark agony.

So, too, Jesus. So, too, every suffering person who lashes out at the God who cannot be found. Deeply influenced by the Flemish mystic, Ruysbroeck, Schillebeeckx speaks of God's presence in suffering as "dark light" and "mediated immediacy."[101] God is the mystical substratum of our life, always already there, even if all we experience is dark absence. Jesus knew this agony in an incomparable way, in inverse proportion to the unique and certain intensity with which he had always experienced God's presence. Thus, he is the guarantor that in every suffering experience of God's absence this felt absence is itself the mediation of God's immediate and absolute nearness.

How can we as Christians know this, or trust this guarantor? How can we trust that God's positive rule is already begun in the earthly words and actions of Jesus? How can we believe that the evil that overwhelms so much of human life really has no future? How can human beings cling to hope in suffering when all seeking of God is met with silence? Schillebeeckx points precisely to the role of silence in dialogue. God is silent in our earthly life, listening to our life story. Full of reverence for our unique personhood and freedom, God listens lovingly and will not interrupt. Only after our death does this divine silence take on a voice and face that we can recognize.[102] "As long as the Eternal One is still listening to our life story of fifty or even a hundred years the eternal God indeed seems to us to be powerless and defenceless. In this there is both a desperate trial for our historical existence and at the same time an experience full of hope and expectation."[103]

Indeed, we may be inclined to temper Schillebeeckx's description of an "experience full of hope and expectation," conscious as we are of how distant hope is from so many who are suffering. Still, Schillebeeckx speaks ultimately from the point of view of resurrection faith. It is only the resurrection that enables us to speak meaningfully of the mysticism of the cross at all. It is only resurrection faith that makes possible the meaning of contrast in the negative experience of suffering. And here Schillebeeckx also gives us a clue as to the role of suffering in forging a profoundly human and authentic experience of resurrection faith. "Within the defencelessness of our own lives we must be able to *experience* the superior power of God: otherwise we accept it with a faith which is presented as purely authoritarian."[104]

The resurrection, then, is the culmination of Jesus' fidelity which is tested in the depths of his own "negative contrast experience." It is, for Schillebeeckx, God's last word and corrective over the negativity of suffering and death. Moreover, it is a corrective whose power lies beneath negativity in the "mercy and compassion of God at the heart of all reality." The resurrection proclaims to us that the redemptive truth that Jesus' death points to is the message of his life's preaching and praxis. Despite all earthly failure, Jesus' fidelity to God and God's to him opens a future beyond death which belongs to all who share in this mission to the *humanum*. The continuity of this mutual fidelity was never broken, though it seemed to disappear from view during the second narrative period of Jesus' life, the period of divine and human defenselessness in the passion. Now, in the third narrative phase, the period after his death, Jesus' identity is clarified by what God does to him. Schillebeeckx remarks that "it is striking how the reader can feel in every verse that here only God is at work . . . although there is hardly any mention of God in the biblical accounts of the experiences."[105] And *we* might remark that Jesus' identification on the basis of what God does to him defines him still as a passive character in the drama. But Schillebeeckx explains,

> Only Jesus, the living one, is the active subject here and himself expresses his identity: he restores the relationship between "this Jesus" (the man from Nazareth) and "the Christ,'" which had become problematical for the disciples. The unexpressed interweaving of "Jesus" and "God" is more evocative here than elsewhere. If Jesus' own initiative disappeared in the previous sequence (the passion narrative), in the resurrection stories everything again happens on the initiative of Jesus, which *coincides with* the absolute initiative of God: only Jesus' appearance (in the account of the resurrection appearances) suggests that God is actively at work here. The composition is masterly, but at the same time unique in its theological concentration. Jesus himself, the man from Nazareth, is the presence of the action of God with us, during his life and also after his death. What seem to be failure and disaster "by human standards" (*kata sarka*, II Cor. 4.11; cf.4.16), and indeed are so on this level, become redemption and victory when seen in the spirit.[106]

This passage evokes the very heart of Schillebeeckx's christology vis-à-vis the question of human suffering. In fact, we may extrapolate that there simply is no other human context for understanding the nature of christology apart from suffering. Schillebeeckx has repeatedly shown that the only glimpse we have of salvation is through the longing that emanates from negative contrast experience in suffering.

> In a word, *christology*, the identification of the person of Jesus in faith, is the specifically human answer to the life-sized problem of human failure. It is the resurrection which gives the lie to the failure of the message and the life of Jesus, and at the same time to merely human conceptions of what 'real success' can and must mean.[107]

The continuity of our life praxis with the life praxis of Jesus, *orthopraxy*, is, then, an essential component of Schillebeeckx's understanding of the resurrection. The ongoing experience of discipleship, the life of the Church, flows from and toward the resurrection experience. Schillebeeckx distinguishes the scriptural accounts of resurrection appearances as *models*. In the completed New Testament texts, the conversion process of the disciples after the death of Jesus became encapsulated in appearance narratives. The reality of the *kerygma* behind these texts is not in question for Schillebeeckx. What is in question is the way the appearance narratives have traditionally been understood. And here we encounter perhaps the most radical import of the influence upon Schillebeeckx of hermeneutics, critical theory, and modern biblical exegesis. What emerges is an indication of the precise way in which the human experience of suffering is a privileged locus of revelation. That is, Schillebeeckx's own, intuitive analyses of the resurrection accounts model in unique and compelling fashion how particular experiences of suffering give rise to the graced knowing that is faith's ultimate authority.

The Role of the Experience of Suffering in Resurrection Faith

The appearance narratives that express resurrection faith arise from a source experience in which Jesus was disclosed to the disciples as living beyond death. Schillebeeckx describes the Easter experience as a process of conversion that became articulated in New Testament texts in the mode of traditional Jewish conversion models. Each instance of Jesus' appearing was unique, intimate, and marked by a renewal and transformation of life after hope had been lost. Along with the alleviation of suffering, in each instance the disciple experienced in greater fullness a joy and sense of self that had been fragmentarily known in relationship to the earthly Jesus. This does not mean that Schillebeeckx interprets the resurrection as a purely subjective experience on the part of the disciples. Yet, he decries the broadly assumed, albeit unreflective, notion of resurrection as an encounter with a "resuscitated corpse." Schillebeeckx maintains that

> the objective cannot be separated from the subjective aspect of the apostolic belief in the resurrection. Apart from the faith-motivated experience it is not possible to speak meaningfully of Jesus' resurrection. It would be like talking about "colours" to somebody blind from birth. Without being identical with it, the resurrection of Jesus—that is, what happened to him, personally, after his death—is inseparable from the Easter experience, or faith-motivated experience, of the disciples: that is to say, from their conversion process, in which they perceive the work of the Spirit of Christ. . . . *Apart from this experience of Christian faith the disciples had no organ that could afford them a sight of Jesus' resurrection.* But besides this subjective aspect it is equally apparent that . . . no Easter experience of renewed life was possible without the personal resurrection of Jesus—in the sense that Jesus' personal-cum-bodily resurrection . . . precedes any faith-motivated experience.[108]

Attention to the italicized sentence in the above passage (italics mine) will bear fruit in this discussion. It is pivotal to any understanding of the nature of Schillebeeckx's insight into the meaning of the resurrection experience. And this insight has everything to do with the epistemological priority of particular experiences of suffering.[109]

The disciples had no organ that could afford them a sight of Jesus' resurrection, because a glorified, resurrected body cannot be seen with earthly eyes.[110] In being raised by God from the dead, Jesus, though living, was transformed beyond earthly seeing. Schillebeeckx does not, as some suggest, deny the bodily resurrection of Jesus. He simply and sensibly asserts that we do not know what this means.[111] We know from the testimony of the disciples that Jesus was encountered after his death as *alive*. We know, too, that there is no separation of body and soul. If the soul is the body's life-principle, then the body is equally the manifestation of the soul. A person's manner of being in the world is in his or her body. How that embodied being is transposed into life beyond death is mystery. All we know—all Schillebeeckx knows—is that incarnational faith entails the integrity of body and soul.

Thus there is no organ for seeing the risen Jesus, unless we understand the *experience of faith* as a manner of seeing. Schillebeeckx's discussion of the kerygmatic tradition reflected in the Pauline letters is helpful here. Paul does not speak of appearances in all of his kerygmatic texts, but Schillebeeckx notes that "where Paul is taking the identity of belief among the Christian churches as the point of departure for a theological argument, the tradition of Christian belief in the resurrection is conjoined with that of Jesus' appearances."[112] In the pre-Pauline tradition and in Luke there is an emphasis on what is called "the appearing." The emphasis turns on phrases to the effect that Jesus "showed himself" or "made himself seen" (1 Cor. 15:3–8). The appearances are described as the initiative of Jesus himself.[113] Schillebeeckx would have us understand that Paul is reacting to a false idea of resurrection among the Corinthians. He wants to establish the common identity of faith among the churches—a universal faith. To this end, he provides, not a list of living witnesses to the resurrection, but "a list of authorities who all proclaim the same thing, namely, that the crucified One is alive; one and the same evidential ground of faith inspires them all."[114]

The primacy of experience as it has developed in Schillebeeckx's theological method is crystallized here. Paul's concern is ours; it is certainly Schillebeeckx's. Whence comes the authority to proclaim the risen Christ? What is the common ground lending Christian faith its universality?[115] What, ultimately, is the basis of revelation? Schillebeeckx's interpretation of Christianity's central doctrine of the resurrection is a pivotal testing ground.

Holding firm to the cognitive value of the experience of faith, Schillebeeckx emphasizes both the subjective and the objective aspects of resurrection faith over against all objectivistic and subjectivistic one-sidedness. This means that the "object"—Jesus' personal and corporeal resurrection and exaltation with God— and the "subject"—the experience of faith which is expressed in Scripture— cannot be separated.[116] Schillebeeckx separates himself from trends identifying Jesus' resurrection with the new life discovered by the disciples, though he asserts this as one dimension of the resurrection experience.[117] He equally denies that resurrection faith is purely interpretative remembrance of the pre-Easter Jesus—although, again, this is an element of the experience. He adds, however, that after Jesus' death there must have been new experiences: a new offer of salvation.[118]

What Schillebeeckx has to say about how the disciples received this new offer of salvation is crucial to our understanding of the experience of suffering in his theology and as a privileged locus of revelation. The impact of the Pauline listing of witnesses noted above is that the experience of the risen Lord is the basis of authority for mission. Experience makes one a witness and issues in narration, opening up the possibility of new life for others.[119] The underlying implication of the naming of a variety of witnesses has to do with the significance of the unique life context of each individual receiving this revelation. This implication becomes an assertion in the contrast between the resurrection appearances to Mary Magdalene and to Peter. In each case, the encounter with the risen Jesus bears the imprint of a uniquely personal experience of suffering.

Schillebeeckx acknowledges that "diverse traditions tell us that Jesus' very first appearance was to Mary Magdalene."[120] (Yet, the first "official" report is attributed to Peter, as the testimony of women in those days was not valid.)[121] Schillebeeckx's reading of each of these accounts has something to tell us about the cognitive value of suffering for particular experiences of faith.

SUFFERING, SITUATEDNESS, AND "SEEING"

Mary's encounter with the risen Jesus reflected the uniqueness of her life experience. Into her present experience of grief and loss comes the real presence of the One whom she mourns.[122] Schillebeeckx focuses here on the significance of the life Mary had regained through the conversion brought about through relationship with the earthly Jesus. In the wake of his death, she questioned again the meaning of that renewed life, "until there came to her the loving assurance that this life regained was stronger than death. This Jesus lived."[123] For Mary Magdalene, the encounter with the risen Jesus was an experience of assurance: confirmation of the fundamental conversion she had already experienced, and empowerment to extend this experience to others in a new era. She and the other women had remained faithful and present throughout the trial, the scandal, the crucifixion. Their fidelity, akin to Jesus' own fidelity to God even through the seeming disintegration of God's plan, was now vindicated.

Peter's experience is a different story. He and the male disciples, for the most part, had not remained faithful and present through Jesus' ordeal. Rather, they had scattered in fear. Their experience of grief after Jesus' death included deep guilt and paralyzing remorse over the memory of their betrayal. Schillebeeckx notes: "Thus, they are in need of conversion: to resume the task of 'being a disciple' and 'imitating Jesus.' But the first condition for that is the experience of having received forgiveness from Jesus—a quite specific experience of grace and mercy."[124]

This "quite specific experience of grace and mercy" is precisely what is entailed in the encounter with the risen Jesus. For Peter and the eleven, this is necessarily experienced as a process of conversion and reconciliation. "Fundamentally," Schillebeeckx asserts, "'conversion' entails a relationship (a) to him whom the disciples had let down: Jesus of Nazareth, and (b) to him to whom they return: Jesus as the Christ."[125] The total picture of their experience with Jesus, in the context of each of their concrete lives, is essential to this process. In his company they had come to know the "God of unconditional mercy and forgiveness." This memory in the midst of guilt's isolation was transforming. It was not, however, the essence of the resurrection experience. In Schillebeeckx's parlance, we might say it was the pre-understanding essential for their encounter with the risen Jesus. It was, indeed, the mode of their faith at that time—their poor faith. For, Schillebeeckx observes, they had not *lost* their faith in Jesus; indeed, they had failed, but it was a failure due to weakness rather than deliberate disloyalty.[126] And the state that failure left them in became the mode of their encounter—albeit an encounter initiated by God in Christ. In this encounter, the offer of relationship is renewed. It is a *new* offer of salvation, and, though unique, it is recognizable on the basis of remembered touchstones. Once accepted, it becomes the means by which relationships among the community of disciples are restored. Thus, for Schillebeeckx, the regathering of the community that is presupposed by the appearance stories is a *result* of the disciples' experience in faith of the risen one. This regathering is the foundation of the Church.

The source experience beneath what have been called "appearance stories" is God's initiative in Christ. *Jesus made himself seen.* That seeing was no earthly seeing, but neither was it a psychological construct on the part of the disciples. The appearance stories point to a real event within the context of salvation-history:

> the "vision" model is a means of articulating an event engendered by grace, a divine, salvific initiative—a grace manifesting itself in historical events and human experiences. In other words, the reporting of what occurred in the guise of appearances indicates the process whereby Peter and his friends were brought together again after their dispersal was felt by them to be an act of sheer grace on God's part.[127]

The disciples' experience of forgiveness is the *disclosure experience* verbally embodied in the "appearance models." Within this disclosure experience is the real revelation of Christ. As Schillebeeckx puts it, "They all of a sudden saw it."[128]

This *seeing* is the kind of experience that is revelatory. And, to paraphrase a popular cliché, what and how one sees depends upon where one is standing. Schillebeeckx would say that the background or horizon against which something is seen becomes "an intrinsic element of one's perception."[129] Schillebeeckx, who repeatedly asserts that all experience is interpreted experience, goes so far as to say that *seeing* is somehow deeper than interpreting. "The element of identification lies in the experience itself."[130] Thus contrasting backgrounds of Mary Magdalene and Peter indicate that their ways of "seeing" Jesus, their respective experiences of the risen one, were unique. They were two different people, with two very different sets of experiences of the earthly Jesus and his ministry. To generalize somewhat, it is fairly self-evident throughout the Gospels that the women, and Mary Magdalene in particular, are more intuitively attuned to Jesus' purposes than the male apostles. Peter, typically, is portrayed as resistant and slow to "get it." Mary and Peter each enter into the Easter experience with a unique memory and in a unique state of being. Mary is grieving, perhaps doubting, but not guilty. She is still about the business of attending to Jesus in concrete ways. Peter, on the other hand *is* in a state of guilty remorse; he is fearful and withdrawn. Thus Mary experiences the encounter with the risen Christ as assurance and rekindled hope. Peter experiences it as forgiveness and reconciliation. Both have encountered the same Lord; both are empowered to proclaim this surprising new life.

"They all of a sudden saw it." And they saw it from where they were standing. As the essential cognitivity of faith, this "seeing" is deeply conditioned by negative contrast experiences engendered through suffering. Ultimately, this represents the central force of the role of suffering in Schillebeeckx's maturing theological method.

CONCLUSION: "EXPERIENCE
WITH EXPERIENCES"[131]

The spiral of Edward Schillebeeckx's own experiences has constituted the matrix of his developing theological method. This chapter has traced, at new levels, the refractory influence of human suffering in dialectical relationship with each of the disciplines crucial to his evolving thought. Schillebeeckx's own experience was gradually transformed in dialogue with contemporary culture. That culture included rich intellectual developments; it also included breakdowns that challenged the structures of common presuppositions about human meaning. Unprecedented societal breakdowns in the wake of unprecedented technological progress led to the crisis of meaning and faith that is the continuing anthropological challenge of Schillebeeckx's theological endeavors. While his assimilation of hermeneutics and critical theory enabled him more effectively to engage the experiences of contemporary culture, it simultaneously enabled him more deeply to engage the original human experiences of divine disclosure beneath the New Testament texts. It is when scripture is experienced as "historied," and experienced thus from within a graced network of relationships in the present, that God's saving acts become known in the midst of present calamities, and a possible future opens up.

The model of Schillebeeckx's own experiencing of the hermeneutical spiral as theologian is important because it illustrates the process whereby suffering plays an increasingly authoritative role in the development of his theology. The indirect, dialectical manner in which the particular experience of suffering reveals God is both cause and effect of his theology's dynamic, relational nature. It is also a source of mistrust for many who do not, in the first place, trust "experience" of any kind as solidly based in objective reality. Schillebeeckx, however, operates out of a relational ontology in which we all participate in the divine reality because we all participate in creation—which is in God. "Experience" is not merely arbitrary feeling. From Schillebeeckx's phenomenological beginnings, it is a way of knowing, a concretely cognitive function.

Suffering experience carries a concentrated, if ambiguous, cognitive force. And here, the resurrection accounts provide a model of how such ambiguous suffering experience becomes authoritative. Indeed, Schillebeeckx calls the appearance stories "models" to emphasize their purpose in giving expression to an event uniquely personal and intimate, yet of universal significance. That event was an encounter of the disciples with a reality clearly "other," clearly inbreaking—and in that sense objective. They recognized this presence as Jesus risen. The reality was clearly other than themselves, and yet in it they recognized themselves in their deepest authenticity. They remembered what had been evoked in them by the earthly Jesus; now, remembering the familiar, yet startled by unexpected newness, they were transformed beyond their hopes or imaginings, and propelled into a new existence. This experience, unique for each disciple, had a common grounding and a common effect: It was initiated by Jesus and it issued in the praxis of a new community of justice and love. And *this* indicates the privileged role of suffering in the authority of human experience. Suffering, unwanted by humans and unwilled by God, nevertheless can forge wisdom and grace, and thus author new life. To understand the formative significance of suffering in the theology of Edward Schillebeeckx, it is necessary to understand and trust the authoritative role of experience as source for theology.

Focusing on these specific resurrection encounters serves to bridge Jesus' experience of the cross and the contemporary experience of the cross in concrete and varied instances of human suffering. Schillebeeckx knows that, if the gospel is to be alive and saving for human beings who suffer and doubt, it is incumbent upon theologians and preachers alike routinely to take hermeneutical risks in uncovering the reality of communion with God and each other in experiences of suffering. Critics who are disturbed by this approach evidently forget its biblical roots. They find this business of encounter with the "other," remembrance and recognition, dialectics and hope, too hard to pin down, too difficult to define, too risky to trust. But that is the very crux of the freedom and authority of a humanity that is the fundamental symbol of God, a humanity whose nature is shared by the second person of the Trinity. Such freedom and authority mirrors the God who risked creating, and then risked entrusting the divine creation to human beings.

When we trust the authority of our human experience, we share in the Creator's own risk. And God has been willing to risk our sin and our failure, even to the point of suffering the evil that our sin has wrought through the ages.

The suffering of the world is evidence that the risk is real, and failures abound. But the other side of God's risky trust in men and women is the divine desire for human wholeness and flourishing. God has risked our total freedom ("blank check") yet refuses to leave us alone with the damage that we do or the failure that we reap. We learn this in an incomparable way in experiences of negative contrast. There we find that the authority of suffering or of any human experience is not an individual property. Our experiencing core (at best, "faith-cognition") is, indeed, uniquely our own. But "experience" is beyond us; it includes a reality much larger than we are, which we encounter in the context of an expansive network of human relationships (and nonrelationships), a reality encompassing continents and centuries and transcending our world. All of this experience *we* experience in the context of the Creator God. But all is not God! Yet, God, who is faithful to our human cause, finds a way to be present even amid the negativity and suffering that the world confronts us with. Schillebeeckx affirms:

> Truth comes near to us by the alienation and disorientation of what we have already achieved and planned. . . . The hermeneutical principle for the disclosure of reality is not the self-evident, but the scandal, the stumbling block of the refractoriness of reality. . . . In such experiences of what proves completely refractory to all our inventions we shall also finally discover the basis for what we rightly call revelation.[132]

In the ordinary spectrum of life, when human beings struggle to find meaning, the positive contours of experience can emerge in fragmentary ways in the dialectic with negative experiences of contrast. There in the fissures and gaps, in the seeming breaks in logic and consistency—there truth emerges. There, for the believer, God shows Godself. There, in those dynamic fissures, experience discloses mercy at the heart of resistant reality.

The nuanced complexity of negative contrast experience emerges here, along with the indirect nature of revelation. Truth is not one-dimensionally revealed in the spaces of contrast between positive and negative experiences, or over against its opposite in the struggle between good and evil. It is revealed, rather, in the genuinely mystical places where reality resists our plans and alienates us from ourselves. "The experience of faith," Schillebeeckx reminds us, "is capable of living with doubt."[133] And so, experiences of suffering, of limitation—the boundaries imposed by "reality"—can be threatening or revelatory, depending upon our capacity to experience reality as a "gift by which God opens a future to humankind." Our own concrete, situated humanity is the sphere in which that future will be opened to us. This, ultimately, is the meaning of Jesus' humanity as salvation-coming-from-God. The cross has meaning in the context of Jesus' whole life-story, which culminates in the resurrection. God's act of raising Jesus from the dead gives the cross its meaning, as it confirms and illuminates the meaning of the whole of Jesus' life praxis. But none of this has any meaning for *our* humanity until we access Jesus' story through our own individual and communal stories. In a mysterious reversal, we then discover our own humanity anew, and find disclosed there the ultimate revelation of God. "In the light of Jesus Christ, the gospel itself is a hermeneutic of fundamental human experience. What speaks to us in Jesus is his being human, and thereby opening up to us the deepest possibilities of our own life, and *in this* God is expressed."[134]

But what about those experiences, of which the world is full, wherein suffering is so great as to deaden hope and the capacity for meaning or value? Early in this chapter the question arose: "How are we to understand the fact of human existence as a promise of salvation when, for so much of humanity, existence itself is overwhelmed by suffering?" Ultimately, it is only from the mysticism of the cross that this enigma can be approached. In the cross God is revealed as present in human life in all those situations where the horror of reality testifies against God's existence. The scandal and horror of the cross cannot be explained away; it remains, even in light of the resurrection. In this same way, the suffering of masses of humankind at this moment remains a scandal: horrible, and not willed by God. And even though such suffering is exacerbated by the deadening of hope, this suffering existence *still* is a promise of salvation: a salvation already begun in the agony of contrast forcing out the most elemental, instinctive resistance in the depths of even the most vanquished of human spirits.

It is easy, Schillebeeckx suggests, to trust in the promise where it is even only fragmentarily fulfilled. "Where good triumphs and suffering and death yield, God is confessed in practice. Certainly," Schillebeeckx counters, "but there is more and also something else: Jesus points out that salvation can also be achieved in suffering and in an unjust execution."[135] It is the cross that both constitutes and answers all of our "buts" at this point. In its dissonance, the cross achieves a strange harmony with the scandalous "remainder" of inexplicable, and especially innocent, human suffering. Citing the New Testament as a theological redefinition of both God and humanity, Schillebeeckx observes:

> Therefore the cross is also a judgment on our own views: a judgment on our ways of living out the meaning of being human and of being God. Here is revealed ultimately and definitively the humanity of God, the nucleus of Jesus' message of the kingdom of God: God who comes into his own *in* the world of human beings for their healing and happiness, even through suffering.[136]

The question asked through the ages, why God permitted the scandal of the cross in Jesus' life, continues to be asked whenever people are confronted with the mystery of suffering. It is framed most forcefully in relation to the sheer disproportion of disaster and violent inhumanity perennially plaguing the masses in some parts of the world, while select regions remain prosperous and free of threat. Schillebeeckx insists, "It was not God but men and women who put Jesus to death; at the same time, however, this execution is the material prepared for God's supreme self-revelation by human beings, as emerges from New Testament belief in the resurrection of Jesus."[137]

In this one statement the central elements of Schillebeeckx's theology are capsulized and the formative role of suffering illuminated. Schillebeeckx's creation-centered theology, in the tradition of Thomas Aquinas, presumes that human beings, participants in the divine nature, are partners in the ongoing work of creation. This ongoing work, in fact, is the work of salvation; for Schillebeeckx, creation and salvation comprise one continuous reality. Essential to that reality are the sovereignty of human freedom and the divine will to human flourishing. These elements formed the context in which human beings put Jesus to death on a cross, and they form the context in which evil and suffering appear today. God will not interfere with human choices or the processes of the natural world. Nevertheless, God's positive will is not thwarted. Human beings, in bringing about the execution of Jesus, prepared the material for God's supreme self-revelation. God did not will the execution of Jesus, but God allowed even that tragic, human-made material to play a part in the work of salvation, weaving it into hope, drawing from it unimaginable new life. That is why, in situations of the most abysmal suffering, where humanity is defeated, damaged beyond recognition, the cross is evoked. It is evoked not to glorify suffering or render us passive: quite the contrary. The cross is evoked as a mute gesture of solidarity with the one who reached the nadir of humiliation and pain without losing trust in the God who had brought him . . . to what? To this awful point of degradation and despair? Experientially, yes; but there was a deeper level of experience vindicated precisely here: Jesus' experience of communion with the One who had made the promise. Ultimately, this communion was his life; it was the life into which he invited others, it was the unvanquishable freedom that the powers of darkness feared and tried to quell. The resurrection is the culmination of this communion and the vindication of the defenseless, superior power of Jesus' vulnerability upon the cross.[138] In the light of resurrection faith, the unmitigated scandal of the cross evokes the depths of Jesus' unbroken communion with God throughout his life, wherein God's reign had already begun. Without the resurrection, the cross remains *only* a scandal, meaningless and absurd.

Both cross and resurrection witness to the force of Jesus' human life of praxis and preaching. It is to that humanity that we, as Christians, continuously return, each time with deeper reverence for the power and import of our own human story. That the human story is "ours" and that it is marked by suffering characterize the dimensions of life lived in continuity with the praxis of Jesus. Communion with God necessarily finds expression in solidarity with other human beings. Solidarity, especially with those who suffer, entails metanoia, which is the deepest meaning of obedience and the heart of political mysticism. Ultimately, it leads to reconciliation, the deepest meaning of the cross, and the meaning toward which all suffering points. The next chapter will consider how metanoia functions as the key to understanding how suffering is a formative factor in Schillebeeckx's theology.

NOTES

1. This point is noted repeatedly in the surveys of the tradition on original sin cited in the previous chapter. See, for example: Henri Rondet, *Original Sin: The Patristic and Theological Background;* Piet Schoonenberg, *Man and Sin;* and Anthony Padovano, *Original Sin and Christian Anthropology.*

2. Schillebeeckx, *Christ: The Experience of Jesus as Lord,* 795.

3. Schillebeeckx, *Christ,* 698–99; Nel Noddings critiques both the Augustinian fall construct and the Irenaean "soul-making" approach, opting instead for a "tragic sense of life" coinciding with a concept of a "more fallible" God. See Nel Noddings, *Women and Evil* (Berkeley: University of California, 1989), 17–26; Christian feminist studies incorporating a similar critique include Kathleen Sands, *Escape from Paradise: Evil and Tragedy in Feminist Theology,* and Marjorie Suchocki, *The Fall to Violence: Original Sin in Relational Theology;* the influence of John Hick's *Evil and the God of Love* is evident in all of these critiques; Noddings distinguishes her own use of the phrase "tragic sense of life" from that of male theodicists rooted in Kant's paradigm of moral self-responsibility; for a contemporary example of the latter, see Keith Yandell, "Tragedy and Evil," *International Journal for the Philosophy of Religion* 36 (1994): 1–26.

4. Schillebeeckx, "Can Christology Be an Experiment?" *Proceedings of the Catholic Theological Society of America* 35 (1980): 1–14.

5. Schillebeeckx, "Can Christology Be an Experiment?" 3.

6. Schillebeeckx, "Can Christology Be an Experiment?" 14.

7. For example, William Thompson outlines the "exclusivist," "relativist," and "inclusivist" christological arguments, himself opting for what he calls a "kenoticist inclusiveness" in line with the patristic *Logos* doctrine; he also addresses the problem that a "male saviour" poses for feminist consciousness, as well as the relationship of Jesus to developing ecological awareness. See William M. Thompson, *The Jesus Debate* (New York/Mahwah: Paulist, 1985), 385–400, and 419–27. More recently, the growing school of eco-feminism has challenged the anthropocentric as well as patriarchal, androcentric nature of traditional christology and soteriology. See, for example, Rita Nakashima Brock, *Journeys by Heart: A Christology of Erotic Power* (New York: Crossroad, 1991), Rosemary Radford Reuther, *Gaia and God: An Ecofeminist Theology of Earth Healing* (San Francisco: Harper San Francisco, 1992), and Sallie McFague, *Models of God: Theology for an Ecological Nuclear Age* (Philadelphia: Fortress, 1987), and *The Body of God: An Ecological Theology* (Minneapolis: Fortress, 1993).

8. Thomas O'Meara, addressing the question of the positioning of Christ in Part III of the *Summa Theologiae,* describes Aquinas's work as a pattern "that flows from God and includes human beings moving toward the eschaton. While Jesus of Nazareth, the Incarnate Word of God, is the pattern and cause of salvation, Aquinas evidently did not want to interrupt the broad sweep of the process of being and life, true of the past and of the present, coming from the Trinity to each man and woman. . . . Aquinas' arrangement

explains why in the Catholic mind Jesus is not the sole actor in salvation and why Spirit and liturgy, saints and sacraments are central." O'Meara counts Schillebeeckx among those contemporary Catholic theologians who reflect this "primacy of grace with a christological center in various degrees before, during, and after Jesus Christ." Thomas F. O'Meara, "Thomas Aquinas and Today's Theology," *Theology Today* 55, no. 1 (1998): 55; see 46–58.

9. Schillebeeckx notes contemporary correlates to the conclusion Aquinas reached at the end of his *quinque viae:* "Within a christian social context, he took as his point of departure the question raised by the world and postulated the need for an 'all-supporting ground,' for a non-christian pre-understanding. He identified this all-supporting ground with God, but this was not a conclusion of his proof of the existence of God, it was a profession of christian faith. From a rational argument, he concluded not to *ergo Deus existit,* but to *et hoc omnes dicunt Deum.* In other words, as a believer, he identified the end of his philosophical analysis, which led him from the empirical phenomena of human experience to an all-supporting point of reference, with the living God. This identification was not a philosophical transition, but a transition made in faith: Thomas indicated the point where christian talk about God becomes intelligible within the context of human experience, at least in medieval times." Schillebeeckx, "Human Question and Christian Answer," in *The Understanding of Faith,* 82–83.

10. Schillebeeckx, "Human Question and Christian Answer," 92.

11. Schillebeeckx, "Human Question and Christian Answer," 94. Schillebeeckx acknowledges German Nazism as the most striking example but cautions against any manipulation of essential human freedoms in service of an imposed ideal.

12. Schillebeeckx, "Human Question and Christian Answer," 94.

13. Schillebeeckx, "Human Question and Christian Answer," 95.

14. Schillebeeckx, *Christ: The Experience of Jesus as Lord,* 733; the published English translation reads *"permanent* human impulses"; Mary Catherine Hilkert suggests*"enduring"* as conveying a dynamism that rings truer to Schillebeeckx's intent. See "The Threatened *Humanum:* Insights from Edward Schillebeeckx," in *Proceedings of the Catholic Theological Society,* 1998.

15. Schillebeeckx, *Christ,* 734.

16. "Questions on Christian Salvation of and for Man," in Schillebeeckx, *The Language of Faith: Essays on Jesus, Theology, and the Church,* intro. Robert J. Schreiter (Nijmegen: Concilium, 1995), 114 see 109–26.

17. Chung Hyun Kyung recently made this assertion in an address entitled "Eco-Feminism and Asian Spirituality" (*Elliott Allen Institute,* University of St. Michael's College, Toronto, June 8, 1998); for elaboration, see her "Ecology, Feminism and African and Asian Spirituality: Towards a Spirituality of Eco-Feminism," in *Ecotheology,* ed. D. Hallman (Maryknoll, N.Y.: Orbis, 1994); for examples of North American perspectives on the evils of globalization as a manifestation of Western patriarchy, see Anne M. Clifford, "When Being Human Becomes Truly Earthly: An Ecofeminist Proposal for Solidarity," in *The Embrace of God,* ed. Ann O'Hara Graff, 173–89, as well as the works of Rosemary Radford Ruether and Sallie McFague previously cited.

18. Schillebeeckx, *Christ,* 736.

19. This may be seen as a further development of Schillebeeckx's roots in the personalist phenomenology of Maurice Merleau-Ponty, evidenced in his early examples of

human relational encounter in the 1959 publication *Christ: The Sacrament of the Encounter with God*, 77–79.

20. Levinas, a prominent influence in postmodern philosophy, was, like Schillebeeckx, schooled in phenomenology, though specifically via Heidegger and Husserl. For him, far more is encountered in a "face" than the individual human other. All human beings are positioned within a totality; that totality "is manifested in a face in which being confronts me." Emmanuel Levinas, *Collected Philosophical Papers*, trans. Alphonso Lingis (The Netherlands: Nijoff Publishers, 1987), 28.

21. Schillebeeckx, *Christ*, 737.

22. Schillebeeckx, *Christ*, 737.

23. Schillebeeckx, *Christ*, 738; this hearkens back to concerns Schillebeeckx expressed in his earliest engagements with hermeneutics and critical theory: see n.8 above; cf. also Schillebeeckx's discussion of dysfunctional relationships and elements of compulsion operating within social structures, "The New Critical Theory," in *The Understanding of Faith*, 113.

24. Schillebeeckx, *Christ*, 65.

25. The experience of powerlessness that Schillebeeckx speaks of as "contingency" and "limit situation" is integral to the redefining of evil and suffering emerging from contemporary feminist ethics. Nel Noddings locates the phenomenological basis of evil in the affective conditions of pain, separation, and helplessness. See Noddings, *Women and Evil*, 129. Elizabeth Johnson gives credence to this analysis in her reflection upon suffering women whose grieving solidarity images God's compassion poured out. Speaking of how women's relational way of being in the world renders them vulnerable to desolation over the suffering visited upon loved ones, Johnson criticizes the Western preponderance of definitions of evil based on disobedience to divine law, and thus on sin. I read this as consonant with (rather than contradictory of) my own interpretation of "obedience" as relational trust and communion in Schillebeeckx's theology. In this rendering, references to "sin" at the root of evil and suffering in Schillebeeckx's understanding have everything to do with the breach of relationship. This relational connotation has been sterilized out of the traditional definitions that Johnson is rightly critical of. See Johnson, *She Who Is: The Mystery of God in Feminist Discourse*, 259; see 246–72.

26. Schillebeeckx, *Christ*, 739

27. Schillebeeckx, *Christ*, 31ff; see also Louis Dupré, "Experience and Interpretation: A Philosophical Reflection on Schillebeeckx's *Jesus* and *Christ*," *Theological Studies* 43 (1982): 30–51; for elucidation of how the interpretive framework is both formed by the history of experience and revised through ongoing encounter with reality, see Mary Catherine Hilkert, "Discovery of the Living God: Revelation and Experience," in Schreiter and Hilkert, eds., *The Praxis of Christian Experience: An Introduction to the Theology of Edward Schillebeeckx*, 37; see 35–51.

28. Schillebeeckx, *Christ*, 739.

29. Schillebeeckx's intention of critiquing traditions, even those of the Church, in the name of those who suffer is underlined by William Portier in a comparative analysis of the anthropological approaches of Ratzinger and Schillebeeckx. He classifies Schillebeeckx's approach as "more contextual" than Ratzinger's "concrete anthropological" one. See William L. Portier, "Mysticism and Politics and Integral Salvation: Two Approaches to Theology in a Suffering World," in *Pluralism and Oppression: Theology in World Per-*

116   *Chapter Three*

spective, The Annual Publication of the College Theology Society, vol. 34, ed. Paul Knitter (Lanham, Md.: University Press of America, 1991), 261; see 255–78.

30. See Schillebeeckx's explanation of his *hermeneutics of history* in "Towards a Catholic Use of Hermeneutics," in *God the Future of Man,* esp. 21–35; for a systematic development of this evolving dimension of Schillebeeckx's work, see M.C. Hilkert, "The Hermeneutics of History in the Theology of Edward Schillebeeckx," *The Thomist* 51 (1987) 97–145.

31. Schillebeekx, *Christ,* 740.

32. Schillebeekx, *Christ,* 740.

33. Schillebeekx, *Christ,* 741.

34. Schillebeekx, *Christ,* 740; cf. also Schillebeeckx's distillation of the negative dialectic of E. Bloch and P. Ricoeur in a foundational expression of negative contrast experience: "A sphere of meaning is revealed in the negative experiences of contrast in our personal and social life. . . . What is positive in it, however—the sphere of meaning—is only expressed in critical opposition to what is inhuman in the situation, while the positive expression of it disintegrates at once into pluralism." *The Understanding of Faith,* 65.

35. Schillebeekx, *Christ,* 742.

36. Schillebeekx, *Christ,* 743.

37. Schillebeekx, *Christ,* 671.

38. Schillebeekx, *Christ,* 672; this statement might well be challenged by secular philosophers and ethicists grappling with issues of evil and suffering. On the other hand, the fact that some thinkers find it necessary to eschew traditional notions of God in order to realistically address suffering may indirectly prove Schillebeeckx's point. See, for example, Nel Noddings' preference for a fallible, developing god, "a god we can live with," in *Women and Evil,* 16–17.

39. Some of the most current perspectives in the burgeoning literature of this field are represented in: Werner Jeanrond and Christoph Theobald, eds., *Who Do You Say That I Am?* (New York: Orbis; London: SCM; Nijmegen: Concilium, 1997), and Leonard Swidler and Paul Motzes, eds., *The Uniqueness of Jesus: A Dialogue with Paul Knitter* (Maryknoll, N.Y.: Orbis, 1997); the parameters of the dialogue itself are evaluated in a series of five perspectives on Knitter's *Jesus and the Other Names: Christian Mission and Global Responsibility* (Maryknoll, N.Y.: Orbis, 1996), in "Review Symposium," *Horizons* 24/2 (1997): 267–96; two distinctly different but comprehensive contextualizations of the interreligious dialogue are presented in J. A. DiNoia, *The Diversity of Religions: A Christian Perspective* (Washington, D.C.: Catholic University of America, 1992), and David Tracy, *Dialogue with the Other: The Inter-Religious Dialogue* (Grand Rapids, Mich.: Eerdmanns, 1990; Louvain, Belgium: Peeters Press, 1990).

40. *Summa Theologiae* III, q.2, a.10.

41. J. A. DiNoia argues in *The Diversity of Religions* that salvation, long the crux of interreligious debate, is not in fact a primary concern for all religions. He seeks to project the discussion beyond the frontiers of present "pluralist," "exclusivist" and "inclusivist" models.

42. See, for example, *Jesus: An Experiment in Christology,* 575ff; *Christ: The Experience of Jesus as Lord,* esp. 802–804; *Church: The Human Story of God,* esp. 144–77; "Identiteit, eigenheid en universaliteit van Gods heil in Jezus" *Tijdschrift voor Theologie* 30 (1990): 159–75; and, most notably, "Universalité unique d'une figure religieuse historique nommée Jésus de Nazareth," *Laval théologique et philosophique* 50 (1994): 265–82.

43. Schillebeekx, "Universalité unique d'une figure religieuse historique nommée Jésus de Nazareth."

44. Schillebeeckx describes at length the authority of historical experiences and the authority of the New Testament, citing any question of the priority of one over the other as a "false alternative." See Schillebeekx, *Christ*, 30–77, esp. 71ff.

45. Schillebeekx, "Universalité unique," 273.

46. Schillebeekx, *Church*, 104.

47. Schillebeeckx, "Universalité unique," 276.

48. Schillebeekx, *Church*, 175.

49. Schillebeekx, *Church*, 176.

50. Schillebeeckx speaks of the definitive, enduring value of what Jesus released in history: the "movement he set afoot" as witnessed in the churches. The constant, unitive factor is the "community-fashioning experience evoked by the impression Jesus makes and, in the Spirit, goes on making upon his followers, people who have experienced final salvation in Jesus of Nazareth." See *Jesus*, 18–19, 57.

51. Schillebeeckx, "Universalité unique," 270–71.

52. Matthew 2:1–18.

53. Schillebeeckx, *Jesus*, 182

54. Schillebeeckx, *Jesus*, 182.

55. Schillebeeckx, *Jesus*, 183.

56. Schillebeeckx, *Jesus*, 185.

57. Schillebeeckx, *Jesus*, 185.

58. Schillebeeckx, *Jesus*, 187.

59. Schillebeeckx explains that people articulated their experience of salvation-in-Jesus through preestablished images that they saw as fulfilled in him. Yet, he clarifies that "it is not the prior expectations that determine who Jesus is, but the other way around: starting from the peculiar and quite specific historical existence of Jesus, the already given expectations are of course partly assimilated yet at the same time transformed, regauged, or corrected. This indicates both a continuity and a discontinuity between the question people were asking about salvation and the historically concrete answer that is Jesus." *Jesus*, 21.

60. Schillebeeckx, *Jesus*, 187.

61. Schillebeeckx, *Jesus*, 192.

62. Schillebeeckx notes that in Jesus' presence suffering people experience God's saving nearness; the fact that Jesus' solidarity with sufferers led to his death confirms that "suffering through and for others (is) an expression of the *unconditional validity* of a pattern of doing good and resisting evil and suffering. Anyone who sets no limits to his sacrifice for the suffering of others will have to pay with his life—even today. Jesus came to terms with this." *Christ: The Experience of Jesus as Lord*, 795.

63. Schillebeeckx, *Jesus*, 183–84.

64. Schillebeeckx, *Jesus*, 189.

65. Schillebeeckx, *Jesus*, 193; in a colorful variant of this image drawn from the literature of Zora Neal Hurston, the human history of suffering is depicted as a "damnation train" derailed by Jesus. Katie Cannon's analysis echoes Schillebeeckx: "This fundamental religious lore embodying African-American people's understanding of evil and suffering implies that human sins committed against humanity are in flagrant opposition to

118 Chapter Three

Divine Goodness. The evil that we do unto one another inflicts wounds not only on Jesus but on all of creation." See Katie Geneva Cannon, "The Wounds of Jesus," in *A Troubling in My Soul: Womanist Perspectives on Evil and Suffering*, ed. Emilie M. Townes (Maryknoll, N.Y.: Orbis, 1993), 219–31, 226.

66. Schillebeeckx, *Jesus*, 194.
67. Schillebeeckx, *Jesus*, 195.
68. Schillebeeckx, *Jesus*, 195.
69. Schillebeeckx, *Jesus*, 196.
70. Schillebeeckx, *Jesus*, 196.
71. Schillebeeckx, *Jesus*, 196.
72. Schillebeeckx, *Jesus*, 256–69 and 652–69; on this point, see also Gabriel Fackre, "Bones Strong and Weak in the Skeletal Structure of Schillebeeckx's Christology," *Journal of Ecumenical Studies* 21/2 (1984): 248–77, 257–58; Reginald H. Fuller, "The Historical Jesus, Some Outstanding Issues," *The Thomist* 48 (1984): 380; see 368–82; John P. Galvin, "The Uniqueness of Jesus and His 'Abba Experience' in the Theology of Edward Schillebeeckx," *CTSA Proceedings* 35 (1980): 309–14; John Nijenhuis, "Christology without Jesus of Nazareth Is Ideology: A Monumental Work by Schillebeeckx on Jesus," *Journal of Ecumenical Studies* 17/1 (1980): 125–40, 136. For a critique of patriarchal renderings of the term "Abba" see Mary Rose D'Angelo, "Abba and 'Father': Imperial Theology and the Jesus Traditions," *Journal of Biblical Literature* 111, no. 4 (1992): 611–30.
73. Schillebeeckx states, "Jesus *in his humanity* gets his name from, i.e., is defined by, his relationship to God." *Church*, 121.
74. Schillebeeckx, *On Christian Faith*, (New York: Crossroad, 1987), 5.
75. Schillebeeckx, *Jesus*, 179, 201, 206, 213.
76. Schillebeeckx, *Jesus*, 260–61.
77. Schillebeeckx, *Jesus*, 269.
78. Schillebeeckx, *Christ*, 35–36.
79. Noting that almost all cultures speak in some way of a "school of suffering," Schillebeeckx acknowledges the potential of suffering and sorrow to forge wisdom, strength, and gentleness of spirit. *Christ*, 724; though contemporary feminists decry the classical notions of suffering as designed to bring forth some greater good, many would resonate with Schillebeeckx's rendering; see for example, M. Shawn Copeland, "Wading through Many Sorrows," in *A Troubling in My Soul*, ed. Emilie M. Townes, 109; see 109–29.
80. Schillebeeckx, *The Church with a Human Face: A New and Expanded Theology of Ministry* (New York: Crossroad, 1985), 32.
81. Schillebeeckx, *Christ*, 729; in a recent analysis, Kenan Osborne maintains that the disunity of christology is attributable to the conflict set up by erroneous interpretations through the centuries of Jesus' arrest, trial, suffering, and death. These elements of Jesus' life story, giving rise to atonement theories, have somehow been allowed to fragment and even overwhelm the message that the reign of God has begun, and at the deepest level of reality goodness has triumphed over evil. See Kenan B. Osborne, *The Resurrection of Jesus: New Considerations for Its Theological Interpretation* (New York and Mahwah, N.J.: Paulist, 1997), 160–74. Schillebeeckx himself laments the damage wrought by widespread misrepresentations of Anselm's atonement theory ingrained in the Church's tradition over the course of centuries. The notion that suffering and blood somehow avenge

God's honor weakens and "tames" the critical force of the crucifixion. It has, in fact, created a "mysticism of suffering" that "establishes the existing order in church and society." *Christ,* 700. It would seem that we have here a negative example of what Schillebeeckx means when he says that understanding "must change in changing situations, otherwise the same thing cannot continue to be understood." "Towards a Catholic Use of Hermeneutics," *God the Future of Man,* 31. It would seem that what Anselm wanted understood was the utter gratuitousness of God's mercy, but his rootedness in a feudal culture conditioned his symbolic rendering of this so deeply that it is impossible for us to glean the truth without radical transposition. The hermeneutical failure to transpose has in fact contributed to suffering in multiple ways. See Anselm of Canterbury, *Cur Deus Homo,* ed. and trans. Jasper Hopkins and Herbert Richardson (Lewiston, N.Y.: The Edwin Mellen Press), 130–35.

82. Schillebeeckx, *Jesus,* 294.

83. Schillebeeckx, *Jesus,* 274; for development, see 274–94.

84. Schillebeeckx, *Jesus,* 282.

85. Schillebeeckx, *Jesus,* 293.

86. Schillebeeckx, *Jesus,* 293.

87. Schillebeeckx, *Jesus,* 311.

88. Schillebeeckx, *Jesus,* 310.

89. This meaning is enfleshed today in the plight of peoples who have been given a voice in multiple theologies of liberation throughout the last thirty years, beginning in Latin America. Gustavo Gutiérrez, the "father" of Latin American liberation theology, claimed to owe his *Theology of Liberation* to Edward Schillebeeckx, his early theological mentor. Today, the image of the "crucified people" in so many parts of the world is leading liberation theologians to call the Church to establish a new, contemporary criteria of martyrdom in the Church, incorporating justice stands, the risk of witness and resistance, and the prevalence of innocent victims. Robert Lasalle-Klein cites Sobrino and Ellacuria in this regard; see Lasalle-Klein, "The Body of Christ: The Claim of the Crucified People on U.S. Theology and Ethics," *Journal of Hispanic/Latino Theology* 5, no. 4 (1998) 48–77.

90. Schillebeeckx describes mysticism quite simply as the life of faith, which always incorporates something of a "dark night" as well as experiences of grace in the saving real presence of God with us, mediated always through negativity. Mysticism is "not just a cognitive process but a particular way of life, a way of salvation." Schillebeeckx sees three constants: 1) an illuminating source experience, an experience of breakthrough, of something new; 2) a phase of purgation in which one experiences wounding and doubt about the earlier illumination; 3) a discovery of divine love, in a trace that the beloved has left behind in the being of the mystic. "There remains a mediated 'immediacy'; there is the pure presence of the divine, but also the natural presence of the mystic with God . 'Mystical union,' mutuality. And yet, this is always with a painful feeling of absence: not-seeing." Finally, Schillebeeckx emphasizes, "Authentic mysticism is never flight from the world but, on the basis of a first disintegrating source-experience, an integrating and reconciling mercy with all things. It is approach, not flight." *Church: The Human Story of God,* 70–72.

91. For examples of Schillebeeckx's treatment of the "peculiar cognitive power of suffering," see *Jesus,* 621–23, and *Christ,* 817–21.

92. Schillebeeckx, *Jesus,* 621.

93. Schillebeeckx, *Jesus,* 622.

94. Schillebeeckx, *Christ,* 827.

95. Schillebeeckx, *Christ,* 827; David Tracy, while acknowledging the different readings of the passion narratives and correspondingly different self-understandings of Christian traditions down through the ages, asserts that they are the first place to look "if one wants to know who Jesus Christ is for Christians." This is where "Christians also discover their principal clues to who God is and who human beings as free agents are empowered to become." *Dialogue with the Other,* 114.

96. The narrative sensibility that marks Schillebeeckx's christology has become a theological category in its own right, with a conscious cultivation of the theological imagination. For representative discussions of the indispensability of narrative for christology, see Michael L. Cook, *Christology as Narrative Quest* (Collegeville, Minn.: Liturgical Press, 1997), esp. 46ff.; Richard G. Cote, "Christology and the Paschal Imagination," in *Who Do You Say That I Am?* ed. Werner Jeanrond and Christoph Theobald. For a sustained narrative treatment of the question of suffering from an ethical perspective, see Stanley Hauerwas, *Naming the Silences: God, Medicine, and the Problem of Suffering* (Grand Rapids: Eerdmans, 1990). For discussion of the philosophical sense in which narratives are "true," see Gary Comstock, "The Truth of Religious Narratives," *International Journal for the Philosophy of Religion,* 34 (1993): 131–50; and Don Cupitt, *What Is a Story?* (London: SCM Press, 1991). For analysis of the rival Yale and Chicago schools of narrative theology vis-à-vis the question of salvation, see Scott Holland, "How Do Stories Save Us? Two Contemporary Theological Responses," *Louvain Studies* 22 (1997): 328–51.

97. Schillebeeckx, *Christ,* 829.

98. Schillebeeckx, *Christ,* 827; in *Christ,* Schillebeeckx's analysis of the Johannine exaltation of the cross is an extended reflection on Jesus' glorification precisely in the hour of suffering and defeat. "In John's gospel, christological statements are always simultaneously soteriological statements" (410); "Glorification is . . . the revelation of the union of love between the Father and the Son who has been sent" (411); we might extend this focus on communion into the pervasive significance of relationship as the fundamental meaning of the cross and suffering in human life. This will be elaborated below in chapter four; cf. also Schillebeeckx's explanation that eternal life does not coincide with the resurrection as it does for Paul. It has already begun now, with death being an element in the ascent to God and the beginning of glorification (*Christ,* 425). The kingdom of God ushered in by Jesus is manifest in visible new relationships in the context of creation (*Church,* 112).

99. Schillebeeckx, *Jesus,* 620.

100. Schillebeeckx brings the tools of critical theory and hermeneutics to bear upon the theme of suffering in biblical history, illustrating in contemporary terms how "critical, selective remembrance is put at the service of the future. . . . The basic moods of human life—anxiety and despair, joy and hope—are evidently bound up with the temporal structure of remembrance and expectation. Therein lies their critical and productive force" (*Christ,* 664–65); later, Schillebeeckx's discussion of temporal awareness leads him to say, "Anyone who believes in God knows that, in some way or other, he holds us in his hand" (*Christ,* 807). The image of God holding the sufferer's hand is one that continuously recurs across the spectrum of his works, and finally evokes Jesus' own experience of God on the cross. See Schillebeeckx's discussion of the term "third day" as "an expression of Jesus' self-understanding: an awareness of having to go through the deepest distress, but in the firm conviction of knowing that he was in God's mighty hand, come what

may" (*Jesus,* 529); cf. also his early article, "The Death of a Christian," as analyzed in chapter two above.

101. Schillebeeckx, *Church,* 70.

102. Schillebeeckx, *Church,* 131.

103. Schillebeeckx, *Church,* 131.

104. Schillebeeckx, *Church,* 131.

105. Schillebeeckx, *Christ,* 828.

106. Schillebeeckx, *Christ,* 828; Schillebeeckx's understanding of Jesus' identification with God, and especially his persistent thread of obedience as communion, is reinforced by C.F.D. Moule. Reflecting on the title "The Son of Man," Moule notes the appropriateness of the Danielic vision of "the human figure" to the ministry of Jesus. On this showing, it is not a title, "but a symbol of a vocation to be utterly loyal, even in death, in the confidence of ultimate vindication in the heavenly court. Jesus is alluding to 'the (well-known, Danielic) Son of Man' in this vein." Moule further notes that in the Marcan account, the authority of the true Israel, and so of authentic humanity, is obedient to God's design. *The Origin of Christology* (Cambridge: Cambridge University Press, 1977), 14.

107. Schillebeeckx, *Christ,* 829.

108. Schillebeeckx, *Jesus,* 645.

109. This increasingly defining principle of postmodern theology is elaborated in an article to which Schillebeeckx refers on at least two occasions: see Lee Cormie, "The Hermeneutical Privilege of the Oppressed," *Proceedings of the Catholic Theological Society of America,* 33 (1978): 155–81.

110. For a recent analysis and discussion of the context of Schillebeeckx's understanding of the elusive meaning of the Greek *opthe* vis-à-vis critics who judge him as failing to maintain the objectivity of the resurrection, see Peter Philips, "Seeing with Eyes of Faith: Schillebeeckx and the Resurrection of Jesus," *Blackfriars* May (1998): 241–50.

111. Schillebeeckx defends his resurrection analysis, among other disputed issues, in *Interim Report on the Books* Jesus *and* Christ (New York: Crossroad, 1980). On the question of bodily seeing he explicitly states: "(I) kept silent about possible visual elements in the process of conversion or the Easter experiences. My intention here was to relieve this visual element of the deep dogmatic significance which people attach to it, namely of being the foundation of the whole of Christian faith" (82); for a recent cataloguing of the body of contemporary scholarship affirming Schillebeeckx's intentionality, see Osborne, *The Resurrection of Jesus* (New York and Mahwah, N.J.: Paulist, 1997).

112. Schillebeeckx, *Jesus,* 347.

113. Schillebeeckx, *Jesus,* 347.

114. Schillebeeckx, *Jesus,* 348.

115. Schillebeeckx maintains that the universality of Christian faith lies in its rapport with the general human question of the universal meaning of history; this must be expressed in transformative action toward a human vision of justice rooted in personal transformation. Any affirmation of the unique universality of Jesus depends upon the believer's continuation of Jesus' praxis on behalf of the *humanum.* See "Universalité unique d'une figure religieuse historique," 275–77; cf. also *Church: The Human Story of God,* 262–72.

116. Schillebeeckx, *Interim Report,* 79.

117. Schillebeeckx, *Interim Report,* 78.

118. Schillebeeckx, *Interim Report,* 90–91.
119. Schillebeeckx, *Christ,* 37–38.
120. Schillebeeckx, *Jesus,* 344.
121. Schillebeeckx, *Jesus,* 388. Schillebeeckx also notes, in an aside, that "it is thanks partly to the experiences of these women that the whole Jesus affair got under way"(345). He does not pursue the significance of official validating of experiences, or the question of how truth is obscured or suffering inflicted when the experience of women and others on the margins, past and present, is dismissed. In *Church: The Human Story of God,* he expresses indignation over the Church's oppression of women and others. He does not, however, develop this critique in a full or satisfying way. An "actualizing" of Schillebeeckx's experience-based theology has yet to be extended in these areas.
122. Gabriel Fackre notes Schillebeeckx's claims that ontological assertions about the "real presence" of the eschatological Jesus have the same decisive weight as the "change in being" motifs in eucharistic theology. Fackre refers to Schillebeeckx's three-level distinctions of datum, ontological affirmation, and theological reconstruction in his *Eucharist* book for help in classification, but disagrees with Schillebeeckx on the basis that (in Fackre's judgment) his handling of the resurrection accounts reduces them to third-level experiences of grace. (Schillebeeckx himself is emphatic that we have to do here, both eucharistically and eschatologically, with the Real Presence of Jesus.) "Bones Strong and Weak in the Skeletal Structure of Schillebeeckx's Christology," *Journal of Ecumenical Studies* 21, no. 2 (1984): 260; see 248–77.
123. Schillebeeckx, *Jesus,* 344.
124. Schillebeeckx, *Jesus,* 381.
125. Schillebeeckx, *Jesus,* 382.
126. Schillebeeckx, *Jesus,* 382.
127. Schillebeeckx, *Jesus,* 390.
128. Schillebeeckx, *Jesus,* 391.
129. Schillebeeckx, *Christ,* 53.
130. Schillebeeckx, *Christ,* 53.
131. Schillebeeckx uses this phrase, for which he is indebted to Eberhard Jüngel, to denote the relationship of the experience of faith to the broad spectrum of human experiences which is faith's mediating context.
132. Schillebeeckx, *Christ,* 35.
133. Schillebeeckx, *Christ,* 39.
134. Schillebeeckx, *Christ,* 76.
135. Schillebeeckx, *Church,* 126.
136. Schillebeeckx, *Church,* 126.
137. Schillebeeckx, *Church,* 126–27; cf. also Schillebeeckx, *The Church with a Human Face,* 33.
138. Schillebeeckx describes Jesus' defenseless vulnerability as God's own; in God, this powerlessness becomes a superior power, God's absolute nearness as presence of pure positivity. He alludes to Paul, who "says that 'the foolishness of God is wiser than men, and the weakness of God stronger than men' (I Cor.1:25); God's presence was near in power, but without the misuse of power" (*Church: The Human Story of God,* 128); cf. also "Doubt in God's Omnipotence: 'When Bad Things Happen to Good People'" in Schillebeeckx, *For the Sake of the Gospel* (New York: Crossroad, 1990; Baarn: Nelissen, 1988), 91, 95–97.

Chapter Four

Political Mysticism

The understanding of the term "political mysticism" in the context of Schille-beeckx's theology has everything to do with the mysticism of the cross as elaborated above in chapter three. Moreover, this mysticism returns in a deepening spiral to Jesus' unbroken communion with God. The centrality of this relationship is revealed as the defining paradigm for every aspect and application of Schillebeeckx's theology. The paschal event reveals this relationship as the essence of Jesus' proclamation and the substance of God's rule. The truth that Jesus both proclaims and embodies is, in fact, this living relation, this trust, this obedience, this unbroken communion. The mission of Jesus does not exist apart from this truth. Integrity of relationship with God, with others, and with creation is part and parcel of justice; there is no "objective" justice or truth that does not participate in this relational integrity. And ultimately, human experiences of suffering have meaning only within this context of relationship. The essence of mysticism uncovered by the cross is the existential, conscious, lived experience of divine/human relationship. This experience of mysticism by definition entails politics, which Schillebeeckx has described as "the difficult art of making possible what is necessary for human salvation."[1]

SOLIDARITY AND METANOIA:
A RECIPROCAL RELATION

The "art of making possible what is necessary for human salvation" entails a deep understanding of the fullness of the *humanum* as an eschatologically open reality. The previous chapter showed how Schillebeeckx establishes a common ground between this anthropological hope and what Christians call salvation in Jesus Christ. Jesus is much more than the paradigm of humanity, but he is at least that.[2] In fact, Schillebeeckx has made clear that Jesus' humanity *is* God's presence in the world. It does not merely cloak God's presence; human flesh is not simply a vehicle that God "uses" in order to act in the world. These are ancient heresies that still afflict and restrict us. God *becomes* human in Jesus, making human nature itself divine.[3] The humanity of Jesus is itself a manner of being in the world of the eternal Word. The ceaseless thrust of Schillebeeckx's work is to convince believers and non-believers alike that human nature is sacred, worthy of our deepest reverence and highest commitment. It is for *this* that God chose to come among us as human; it is for *this* that Jesus lived and ultimately died; and it is because of this that God raised Jesus up in the resurrection. Schillebeeckx never tires of asserting that Jesus' unfaltering commitment to humanity *is* his unfaltering commitment to God, and vice versa. This is the gospel that the Church exists to proclaim throughout the world, and it is challenged today wherever it is not rooted in genuine, personal mysticism. Explaining how the Church's belief in God's unconditional love of humanity must inform secular life, Schillebeeckx states,

> Included in this, however, is the irreplaceable meaningfulness of *dwelling upon* the personal mystery, since it is only within this personal mystery that human life in the world becomes ultimately and definitively meaningful as *personal* life in a *community,* and it is to this personal mystery that man [*sic*] knows himself to be ultimately responsible in his work in the world.[4]

Now, it is from this base of the divine/human relationship that we turn to the concrete reality that takes shape in the world of politics but which is *given* shape in the experience of mysticism. Mysticism,[5] in Schillebeeckx's understanding, is this fundamental relationship existing at the core of authentic human solidarity. It is this relationship that determines one's attitude toward one's neighbors in the human community, and thus it corresponds, in practice, to the domain of ethics.[6] To be human is to be human-for-the-other. But the essence of this "being human" is not a reality that can be abstractly defined; rather, each person's "individuality determines 'being human' from within."[7] Schillebeeckx continues,

> Only and exclusively as intrinsically individualized is "being human" a reality and can it be the source of moral norms (which in religious parlance, we can rightly describe as the will of God). Therefore, there is only one source of ethical norms, namely, the historical reality of the inviolable human person with all its bodily and social implications. That is why we cannot attribute validity to abstract norms as such. Moreover, no abstract statement can produce a call or invitation.[8]

Schillebeeckx in no way intends to do away with abstract, generally valid norms; instead, he wishes to emphasize their appropriate function as "an inadequate yet *real* pointer to the one real, concrete ethical norm, namely, this concrete human person living historically in this concrete society."[9] This kind of reverence for human particularity is precisely the worldly expression that the Incarnation was meant to effect. And it is only from within the space of this reverence that an individual can experience a living call or invitation to a truly human, that is, moral, life. It is, in fact, when this is forgotten that the suffering both of individuals and of communities is exacerbated.[10] When this is remembered and honored, a situation is nurtured in which the union between the inner and outer dynamics of mysticism and human solidarity can bear fruit. The inner orientation of the individual is affected by the "other," whose existence invites response in relationship. In a simple, positive sense, this is the beginning of solidarity.[11] Particularly from a Christian perspective, this is the extension in the world of Jesus' communion with God and with his human companions.

The "other," of course, is multiplied infinitely across the spectrum of society. But even before the numbers are multiplied, the reality emerges that the human "others" who make demands on us are suffering others. And it is here that we are challenged by the meaning of the mutual, reciprocal relationship between solidarity and metanoia. With Schillebeeckx, when we use the term "solidarity" we are speaking of the deep communion that is inseparable from the experience of mysticism. We have seen how, in his early writings, Schillebeeckx spoke of the solidarity of human beings in grace and in sin.[12] The primordial solidarity of the race is found in the state of original justice in which we were created. At the core of this solidarity is the personal relationship with God, which Schillebeeckx speaks of in terms of "obedience" in his early work, and later, especially in his christology, in terms of "trust" and Jesus' own "unbroken communion with God." Unfortunately, our knowledge of this positive solidarity too commonly arises by contrast via its negative manifestation in "the universal solidarity of humankind in sin."[13] The concrete reality of suffering and sin that reminds us of our solidarity in the negative dimensions of the human condition, can also give rise to the lived experience of "the human community in personal intimacy with God" through personal and communal metanoia.[14] In fact, genuine solidarity is rooted in the metanoia integral to the experience of mysticism.[15]

The personal experience of metanoia to which Schillebeeckx gives sustained treatment in "The Death of a Christian" finds its mature expression in the political mysticism of his later works. This does not imply a merely logical progression of cause and effect. The personal and communal dimensions of mysticism and solidarity are present at the beginning and at the end of Schillebeeckx's corpus. With his well-known methodological "shift" came a gradual and developing shift of emphasis, which embraced more and more of the world's diverse reality as well as salient dimensions of critical and scientific discourse. It is the dialectical movement within the densely organic process of the hermeneutical spiral that gives rise to the new and compelling political emphasis.[16] Simply stated, this is the reciprocal dynamic of metanoia and solidarity in Schillebeeckx's work in which the reality of suffering is pivotal. Here is the inevitable fruition of Schillebeeckx's fundamental incarnational principle, namely that humanity is God's chosen manner of being in the world. The overwhelming constancy of *suffering* in the history of humanity also informed the substance of God's solidarity with us in Jesus Christ. This is the meaning of the paschal mystery from "the under-side." God's choice to become one with humanity was also a choice to allow the vagaries of the human condition to contribute to the contours of salvation and redemption. Thus, Schillebeeckx describes the basic creed found throughout the New Testament as "Jesus' *solidarity* with suffering and sinful man [*sic*] as a result of a radical fidelity to God to the point of death, the giving up of his life, and God's creative and affirmative acceptance of such a life in solidarity and faithfulness."[17]

Methodologically speaking, it is clear that the development of Schillebeeckx's christology and soteriology from the late sixties onward is profoundly affected by his lecture tour of the United States in 1967. This experience awakened in him the sense of secularization as a positive phenomenon and an urgency about find-ing a way to proclaim the gospel in its context. The civil rights movement and the antiwar protests of the Vietnam era were for Schillebeeckx an experience of negative contrast, in which the shocking struggle of resistance laid bare the extent of suffering caused by oppression and injustice in the very nation that was the world's primary symbol of democratic freedom and prosperity. It was not just an experience of the way things were in America; it was the experience that would complete a paradigm shift for which the foundations were already well estab-lished in Schillebeeckx's thought. Suffering, and the sin at its origin, began from that moment to take on an increasingly global significance that informed the direction, method, and content of Schillebeeckx's theological project. Correla-tively, the disciplines with which he entered into dialogue were concerned with human experience and knowledge from socially critical perspectives.[18] Yet, the personal mysticism and its relationship to spiritual and physical suffering in his early works does not leave the stage. It remains as the powerful embryonic core of a theology expanding to encompass personal human experience in its commu-nal and societal dimensions, especially when it is ravaged by the very structures designed to uphold human freedom. In particular, the impact of this development on Schillebeeckx's christology reveals that the fullest appropriation of incarna-tional faith necessarily entails the essential *unity* of the experiences of turning toward God and turning toward the human "other." This, ultimately, is what dis-tinguishes political mysticism in Schillebeeckx's theology from mere politics.

Thus the metanoia that implies a personal turning away from sin and toward God is manifested in the outward turning toward the other. On this basis, it is also true that the initial turning is often engendered by the call, the invitation that the demand of the suffering "other" effects. In any case, the experience of soli-darity leading to concrete care for the "other" in turn deepens the experience of metanoia, furthering personal conversion and increasing its fruits in community and society, simultaneously increasing holiness and advancing justice in the world. And this, ultimately, is the substance of salvation. Time and again Schille-beeckx insists that any view of "salvation" which has no concrete manifestation in this world has no relationship to the gospel. Jesus' manner of life testifies to this. Whoever came into contact with Jesus in an attitude of trust experienced wholeness in an immediate way. At the same time, we have noted Schillebeeckx's observation that every miracle of physical healing Jesus performed was undergirded by the summons to metanoia, a change of heart. In those situations where Jesus was powerless to effect healing, Schillebeeckx maintains that those in need of it were not open to this summons.[19] And this indicates that the significance of metanoia holds the clue to understanding the essence of suffering as well as the essence of true healing.

METANOIA AND EXPERIENCES OF
NEGATIVE CONTRAST

In Schillebeeckx's christology, Jesus' concern for people's concrete suffering always penetrates much deeper than any external affliction. The healing of physical illness, while important, is always a sign of the deeper healing that Jesus is able to bring about only when a person entrusts his or her suffering to him. It is this surrender in faith, this letting go in vulnerability, that is itself the beginning of the essential healing. The act by which a person chooses to depend upon God in relationship is the beginning of the transformation to wholeness that is salvation. It is what Jesus means when he says, "Go now; your faith has saved you." By this active choice, a person moves out beyond the limits of his or her life into the space of liberation where a new kind of living is possible. Those limits themselves provide the challenge that becomes part of the material of salvation. In the case of Jesus' physical healings, for instance, it is the limit imposed by illness, which the sick person instinctively resists and seeks to overcome. Sometimes the resistance and struggle has absorbed the person's energy and resources over a span of many years.[20] The illness, the physical limitation, the pain suffered can become the defining factor of a life, either in itself or in the constant experimentation with remedies that it provokes. The miracles of the New Testament mark those occasions when a person caught in the illusion either of control or of helpless passivity leaves familiar terrain behind to risk the approach to Jesus. The saving element is the act of trust in God embodied in the active turn toward the person of Jesus. In that divine/human encounter a transformation takes place that signifies more than the alleviation of illness. The restoration of physical faculties always signifies the deep spiritual restoration of the person.

The relationship that this kind of personal restoration bears to metanoia is clear. But what relationship does it bear to political mysticism? The answer lies in the experience of negative contrast, which is the ground of both personal and political transformation. The next and final chapter will explore the particular personal suffering of illness in greater depth. Now, however, the discussion turns to the dynamic of negative contrast experience revealed in Jesus' healing miracles, which also holds the key to how metanoia operates in the social, political process of transformation.

When Jesus is approached by a suffering individual, he does not only attend to that person's need for healing. In and through the depths of a personal response, Jesus sheds light on the sources of affliction, oppression, marginalization. He does not directly address the social and political structures that may be responsible for the suffering person's plight; nevertheless, Jesus' response illuminates what is wrong in the wider society through his implicit proclamation that "this should not be."[21] Sometimes his healing praxis is accompanied by words, as when, in John's gospel, he proclaims that the blind man's affliction is due neither to his sin nor to the sin of his parents. In doing so, he pronounces a judgment on the religious and social structures that ostracized the physically disabled by associating suffering with sin.[22] In fact, most of Jesus' pronouncements of judgment had to do with the hypocrisy of authorities who styled themselves "righteous" while increasing the burdens of the poor and those who suffered.

Undergirding Jesus' "this should not be" is the positive vision of what God wills for humanity: happiness and peace, freedom and charity, a community of sharing where the "other" is neighbor, and where the neighbor's need is the standard for acting. In such a community, the reciprocity between solidarity and metanoia is clear.[23] It is the experience of salvation-in-the-flesh, here and now.

Some would say such an experience is a "utopia," not realizable in human society. Such visions and utopias, however, arise from the yearnings of the oppressed; they depend upon solidarity for their fulfillment, and they fail, often tragically, when fear-based possessiveness holds sway. In many parts of the world, at every point in history, the dream of such a utopia has inspired revolutions. And, throughout history, there have been those willing to carry out both revolutions and conquests under a banner exalting Jesus as "revolutionary hero" or "triumphant king." Scripture has been used to claim Jesus' authority for every type of social/political agenda. Edward Schillebeeckx maintains, however, that Jesus cannot be aligned with any political agenda; to do so is to make a limited vision absolute. Schillebeeckx cites the murderous visions and utopias in history that have sent millions to their deaths for religious ideals, as well as for enlightened, secular ideals, in our modern age. The Holocaust is emblematic of the horrors of a vision made absolute. "A 'vision' has a dangerous Janus' head." Schillebeeckx continues:

> Where the fanatical ideal of the *distant* absolute is held up in the hands of finite beings, somewhere *nearby* a Jesus of Nazareth is being nailed to the cross. Absolute ideals are fatal unless they are a vision *of love,* that is, of selfless involvement, even if they carry freedom and humanity on their banner. These concepts are already as stained with pollution as the name of God has been dishonoured down the ages.[24]

Correspondingly, Schillebeeckx criticizes Christians who use the New Testament either to defend their political positions, even positions of liberation theology, or to prove that Christianity should occupy a realm apart from politics:

It is striking that both approaches put their questions to the New Testament with a specific interest;. . . . Both positions seem to me to be a kind of fundamentalism—to the left or to the right; they forget to analyze the historical conditions.[25]

An historical analysis of New Testament texts reveals the unique and complex relationship of each Christian community to the social and political structures of the day. Each gospel, each letter is conditioned by its own milieu in such a way that we must allow the scripture's deep truth to emerge in the dialectic between the early Christian community's situated reality and our own. This is the essence of Schillebeeckx's historical hermeneutics, which he posits as necessary for the same truth to be understood in a true way in every age.[26] To understand the experience of New Testament Christians in historical terms is to understand that the gospel's appeal to the heart, to inner *metanoia,* is primary; the building of a new society upon this basis is taken for granted, but it is not pursued publicly and politically. As a vulnerable minority within the Hellenistic Roman empire, the Church could not even conceive of active social reform. Peaceful coexistence with this quite alien society was all that early Christians generally sought, and even this proved tenuous and short-lived.[27] But this neither signifies nor justifies an individualistic approach to religion. "In the New Testament, both the person and the structures are subject to the demand for repentance which is provoked by grace."[28] Portraying the ancient world's integration of person and institution as unafflicted by our modern tendency to contrast the two, Schillebeeckx explains:

> For that very reason, the New Testament Christians understand the summons to metanoia or repentance as an implication of the coming kingdom of God, not simply as a mere internal renewal of life but also as a socio-political alteration in the structure of society. However . . . they do this only within the community of God, to which they give just structures with the norm of the kingdom of God in mind. The New Testament was concerned that the structure of a better world and a new society should be realized *alongside* the greater society in the "enclosed garden" of the church communities.[29]

This approach arose against the background of the pervasive pessimism of the ancient world. Schillebeeckx calls attention to New Testament images of heaven as the true homeland, believers as exiles on earth, sojourners in a strange land, the Christian community as an exodus community. "The 'earthly vale of tears' and the 'world above' . . . is a feeling about life which is general throughout late antiquity."[30] In such an environment, early Christians experienced the personal call to metanoia as also a challenge to make real in the world the approach of God's reign. They understood that the gospel was a summons to transform the world as well as to be transformed. But because the political reality made that an impossibility, they focused their efforts on the transformation of social structures and relations within their own communities.[31] Only later, when the church had grown beyond its peripheral, minority status, could it begin the work of incarnating God's rule in worldly structures.

There is neither a disjointedness, nor, for that matter, even a strictly linear quality to the way in which this relationship between grace and politics develops. Though Schillebeeckx does not use the word, his explanations seem to suggest an embryonic kind of growth, expansion, and development. He speaks of looking for "symptoms" of this inner connection between grace and politics, and cites Paul's letter to Philemon as the only text which seems to offer them.[32] In the process, he deals with an issue which has been the source of much suffering in history, and to which, in different historical times and places, the Church's official relationship has often been murky. The issue of slavery emerges multiple times throughout the Pauline corpus, and it is dealt with according to the particular social situation in each case. In examining the letter to Philemon, Schillebeeckx demonstrates how Paul's handling of a particular circumstance within the Christian community illuminates the political responsibility of Christians vis-à-vis corresponding issues today.

Paul's brief letter to Philemon seems to accept, perhaps even condone, the social structure of slavery in place at the time. In fact, this letter is not about slavery, per se. It is about the kind of relationships that should prevail in the Christian community. Paul does not speak against the accepted social structure of slavery; he speaks, rather, in light of the mutuality of relationship that must prevail in Christ. He has developed an affection for the runaway slave, Onesimus, whom he has converted to Christ and to whom he is now related in faith. He sends him back to his friend, Philemon, also a Christian, out of respect for the civil legality of slavery. But he sends him back transformed, and he summons Philemon to acknowledge the transformation of the master-slave relationship in Christ. Schillebeeckx develops Paul's nuanced understandings of authority, but my concern here is with the transformation of relationships in Christ. In and through the personal transformation of relationships, the flourishing of mutuality and freedom among brothers and sisters, earthly reality itself is transformed. This was a situation where Christians abided by the civil law, were powerless to change political structures even when they recognized these as oppressive, and were conditioned by the social system in which they were participants when they came to accept the gospel. Under these conditions, the experience of metanoia took root in ways that remained socially hidden for a time. As grace transformed the relationships among the members of the church who were also members of society, it would seem that the appearance of the master-slave structure merely cloaked a reality of mutual relationship. Gradually, even the appearance began to change, so that what Christians were living in the midst of society emerged as a living challenge to that society's political reality. "In the long run, as a result of historical circumstances, this social renewal within the church will also have outward consequences."[33] And yet, in the particular case of Philemon, Schillebeeckx points out that Paul is not concerned with matters of principle. He is, in the most personal of ways, concerned with relationship. He quite simply cares about Onesimus and has, himself, come to rely on him for help with the work of evangelization. In a quite literal way, he wants him free for the gospel. And, to this end, Paul goes so far as to uncharacteristically persuade his friend to free the slave even in social terms.

However disappointing it may be that Paul does not take up the issue of slavery on the basis of principle, there is something important to be gleaned from his attitude in the letter to Philemon. There is a primacy accorded to human relationship in Christ, and an acknowledgment that, even when civil structures are respected, the relational reality beneath those structures transcends political boundaries. This reality is more important than the fact that Paul may be manipulating a situation to his own advantage; in any case, his own advantage is at the service of the gospel.

In other passages dealing specifically with the condition of slavery, Paul chose to focus on the interior transformation of the social structure.[34] The Christian reality of nondiscrimination between slave and free that Paul proclaimed did not stop him from making such contradictory demands as urging slaves to continue as they were when called by Christ (1 Cor. 7:21ff). "Here," Schillebeeckx notes, "Paul speaks on the basis of a Christianized Stoic concept of inner freedom."[35] Schillebeeckx cites Seneca's observation that, after the democratic Greek *polis* collapsed, philosophy lost its role of social critique. Stoic philosophy, thus depoliticized, focused on interior meaning in the midst of an oppressive culture. Civil, political freedom was replaced by an emphasis on the inner freedom that no oppressive structure can take away. Seneca's philosophy anticipates Paul.[36] So, too, the Christian gospel "is by nature relevant to politics and society, and must become politically effective, except when historical or particular situations make this impossible. However, where it is possible, it must come about."[37]

From this we may glean a recognition of the power of inner metanoia even in those circumstances where its outer manifestation is impossible. We can find historical and contemporary parallels in all those circumstances where personal mysticism survives and transcends the external defeat of efforts to resist and remove the social causes of suffering and oppression.[38] Certainly, we find the basis and model for the mutual reciprocity of metanoia and solidarity in Jesus' unbroken communion with God and commitment to human beings. In Jesus,

the messianic coming of God, before which evil yields, is not a coming in power, which will shatter evil with nationalistic and messianic force of arms. It works through *metanoia*, repentance. It is a victory over evil through obedience to God, and not through human force.[39]

Obedience to God , the heart of metanoia, is communion. It is the divine/human communion that manifests itself in the world through human relationships of solidarity, especially solidarity with those who suffer.[40] We have already seen that Jesus' farewell meal before his death proclaims the sacredness of relationship as the substance of God's reign *beginning now.* Wherever such relationships prevail, the victory over sin, evil, and suffering has already been won, despite earthly evidence to the contrary. This is the essence of the rule of God that Jesus embodied.

Jesus' concern, then, was not with earthly structures *per se,* but with proclaiming the rule of God.[41] It was from this positive proclamation grounded in the eschatological promise that Jesus lived, spoke, and acted. Any judgments he passed were passed on those realities that did not conform to God's rule. Jesus addressed persons—sinners, prostitutes, Pharisees, tax collectors, women and men, ordinary peasants and wealthy landowners. All of these represented or were affected by social structures, but the implications of their relationships to those structures are for us to interpret. The closest Jesus comes to formally addressing structures are his diatribes against Pharisees and lawyers who have gone too far in yoking simple people with burdens of religious legality without ever acting to ease their lot. Jesus' incessant concern is the suffering plight of the concrete person before him. In speaking and acting, his aim is the human heart. And yet, by touching a leper, speaking to a woman, eating with a tax collector, he dissolves socially constructed barriers in his person and by his presence. It is precisely through Jesus' free initiation of relationship that the social structures/mores against which he offends are indicted. All of this occurs in and through Jesus' personal response to suffering individuals with whom he enters into solidarity.[42]

Jesus' mission is the proclamation of God's rule of justice and love. Faithfulness to that mission draws him into relationships of solidarity with the most vulnerable groups of his day. That chosen solidarity is experienced by authorities as an affront to the status quo, simply because truth lived and proclaimed functions as judgment in the presence of the powerful who manipulate truth to their own ends.[43] Faced with the judgment arising from this clear experience of contrast, we who engage in a contemporary hermeneutic are inescapably drawn into the realm of politics. The light of Jesus' life showing up the darkness underlying the authoritative structures of his own day penetrates through history to our own concrete situation. Jesus had no political agenda, but we who live by his light are compelled to engage in the concrete negotiation of structures and forces that condition and impact human life within our society. We find ourselves in the midst of the immediate experience of negative contrast. It is not a matter of choice; it is a matter of consciousness. Once such consciousness is awakened, we have no choice but to act. The contrast created by the recognition of human suffering against the horizon of the eschatological promise transforms personal consciousness into a call to political praxis. And this is the essence of political mysticism.

Jesus' miracles of personal healing and liberation thus lead to political mysticism on the common ground of negative contrast experience. "Political mysticism" appears in all those situations in which experiences of injustice, oppression, and suffering give rise to protest and the ethical imperative toward active transformation. Schillebeeckx emphasizes,

> these contrast experiences show that the moral imperative is first discovered in its immediate, concrete, *inner* meaning, before it can be made the object of a science and then reduced to a generally valid principle. . . . The initial creative decision which discovered the historical imperative directly in its *inner* meaning in the very contrast experience *is,* for the believer, at the same time the charismatic element of this whole process.[44]

For the believer, this inner, charismatic element is the essence of metanoia. It is first of all personal, inhabiting the realm of mysticism. It corresponds to the depths of the Word which the Scriptures, old and new, have urged people to recognize as "very near to you, on your lips and in your heart." It is the Word that Paul likens to a two-edged sword, living and active, probing the thoughts of the heart. In Schillebeeckx's theological development, it becomes increasingly evident that it is frequently suffering that activates the process of metanoia. Schillebeeckx illustrates the personal process whereby this occurs in his early article, "The Death of a Christian," where the individual's encounter with life's limits in death illuminates the centrality of the ultimate call to surrender in obedience to the divine mystery. The facing of one's own limits in illness or in any experience that evokes the inevitability of death elicits a spectrum of responses, beginning often with denial, followed by resistance, and requiring, ultimately, some form of reconciliation.

In the societal realm, awareness of human limits in the face of structures that create suffering similarly evokes denial and resistance. Denial can function as a buffer against consciousness of the scope of systematized injustice when such consciousness would prove too overwhelming to live with, or present a challenge too risky to undertake. In "sophisticated" Western societies, the evil of injustice and oppression is often so insidiously imbedded in accepted structures that it is difficult to isolate, name, and deal with it without so threatening the status quo that the injustice is intensified in reactionary righteousness and indignation.[45] In societies whose infrastructures are weakened by overt corruption and long histories of violence, the sources of evil are concretely evident and widely known. Denial in these scenarios is a means of protection against the violent recriminations that are the common method of maintaining power.

But at the point beyond which suffering can no longer be silently, passively endured, denial breaks forth into resistance and protest. This requires solidarity, among both the victims of oppression and others who align themselves with the truth. For the victimized, the truth is known by contrast in and through the suffering of injustice. For their companions, the truth is known, also by contrast, in and through relationship with those undergoing suffering. The process whereby one enters into compassionate solidarity with another who suffers is the process of metanoia. Many who work for justice on behalf of the oppressed in the secular realm share in a similar experience. Schillebeeckx repeatedly urges religious people to recognize the authentic, transformative power of the commitment of people working for justice on the basis of a purely secular ethic. Whether they call the ideal they are working toward "the reign of God" or not, it can point to the same reality. And yet, in typical "both/and" fashion, Schillebeeckx makes clear that a Christian ethics is distinct in its source of inspiration.

First of all, it is fundamentally biblical, concerned with God's rule; secondly, it is "intrinsically bound up with the person of Jesus, who was able to break through both the specific laws of Judaism and the ethics prevailing at the time."[46]

There are biblical examples of explicitly political critique, by the prophets in the Hebrew Testament. But this is fundamentally a religious critique. In a scenario with a familiar, contemporary flavor, Schillebeeckx points out how social disparity increased with urbanization and the pragmatic appropriation of Canaanite ways among the Israelites. Amos, Micah, and Isaiah never say what society should be like; "they only appeal for a return to the true Yahwism from which people had broken away. Yahweh no longer has any part to play in political decisions (Isa. 31:1–2), the aristocracy and people with official rank enrich themselves at the expense of ordinary folk."[47] What is important is that the basis both of the conduct and of the critique is the covenant, a standard of relationship. The fundamental relationship with God in and through which the Israelites historically had come to know and identify themselves as a people is the standard to which the prophets hold them. "It is because every Israelite is a fully-fledged member of the people of God in this country (Isa. 3:14–15) that the prophets utter their protest: their critique is a religious one."[48] More, it is rooted in zeal for the cause of God, which must be Israel's cause also.

Schillebeeckx expresses the simple proclamation of judgment in this way: "God will not let himself be cornered."[49] That is, the suffering, the injustice, the oppression being visited upon the vulnerable by the powerful is an affront to God and God's power. Despite the fact that the prophets can't say exactly what society should look like, Schillebeeckx says that "a prospect of salvation-from-God does come vaguely into sight," and it is marked by a new and just redistribution of goods according to the design of God, with whom the future rests.[50] The prophets do not, in Schillebeeckx's estimation, indict any particular institutions. Their complaint is leveled at abuse of power and oppression of the poor. And here Schillebeeckx raises the question so frequently raised in religious as well as secular communities and societies today: "Who are the poor?" They are, he maintains, those who cannot stand up for themselves. In the Hebrew scriptures, these were initially the actual poor of society, the victims of structures. Within this, however, there developed a religious implication arising out of the experience of the "remnant" after the exile. The "poor" came to symbolize those sustained by the old Yahwistic spirituality, those living according to the covenant. They are those who have nothing to hope for from human history, and so wait expectantly upon God. "In Jesus' time therefore, the 'poor' among the Jews are people who cannot command justice for themselves and so can only trust in the justice of God." Now, as in Jesus' time, as in the tradition of the Hebrew Scriptures, they are those whom we have come to call the *anawim*.[51]

A Contemporary View: The "Poor" Are Those Who Suffer

If, in response to the question, "Who are the poor?" we in our own day answer that they are "those who have nothing to hope for from human history," then we have, in effect, described the plight of all those who are enduring the extremes of suffering. When we have evoked examples from the masses of people subject to unending eruptions of genocide in places as diverse as Rwanda and Bosnia, to the slave labor through which children are sacrificed to the god of the global economy in China and throughout the developing nations, to the victims of the violence escalating with the drug trade in our North American cities, we have only begun to name the "poor." The "poor" are those who suffer. They are the economically deprived who bear all the complex burdens that attend poverty in its different cultural guises. They are the ones who cannot command justice for themselves. Mere survival demands all their meager resources. In many cases, even where there may be enough energy of spirit for resistance, the stakes are just too high.

The mother of an overcrowded family in China cannot demand safer conditions at the factory where her children labor for fear that she will lose the small wage that helps to keep the family just this side of starvation. Much less will she consider her own welfare at work, if she is so lucky as to have a job. The young girl sold into prostitution cannot protest her plight because, once sent (cruelly or naively) away by her father, she has no other means of survival. And her "arrangement" may be a condition of the survival of her siblings at home.

In the Western Hemisphere, Guatemala and El Salvador are only two among many examples of Latin American countries scarred by long oppressive histories. They teach us, vividly, how a history of suffering marks a people, even when they enter upon a time of "peace." The governments of both El Salvador and Guatemala signed peace accords in 1996. The civil wars that had raged in each country between guerrillas and the military for over thirty years officially ceased. The overt fighting stopped, but the people have been left to deal with the effects of the slaughter systematically perpetrated by government forces. Far worse is the way that violence and brutality have seeped into the blood of the peasants, damaging their collective psyche. They suffer, now, the effects of their own failed struggle of resistance against their oppressors—failed, in large part, because the powers to the north abandoned them, siding with their military governments.[52]

On the terrain internal to each of these countries, the dynamics of solidarity and metanoia essential to reconciliation entail the long, slow grieving that is attendant upon the process of digging up the dead, bringing the crimes of the past to light, and walking the painful path to healing. Each of these countries suffers the scars of long, bitter conflict among its own indigenous peoples. They share with the countries of Africa the still more deeply etched scars of centuries of European pawn-brokering, continued by North America and the current dynamics of the global market. The multiple slaveries of the past have merely changed in form. Politically, socially, and geographically instances of suffering, oppression, and injustice continue to multiply.[53] Here we have merely sought to evoke some crucial elements of solidarity and metanoia in a few well-known scenarios.

Another category of people to take into account when considering the poor who "have nothing to hope for from human history" and who cannot command justice for themselves, includes the vulnerable inhabitants of our affluent societies. Some are merely the victims of our bustling, success-oriented North American culture—those who, somehow, have "dropped out." Primary among these are the members of that complexly varied population we label "homeless," and especially those who have become homeless as a direct consequence of mental illness. They clearly "cannot command justice for themselves," and their increasingly visible presence is an indictment of our structures that value the wealth and success of a narrowing, globally interconnected corporate sector more than the life and health of society's vulnerable members.

Also among society's vulnerable members are many who appear to have every reason for hope, who seem well placed to command justice for themselves. These are the ones who, in their attainment of the "good life," have lost their souls. Victims of the oppressive dynamics and trappings of their own success, they suffer the deepest kind of alienation. They suffer the psychic and spiritual devastation of a life defined by power and an autonomy that, in effect, stands over against authentic freedom.

But there are others, still more vulnerable than these. Those who suffer severe illness, physical or mental, and who find themselves at the extreme limits of life in this technologically sophisticated milieu, are by far the most vulnerable. They are the ones, the "poor," who truly cannot command justice for themselves. Here I refer especially to those at life's beginning and end who are sick beyond hope and find themselves at the mercy of a society whose valuing of nonautonomous life is perilously atrophied. Social platforms often employ the injunction that a society's moral measure is the quality of care it extends to its most vulnerable members. The injunction is usually leveled at legislators in behalf of the disenfranchised, especially women and children, who depend upon a strong social welfare net for survival; this is worthwhile and necessary. Yet, in a society where life's value is measured by worldly success and functional efficiency, the incurably ill and the severely disabled who are also dependent upon the community for survival are the foremost among the vulnerable. Whether rich or poor (the latter incur a double jeopardy), they comprise the excruciating test case of the foundational life principle undergirding a society's ethics.

Such injustices extend far beyond the scope of this study. In fact, every scenario I have evoked poses a moral and ethical dilemma of social or personal justice that is a study unto itself. They serve only to suggest the vast and complexly interconnected network of human suffering in the present age. In a different way in each case it is clear that the very presence of suffering and injustice points by contrast to a possibility of salvation, however vague; it is equally clear that the plight of those who suffer stands as an indictment of the structures of the *status quo* and those who benefit from them. But there is more here. There is a model, differently nuanced in each case, of the reciprocal role of solidarity and metanoia.

The springboard for this contemporary analysis was Schillebeeckx's assessment of the biblical ground for understanding who "the poor" are. In the Yahwistic tradition, the humble who depend upon God were referred to as the anawim. I have further interpreted Schillebeeckx's definition of the "poor" as applying to *all* those who suffer without hope, who cannot command justice for themselves, who are at the edges of life. At this point, the distinction must be made that not all of these "poor" can be classified as anawim. Members of the anawim are the "renewed" people of God. To be counted among them implies that one has entrusted oneself and one's plight to God. This entails a stance of faith consistent with metanoia. We might, then, identify the anawim as the poor and suffering who have experienced metanoia. Those who can hope for nothing from human history, who cannot command justice for themselves, but nevertheless entrust themselves to God and God's hidden future, are the anawim.[54]

But what of the rest? What of those who suffer without trust and those who are self-sufficient and thriving according to the values of the world? All of these are lacking the fullness of human life that is prerequisite to salvation. All of these occupy different dimensions of the arena in which metanoia and solidarity must interact to "make possible what is necessary for salvation." They raise a point that Schillebeeckx makes repeatedly, namely, that Jesus cared not whether a sufferer was righteous. He responded with compassion and was able to effect healing in those whose hearts were open to change, regardless of their personal histories of sin.

While noting that the conversation partner of Western theology in modern times has been the unbelieving humanist, Schillebeeckx points to the different and compelling dialogical ground of regional theologies of liberation, beginning with Latin American liberation theology. "The conversation-partner of this non-western theology is no longer the unbelieving fellow citizen, but the fellow-man [*sic*] who is despised, oppressed and held in subjection: the poor man (believer or unbeliever), the victim of our self-made systems."[55] Theologians who give a voice to the experiences of these people are, as Schillebeeckx points out, bringing *another* theology to life. Theologies that have "matured on another field of experience" must be guarded in their uniqueness even as their participation in the universal saving truth is recognized.[56] The realities of oppression and injustice dominating these particular loci of experience illuminate the prior and intended reality of the eschatological promise. The experience of contrast gives rise to the moral impetus to resist injustice and begin to construct politically the conditions which will make salvation possible.

The reality of suffering has thus shaped not only Schillebeeckx's theological project, but also his analysis of what is required of theology in a new age. He laments that the deepest impulses of the gospel have not yet borne themselves out in the Church's own self-understanding.[57] He makes it clear that the concrete contemporary manifestations of suffering with their corresponding intuitions will reveal the gospel's deepest impulses and provide the material with which to construct new theologies. Jesus himself overturned the biblical preoccupation with the *innocent* sufferer. In our contemporary world, the oppression, exploitation, and injustice imposed on our brothers and sisters by the anonymous forces of political and economic systems render inconsequential the righteousness or lack of righteousness of those who suffer. Schillebeeckx bluntly exposes the moral ambiguity that must be mercifully regarded as part of the substance of today's suffering:

> This constant exploitation seems to make it impossible from the start for the individual to find the strength or the time to become *saddiq* or righteous. He does not suffer in any way *for* the kingdom of God or *for* a good cause. He suffers. And suffers above all *from* something, not *for the sake of* a good cause. Dumb suffering. This is a new situation. . . . more reminiscent of the oldest biblical story of all: the mere fact of the lament of the Hebrews over their slavery (Ex. 2.23–25;3.7f.). *This* caused God to come down to free his people (Ex. 3.8.)[58]

The historical impulses to solidarity with suffering people, on the basis of the rights that are theirs simply by virtue of their *being human,* have arisen in recent times predominantly from secular movements. Schillebeeckx points out, however, that it is incumbent upon Christians to understand their own tradition well enough to recognize its elements in "the solemn concern of others for the *humanum* in accordance with its own value" and "give a hearing to the echo . . . of forgotten truths. . . . from their own experience of Christian belief."[59] Thus will the deepest impulses of the gospel be activated, not "through imitative repetition, but through the creation of new yet nevertheless Christian traditions: a tradition yet to come, albeit from wisdom already acquired!"[60]

The movement of Schillebeeckx's own theology is guided by the increasing realization that the very incomprehensibility of so much of human suffering must somehow become part of the Church's self-understanding, ministry, and preaching. And this is a humbling prospect. Essential to the proclamation of the gospel is the Church's own prior realization that God wills to save *sinners.* Salvation entails the healing of humanity from all its ills. *This* entails repentance and the forgiveness of sins, but does not require an ordering of "steps" in which meta-noia must precede the alleviation of poverty, the securing of food and housing, or liberation from oppressive structures and relationships. In fact, if we are to believe Schillebeeckx, the very conditions of physical, economic, or psychological suffering impede the possibility of interior metanoia. This is what he means when he defines politics as "the difficult art of making possible what is necessary for salvation." Conditions of justice must prevail for men and women to approach the freedom necessary for the turning to God that brings about full human flourishing integral to salvation.[61] Those who suffer *are* the "poor" who cannot command justice for themselves. The link between metanoia and solidarity summons believers into relationship with those who suffer, *especially* in the most incomprehensible situations. It involves them in the concrete, contemporary instances of suffering just mentioned. In each scenario the twofold question arises, "Who has the authority to command justice for those who cannot command it for themselves?" and "How will they be moved to risk such a command?" In each scenario, there is a summons to solidarity that entails metanoia.

The situations in Rwanda and in the Balkans are quite different from each other; each is representative, though, of long histories of tribal or ethnic conflict that plague their respective regions. They share a degree of ongoing, senseless brutality that shocks us, sometimes to the point of numbness. Clearly, within these situations, the only hope for healing is enough compassionate solidarity with those who are "other," who have long been "enemy," to effect a genuine change of heart on the part of victims and oppressors alike. This is especially necessary in situations, particularly in Africa, where the victim and oppressor roles change places regularly. In environments of conflict, "solidarity" usually defines relationships with those who are "on our side" in the struggle. Compassionate solidarity, however, crosses all boundaries in identification with another who suffers. Necessarily, this already entails a degree of metanoia, an openness of heart rendered through grace and entailing a fundamental trust. The mutually reciprocal action of solidarity and metanoia is essential to the reconciliation that these regions cry out for.

The overwhelming effects of human rights abuses in China (to name only one very prominent example) immediately and concretely engages the Western world and, particularly, North America. China serves to illumine the role of solidarity and metanoia in all of the dimensions of human suffering. Because its people are oppressed by no one but their own dictators *and* the enslaving ideal of success exalted by the prosperous leaders of the global economy, China's plight exemplifies the reality of human solidarity in sin. There is no overt conflict here of race, religion, or tribe; rather, there is the unmitigated suffering of a people governed by leaders whose god is economic success and technological progress.[62] Beyond the human rights abuses that we have barely mentioned, there is the ongoing assault on the human spirit of a people whose freedom is restricted, whose life choices are controlled. Perhaps even worse is the plight of those who believe themselves free as they advance along the path of scientific progress. They share with their successful Western counterparts the elements of experience that ultimately lead to the suffering of the soul's alienation. The summons to solidarity and metanoia, in this case, cuts across the globe. To perceive the truth of China's suffering is to perceive the truth of the sins of the West.[63] It is to recognize that our exaltation of profit enslaves the children in Chinese factories as surely as the chains that some of them wear. To ask the question "why?" when we look with horror upon the manifold slavery of children is to be led back to our own doorsteps. As surely as we participate in the goods of our prosperous society, we participate in the enslavement of a world-wide "underclass." Even the most searing consciousness cannot extricate us from this dark underside of our human solidarity. But it can evoke in us the solidarity in grace that arises from and furthers metanoia.[64]

Guatemala and El Salvador present a quite different scenario, one in which the dynamics of solidarity and metanoia essential to reconciliation entail the long, slow grieving that is attendant upon the process of digging up the dead, bringing the crimes of the past to light, and walking the painful path to healing. Each of these countries suffers the scars of long, bitter conflict among its own indigenous peoples. They share with the countries of Africa the still more deeply etched scars of centuries of European pawn-brokering, continued by North America and the current dynamics of the global market. The multiple slaveries of the past have merely changed in form. Politically, socially, and geographically multiplying instances of suffering, oppression, and injustice continue to multiply.[65] Here we have merely sought to evoke some crucial elements of solidarity and metanoia in a few well-known scenarios.

Thus the vast extent of global suffering requires the dynamics of solidarity and metanoia at multiple levels. The recurring evidence indicates that the privileged (and we of the West are privileged simply in our freedom and capacity to reflect) are those summoned first, foremost, and most urgently to solidarity and metanoia. It begins in that kernel where we first experience the indignation that operates as moral impulse, that tiny cell where conversion begins and allows us to enter the space beyond our own life's limits where the "other" dwells, so as to be challenged at increasingly complex and inclusive levels of our being, our choosing, and our relating. That is the beginning of the solidarity that perpetuates the process of metanoia and extends it in the widening and deepening spirals of community and society. It is the place in which we come to an awareness of truth in interior freedom with sufficient exterior freedom for embodiment in love. And it seems that, religiously and ethically, we have to come to this place before we can ever begin to deal with the question of those we have called the "foremost among the vulnerable" in our own society.

In approaching the questions raging in the field of ethics *vis-à-vis* those who are sick beyond hope, those who can no longer determine their own lives, one enters the arena of suffering that demands the care that can only come from the place of solidarity that entails metanoia. When life is at its most vulnerable, when all superficial values are shorn away, the ultimate meaning of suffering is revealed in a manner that exposes the foundations of the life principles of a society.

ORIGINAL JUSTICE REVISITED

The foundations of a society's life principles are positively identified, in Christian thought, with what has traditionally been called "original justice." Chapter two analyzed the Thomistic notion of "original justice" as the image of the solidarity in grace in which human beings were created. This truest foundation is too commonly recognized in human experience negatively, through the lens of primal loss that we call original sin. Original justice is that mythic configuration of earthly perfection and balance that closely evokes the salvation human beings long for. It is the primordial and intended reality to which suffering and sin pose so much evidence to the contrary in human life. It is, in the language of Schillebeeckx's later theology, the eschatological promise made vivid by the memory of suffering.

The essence of personal suffering in the individual's encounter with death is the relinquishing of life, especially as life is made tangible in relationships. The reality of solidarity is evident in the implication that one's self, one's personal being, inheres in those earthly relationships. Such a letting-go calls for total self-abandonment into God's hands, trusting God to keep one's life. The personal mysticism that is illumined in the believer's encounter with death simultaneously illumines and is illumined by the believer's encounter with the universal human solidarity in suffering that, like death, is the manifestation of sin in the world.[66]

The utter self-abandonment in trust made possible by the encounter with death can also be wrought through near, personal encounters with suffering of a nature that magnifies our human helplessness in the face of so very much of the world's evil. The absence, failure, or betrayal of trust is the common element in the numberless concrete instances that constitute the dense web of suffering that we have only fragmentarily represented. Even if we forget history and limit our consciousness to the present moment, it is difficult to consider in one category such distinct scenarios as the suffering of a successful, comfortably situated North American faced with the physical and psychic pain of a terminal illness; the millions of people throughout the world who regularly suffer the devastation of natural disasters; the multiple victims of the addictions that spiral through all cultures and classes, giving rise to cycles of abuse and violence in which the perpetrators themselves are victims of their own environmental histories; the agony of a mother without the means to adequately care for her children; the suffering of those affected by AIDS, not least of which is the pain of society's fear and rejection.

Such a catalogue of sufferings holds little hope of completion and could never be adequately treated, much less resolved, in this space. My point, in conformity with Schillebeeckx, is to show the inextricable connection between the single most painful dimension of all these scenarios and the healing dimension of salvation. However incomparable these scenarios might be, and however incomprehensible some may remain, they have this in common: they illuminate the power of trust through its absence or its violent betrayal. At the core of every experience of suffering, the role of trust is revealed as pivotal. However incomprehensible the situation, whatever its origins, there is no experience of suffering that is not rooted in or exacerbated by the lack or the betrayal of trust, or in some way alleviated through an act of trust.

On the surface, this statement may seem somewhat sweeping; it may raise questions as to what trust has to do with natural disasters, with sudden physical injury, or with the onset of terminal illness. Of course, a lack or failure of trust does not cause such sufferings—unless we transpose such scenarios via the metaphorical consciousness required for a contemporary rendering of the symbols of original justice and original sin. Failure to trust may be straightforwardly at the root of the suffering incurred by civil war. It is not straightforwardly at the root of a diagnosis of cancer. It is not straightforwardly at the root of a devastating earthquake. Failure to trust is, however, *metaphorically* at the root of such sufferings, in the same symbolic way that original sin is at the root of death. In "The Death of a Christian," Schillebeeckx observes that the agony of death indicates that something is unstuck at the heart of things in the world. He elaborates:

> The death of an innocent child, fratricide, the death of a beloved mother whose love and care is woven into the texture of the whole of life, any death at all, proves only that there is something unstuck somewhere in the world, that something is maimed—something that cannot be explained by pointing philosophically to the limitations of humanity.[67]

Death and all suffering are somehow rooted in the primordial severing of divine/human relationship symbolized by original sin. This root is alienation, the diametric opposite of trust. Saying this simply gives voice to the absurdity that Schillebeeckx acknowledges when he speaks of suffering as ultimately mysterious, pointing to suffering's root in original sin. This picture has been negatively filled out in contrast to the horizon of Jesus' own life, marked by trusting surrender to God.

Schillebeeckx's rendering of Jesus' life and mission reveal the ways in which trust in the promise makes possible God's reign. Certainly, in the whole of the Christian tradition, salvation is known in the love of God made visible in Christ and available to Christians through our communion with one another in the Holy Spirit. But too often in our human experience that communion is blocked or negated by our inability to trust God and one another. In this sense, trust is the material of salvation and the essence of solidarity. It is the basis of authentic relating; even more, it is the substance of relationship, which increases dialectically through the process of metanoia. Trust is essential for the final letting go in vulnerability that transforms death itself into a free act.[68] The absence of trust makes of life a hell; the degree to which trust is present is the degree to which salvation is experienced even here, even now, even in the midst of suffering. Such trust in its fullness is what Schillebeeckx has called Jesus' "unbroken communion with God."[69] It is the obedience at the heart of the paschal mystery, the living relation that sustains death and issues in the resurrection. The gift of the resurrection is the extension of Jesus' communion with God and his earthly companions to the whole company of believers down through the ages.

Thus, it is the lack of trust which breaks communion, impedes solidarity, negates salvation. And whatever negates salvation is sin. The sin of the world is inextricably bound up with the lack of trust. This deficiency, rooted in the original human refusal to "walk with God in the garden," is both the essence of sin and, dialectically, the source of evil and suffering; frequently, it is its own suffering. The failure to trust is the failure to remember the original justice in which we were created; equally, it is the failure to believe in the promise of the future secured in the resurrection. Ultimately, it is the refusal of grace. Yet, paradoxically, even in this we are not deprived of grace. In the overwhelming experience of powerlessness we are faced simultaneously with our own sin and God's unconditional love offered yet again.

At the beginning of this chapter, I noted that the essence of mysticism uncovered by the cross is the existential, conscious, lived experience of divine/human relationship. This experience of mysticism is, in simple terms, the reality of trust. For Schillebeeckx, this is a profoundly theological reality, which is prior to politics as it is prior to ethics. And yet, it entails both of these. Further, when mysticism gives rise to ethical, political action, it is deepened in its spiritual reality precisely in and through its worldly realization. While distinguishing the theological from the ethical, Schillebeeckx maintains that they cannot be separated; we must take account of the ethical dimension of theology as well as the theological dimension of ethics.[70]

In speaking of the centrality of trust, I have identified the effects of its absence or betrayal with sin. At the same time, I observed that the failure, absence, or betrayal of trust constitutes its own substantial suffering. Schillebeeckx clarifies the language of sin as he elaborates the relationship between ethics and theology, that is, the secular and religious spheres. The language of sin has come into secular usage sometimes frivolously and to the detriment of its true meaning. Even when it is employed to name real ethical evil, its deep meaning is often missed. Schillebeeckx points out that, in Christian understanding, the language of sin only has meaning in the context of relationship to God. But if we understand that the violation of human beings is by that very fact a violation of our relationship with God, Christians have common ground for dialogue between believers and nonbelievers or other-believers.[71]

At the same time, the theological perspective recognizes the ontological import of the events that destroy or damage human dignity and well-being.[72] Thus is Schillebeeckx able to speak of a *specifically Christian* ethic which is not exclusive to Christianity. The Christian inspiration that leads to a particular, yet universally communicable ethical judgment and practice is the knowledge arising from the experience of grace. This is a "discerning of spirits . . . both contemplative (mystical) and ethical . . . in and through the daily affairs of an ethically oriented life."[73] Schillebeeckx cites, by way of example, the "utopian-critical force" of the Sermon on the Mount, which can never be legalistically codified. "For the believer, the gospel can exercise a binding power which leads to an ethical decision, but which can never be prescribed by a commandment or a prohibition."[74]

It would seem that Schillebeeckx's fundamental view of ethical Christian life depends upon the centrality of trust, which is beginning to look more and more like grace. It takes a measure of trust even to accept his hermeneutic, which presumes the operation of grace in the depths of human experience. But, as we have already noted, that is a risk that God took first in creation. As human beings, we are fully entrusted with the care of the world and of each other. Created in God's own image, we are challenged to mirror the divine initiative of "risky trust."

THE HUMAN VOCATION
TO MEDIATE GRACE

In his early view of "original justice," Schillebeeckx characterized "original sin" as the human failure in the vocation to mediate grace.[75] This is the communal side of the human "refusal to walk with God in the garden."[76] In his more recent theology, he speaks of the religious challenge constituted by ethics, and I have outlined how the formative impact of suffering upon Schillebeeckx's theological development is implicit in the dynamism of negative contrast experience, with its capacity to give rise to a moral imperative. It is also clear that the root of the moral imperative is the inner dynamic of metanoia, the substantive thread of mysticism underlying and sustaining every movement in Schillebeeckx's theology.[77] That "root" is the very essence of struggle in contrast, the struggle that is so often experienced as suffering. The resistance entailed is sometimes manifest externally, even politically, in protest, and followed or accompanied by positive action for good. Salvation is concretely attained in fragmentary ways when such efforts bear fruit in visible transformation of persons and structures. Very often, however, whether in politically oppressive situations where people suffer the weight of powerlessness, or in personal situations such as illness, the "resistance" is an internal one that resolves into a will to endure. It may look like passive acceptance. In fact, it is the obedience that acts justly and faithfully on behalf of the fullest possible humanity within life's current contingencies, while entrusting the hope of life's final flourishing and ultimate truth to God.[78]

The core of such metanoia is the relational depth of personal communion with God. This is the only possible basis for the kind of human trust essential to the solidarity for which we were created, the solidarity that mirrors God's own being. This trust is the embodiment of grace, the essence of what was "lost" at the metaphorical origins of our race. While still very close to his early Thomistic training, Schillebeeckx wrote: "It is only in the warmth of God's saving love, to which (perhaps only implicit) consent has been given, that our humanity becomes a grace. It is in this way that we become an offer of grace for each other or the concrete form of the *initium fidei* which through God's grace also feels its way in our fellow men and women."[79] This early assertion that it is God's love that renders humanity itself a grace underlies his later and increasing insistence upon the concrete human person as the norm of ethical praxis. It develops into a nuanced expression of the political and social requirements of a mysticism formed by faith in the God of humanity. Created in the image of the relational God who exists for us,[80] human beings are structured as mediators of grace for one another. But Adam's mythic refusal lives on, in the inclination to withdraw from mediatorship that continues to mark the human condition.[81] It is one thing to say that God's reign (creation's flourishing) is advanced on earth to the degree to which we respond to our human vocation as mediators of grace, and diminished to the degree that we fail to respond. It is quite another to recognize the complex relational and structural context that makes neither response nor refusal so clear-cut an act, either of grace or of sin.

Precisely this ambiguity of the human condition leads Schillebeeckx in his later theology to acknowledge that human beings are not only grace, but also threat to their fellow men and women. The ethical demand placed upon an individual in encounter with the human "other" is a basic standard which Christian praxis shares with many secular philosophies of ethics, and one upon which Schillebeeckx places a very high priority. It underlies the critical social theories so important to Schillebeeckx's development. It is a demand framed in compelling terms by Emmanuel Levinas, with whom Schillebeeckx frequently enters into positive dialogue in his writing. Levinas's central thesis inheres in the ethical claim of the "other" upon one's freedom. Though all of Schillebeeckx's writing affirms the human cause as the highest priority, his affirmation presumes God's ultimacy in and through humanity. For Levinas, the face-to-face with the human other remains the ultimate situation, and this, Schillebeeckx maintains, "leads to a cul-de-sac or aporia,"[82] precisely because of the threat human beings can pose to each other in their freedom. Drawing upon Kant, he emphasizes that it is dangerous to make the human the ultimate source of meaning and value because "then there is no guarantee whatsoever that evil will not have the last word on our existence as ethically responsible beings."[83] This is most threateningly true in asymmetrical ethical relationships between parties of unequal power. We have only to think of the political as well as personal structures of injustice wherein the dominance of power determines, limits, or abuses the freedom of the weaker party.

A general feeling of hopelessness attends many of the scenarios of suffering in our world. The incredible imbalance of power in so many human spheres damages and distorts trust by manipulating human freedom. It even invades the most personal sphere of suffering, as when individuals, believers or not, are conditioned by such experience to perceive God or ultimate reality as cruel or manipulative. The pervasive misuse of power and thwarting of freedom cripples men and women in their capacity to respond to their vocation as mediators of grace. This, indeed, is the contemporary manifestation of our "universal solidarity in sin." This is the realistic, contrastive expression of the mystical centrality of trust at the heart of the experience of suffering.

It certainly does seem that the universal solidarity in grace manifest in personal and structural relations of mutual trust has been forfeited forever with the loss of "original justice." And yet, this almost tangible memory of loss is not only restored but transcended in the proclamation of the reign of God. What does this mean for human beings who risk the threat of evil in responding to the ethical demand? Schillebeeckx attempts to answer this question through an illustration of heroic ethical action to which he admits a variety of legitimate interpretations. He tells the story of a soldier required to kill a hostage. The soldier refuses to do so, knowing that he will be killed as a result, and the hostage will be killed in spite of him. At one level, this is a "disarming act of conscience" which, in Levinas's terms, "demonstrates the 'end of the powers.'"[84] It is a moral gesture that is unquestionably absurd in its finite ineffectiveness. In this sense, it leads to the aporia or cul-de-sac that evoked Schillebeeckx's critique of Levinas. Schillebeeckx suggests two possible solutions to this aporia, one humanist and one religious. Both cling to the ultimate value of the *humanum;* the agnostic humanism of Sartre or Camus and the religious faith of the believer equally recognize the victory of the "gratuitous heroic action" over the "empirical triumph of the facts."[85] But Schillebeeckx points out that the most profound humanist "does not know in the end whether reality itself will prove our ethical conviction of standing on the side of justice to be right!"[86] This is precisely where the deepest truth uncovered in the experience of suffering comes to the fore. The suffering victims of history arise in overwhelming, silent witness to the reality of a different ground of hope for the eventual triumph of the *humanum.*

Solidarity with the *Threatened Humanum* as Martyrdom

If hope for the future rests only on ethics, then the victims of the past, including those who offered themselves in heroic ethical acts, are all lost in an oblivion of absurdity. If this is true, then the cherishing of an individual human life as precious is itself absurdity. Human life is reduced to a principle, a principle of some ideal, abstract future when life will have a higher quality. This is fundamentally anti-incarnational; in the light of the gospel, no concrete, particular human life can be sacrificed for an ideal. The universal good can never be separated from the intrinsic worth of every individual in his or her particularity.

Schillebeeckx speaks here on the basis of a delicate but essential differentiation between the humanist who is more than a pragmatic ethicist, who perceives the deep, nonempirical value at the depths of the *humanum,* and the religious believer. For the former, there is meaning in the ethical act of the soldier because it testifies to the priority of the praxis of justice, even where it is sure to be empirically defeated. But the sacrifice of the soldier's life has no meaning beyond the witness to an ideal, which may inspire others to create conditions for a better humanity in the future. This is good, but it is not enough. The humanist valuing of justice sustains hope for an earthly future, but it does nothing to redeem the past; it offers no hope or redemption for the particular life of the soldier.[87] In the Christian view, this is not satisfactory. There must be hope and a future even for those swallowed up by earthly defeat and failure.[88] The religious ground for hope lies in the fact that the believer who thus experiences reality's absolute limit experiences it as God's personal, absolute and saving presence. Reprising his constant anthem, Schillebeeckx insists that the absurd is not argued away; rather, believers entrust the absurdity to God, the source of pure positivity and the mystical foundation of ethical commitment. The religious, and especially Christian, distinction lies in the meaning of the martyr's death; "this act itself is praxis of the kingdom of God and bears within itself the germ of resurrection."[89]

Martyrdom is the expression of "God's defenceless victory" that brings us to the crux of the human vocation to mediate grace. The trust necessary to this mediation is so often violated in human experience that our human solidarity in sin is more familiar to us than our solidarity in grace. Yet, paradoxically, our human solidarity in grace is the foundational and transcendent reality from which and toward which we live. We know this most clearly through the suffering wrought in personal or structural relations by the absence or betrayal of trust. It is the startling effect of trust's violation that is revelatory of a different, positive fundamental expectation. It may be argued that even the cynicism of those hardened against the possibility, or even the wisdom, of any human mutuality in trust is due to the existence of a positive, primordial expectation soured by too much evidence to the contrary. This itself is a suffering, the suffering of alienation arising from that most original sin and contributing to further sin and suffering. And so continues the most negative strand of the spiral of human experience. Still, as the paschal mystery proclaims, the persistence of God's original intent in creation can weave the darkest strands of human existence back into the pattern of redemption.

Precisely the supreme violation of human trust that martyrdom represents reveals, by contrast, the sure and positive ground of the human vocation to mediate grace. That positive ground goes beyond the sustaining, but always fragile, force of human trust in God to the unassailable foundation of all human trust— God's own trust in humanity. The divine trust invested in creation transcends all our human failures to mediate grace, turning even the material of our failure into a renewed invitation to solidarity. Political martyrdom makes visible the power of authentic trust in those situations where conflicting ideologies and the confusing claims of violent factions cloud the real nature of suffering. True martyrs are those whose solidarity with the *threatened humanum* even unto death bears witness to God's absolute saving presence in the midst of oppression and injustice. It is only grace, Schillebeeckx says, that "gives us a moral capacity to the death."

The contrast experience of martyrdom throws into vivid relief the mix of pain and liberation entailed in the authentic trust essential to solidarity. The extremes of life and death at stake in the volatile political strife in so many parts of our world have proportionate counterparts in local societal structures as well, right down to the most interpersonal relational dynamics. The quality of freedom inherent in authentic trust becomes evident in all of these arenas. Schillebeeckx describes such freedom in a manner that illumines trust's centrality in the creation or alleviation of all kinds of suffering: "The Christian freedom of the gospel is a freedom in solidarity, in which the freedom of one person is not a threat to another, as often was and still is the case with liberal, bourgeois freedoms, and also with communist freedoms."[90] The essence of trust, then, inheres in this "freedom in solidarity in which the freedom of one person is not a threat to another." And the essence of so much human suffering inheres in the reality that, even where such nonthreatening (and unthreatened) freedom is prized, it is, at best, only fragmentarily realized. Whether the subject is nations, groups, or persons, that the freedom of the "other" can be experienced as threat is testimony to the deep wound of original sin. "Original justice" was forfeited in the refusal to "let God be God." What is imaged as a freely chosen refusal has become the wound of fear crippling humanity's capacity to trust on the one hand, and giving rise to the evil that increases the reality of threat on the other. This is the human condition of grace and sin, the condition in and through which we seek salvation. This is in the depths of the human heart, where even the most globally conscious dimensions of Schillebeeckx's theology must begin and end.

The complex demands of trust return the discussion to the center of the hermeneutical spiral, to the mysticism of the cross experienced in each personal "turning" or metanoia. Life's pervasive threat to the gospel image of freedom in solidarity reaches beyond the woundedness of original sin to the creation in original justice. The capacity of human beings to threaten and be threatened by one another's freedom can only be healed through the action of reconciliation, which both depends upon and furthers metanoia. Such action must invoke our memory of original justice in the concrete imagining of that "freedom redeemed from egoism and power, freedom which rests on the fact that all are accepted by God, even before they begin to act."[91]

Reconciliation as Gift and Task

The dimensions of suffering as mystery and as challenge find correlates in the nature of reconciliation as gift and as task. Certainly, the dimension of "gift" is evident in the human need for grace, the dependence on the initiative of divine forgiveness in every human act of reconciliation. Beyond this, however, Schillebeeckx comes to understand reconciliation as a gift given by God in creation; he understands this in terms of the reality underlying Thomas's construct of original justice, but with new implications. Drawing upon Ambrose's commentary on Genesis, he links God's creation of humanity, the sabbath, and reconciliation in a way that suggests the mutually permeating qualities of "gift" and "creative task." After all the elements of the world were created, God created humanity; only then, after creating the one upon whom the divine forgiveness could be poured out, did God rest.[92]

The point here is not that human beings were bound to sin so that they could be forgiven. The point is, rather, that mercy is God's most self-revealing feature; compassion is the essence of God's being. It is of God's essence to pour out mercy and forgiveness; this is the identity of the God in whose image we were created. Thus, it belongs to our being as creatures both to receive this merciful forgiveness and to pour it out to others. To do so is to become who we most truly are.[93]

This gift of reconciliation given in creation is also a task. It is a creative task whose necessity and demand is conditioned by the concrete particularity of human structures and relations. It meets its greatest challenge in all those places where threat damages, undermines, or replaces trust. This is the meaning of sin, and, as Schillebeeckx emphasizes, sin must be clearly named. When recognized and named, sin itself calls down God's forgiveness, not from on high, but through the mediation of our fellow men and women. The very conditions of threat, of suffering, of sin become the conditions of salvation. Reconciliation is the earthly means of salvation.

"God Is in This Place and I Did Not Know It"

There is danger, Schillebeeckx warns, in preaching redemption as though religious love freed evil of its calamity, its sinfulness, its suffering. The gospel of freedom, the forgiving love of God in Jesus Christ, is rendered mere ideology if it is naively proclaimed without reference to real human experience. Worse, religion becomes an enslaving burden, binding people in chains of guilt, damaging and alienating them from themselves. This is the "un-gospel of humanity," the enemy of the rejoicing God desires, and as such, the deepest expression of sin. This is what damages the honor of God.[94] And so, it is precisely in the midst of human sin and suffering, in the place where the darkest portent of human creaturehood is revealed and all hope of trust seems extinguished, that God shows forth as most truly God.

The worst scenarios of sin and suffering reveal to us, by contrast, the deepest possibilities of being human and of being God. In all those places where the need of mercy is so great as to seem hopeless, God's own compassion is revealed in the human capacity to forgive and be forgiven. The point here is that this is true *especially* when every concrete fact indicates the contrary. Even where men and women fail most miserably to mediate grace, the failure itself points to a possibility on the horizon. It arises—if only here and there—out of the deepest human recesses where the creature and creator meet, giving rise to that spark of being that makes the possibility real in the world.[95] Here, in this place, the reality that God's own forgiveness can be poured out through human mediation comes to us as a truth from the farthest reaches, but yet still an audible and thus decipherable sign of the all-surpassing possibility of divine forgiveness.

Over and over again, Schillebeeckx proclaims that humanity is the fundamental symbol of God in the world. This is not negated by the fact that human beings are flawed, sinful, and often at war with one another. It is not negated by the fact that human beings are so often the cause of one another's suffering. God has found a way to be present even here, *especially* here. This is what Schillebeeckx means when he speaks of reconciliation as a gift given in creation. It is what he means when he speaks of the fullness of God's identity in the very pouring out of forgiveness that our sin requires. In this is humanity's deep suffering relieved; in this is sinful human solidarity transformed into solidarity in grace, fragmentarily incarnated.

The presence of suffering, brokenness, and alienation in our world illuminates human powerlessness, revealing the gratuitousness of salvation. Reconciliation from the vantage point of much human experience is possible *only* as pure grace and gift. The risen Christ, whose life we share, *is* this grace. And this is not to contradict Schillebeeckx's assertion that reconciliation is a gift given in creation, for creation, covenant, and redemption are all mediated through Christ. Schillebeeckx emphasizes the New Testament understanding in which creation and salvation are components of a single plan in which everything can become grace. Thus, "failure, disaster, and particularly unnecessary and alienating suffering (above all in the tradition of Mark, I Peter, and Hebrews) are given a dimension of grace in Christ."[96]

This mysticism of grace through suffering joined to Christ evokes the cosmic dimension of reconciliation. But Schillebeeckx reminds us that, in the New Testament, reconciliation as gift or grace is not separate from reconciliation as creative task. The New Testament proclaims salvation and glory achieved "thanks to the forgiveness of sins, that means not through a cosmic but through an anthropological reconciliation, and therefore through an ethical life in this world."[97]

The ethical life, for Schillebeeckx, is the public manifestation of the life of grace. It is shaped by reconciliation received as gift and undertaken as a creative task—not in linear fashion, but as a single, spiraling, movement. The creative task of reconciliation requires the freedom and fluidity of imagination that alone can transcend the often graceless lines of reason. Transcendent, liberating images already abound in scripture. Reaching back into the Old Testament, Schille-beeckx shows us the possibilities for imaginatively proclaiming a praxis of recon-ciliation in his own interpretation of the twin stories of Jacob's struggle with God's angel and his confrontation with the cheated Esau. The two stories, he maintains, are really one; the meaning of each inheres in the other. Jacob wrestles with the angel, sees the face of God, and reconciles with his brother, *in whose open welcome he sees the face of God.* These two experiences of "seeing" are, for Schillebeeckx, one graced event.[98] In the very struggle to be reconciled with another, we encounter God. More truly, God encounters us, doing what we can-not do for ourselves.

Reconciliation among humans, therefore, "has something to do with reconcili-ation with God from God's side."[99] This inevitably evokes the experience of mysticism, which Schillebeeckx calls "mediated immediacy." That is, from our side, all experience of God is mediated, but God from God's side is immediately present, absolutely near to us in grace. People experience this profoundly in all those situations in which they realize that they can never completely overcome the personal or social suffering and alienation of the world. They experience it in those "dark nights" in which the experience of God's absence is the only media-tion of God's presence.[100] This dark night seems, at times, to have permanently descended upon whole areas of the globe, as well as upon suffering men and women who are very near. But there is no knowledge of God's absence that does not depend upon the memory (however distant) of some positive experience of God's presence in justice and love. God is mediated also (and primarily) through goodness, through the human experiences of joy that can rise up not only along-side of but in the very midst of suffering.

Joy gives rise to praise and gratitude, to a heightened relishing of relationships with one another and with God. In other words, it gives rise to prayer and the deepening of communion and solidarity. Suffering, too, gives rise to prayer. It lays bare our dependence upon one another and upon God. It can uncover the roots of sin and draw forth deep, transforming sorrow. It can lead to the humility that opens the way to reconciliation. It can forge the wisdom and grace that enable the most damaged soul to choose to love again, restoring the bonds of communion and solidarity.

Suffering *can*, through the whole complex dynamic of negative contrast as here examined personally and politically, become thus an experience of earthly salvation and spiritual redemption. All of this seeking, all of this ethical praxis, is itself prayer. It is itself the ambiguous experience through which God is dis-closed as mercy at the heart of reality. But it leads still further into the explicit praying that Schillebeeckx says is "the most difficult metanoia or conversion of our life."

Schillebeeckx's painful cataloguing of the human history of suffering, his stringent critique of structures and beliefs that diminish humanity for any reason, and his exhortations to unceasing commitment to ethical praxis incarnate the principles of political mysticism but do not exhaust them. The alleviation of some suffering, the conversion of some sinful structures through successful praxis, make grace visible here and there, and for a time. That leaves much suffering untouched, and much sin unconverted—including sometimes, on both counts, our own. All of this, ultimately, is the reconciling work of God's grace. And we are thrown back upon God's free initiative in grace when we experience the limitation of human efforts in the face of suffering and sin, both the world's and our own. We are thrown back, quite simply, to mysticism. Which is not to say that this is where political praxis ends. It is a deeper rung of the spiral, and it will merge, eventually, into further political praxis. It is prayer, Schillebeeckx concludes, that "gives Christian faith its most critical and productive force."[101]

CONCLUSION

This chapter began with the recognition that political mysticism inheres in the mysticism of the cross, leading in a deepening spiral to Jesus' unbroken communion with God. It has explored the significance of Schillebeeckx's grounding in the Thomistic constructs of original justice and original sin for the role of suffering in his developing theology. It has shown the centrality of trust for the relational integrity essential to human salvation, even as it touched upon the overwhelming evidence of evil and suffering arising from trust's absence or betrayal. It has examined some of the concrete ways in which our human failures to mediate grace contribute to personal, communal, and global suffering. Although Christians are ever challenged to engage the political art of "making possible what is necessary for human salvation," our failures reveal the necessity of reconciliation. The significance of suffering for Schillebeeckx's theology is precisely that it leads us to this point: the experience of our utter human need for the grace of reconciliation. Personally, politically, or as a race we may or may not succeed in the external achievement of reconciliation, but that is not the point. The point is that, in willingly embracing the task of reconciliation, we come to know its utter gratuitousness. And this is the gratuitousness of salvation. Whatever leads men and women to experience this gratuitousness restores the relationship of faithful trust in God which must take place in each human heart. "In the prophet Jesus, mysticism and the healing of men [*sic*] came from one and the same source: his experience of the contrast between the living God and the history of human suffering."[102]

The mysticism capable of living from the place of contrast returns again and again to the praxis of solidarity with those who suffer. The living and articulating of such mystical praxis requires a narrative continuity with the story of Jesus, whose unbroken communion with God is the source of all our trust. In the next and final chapter, I will explore the implications of a "practical theodicy" and a "discipleship of presence." In doing so, I will return to the problem of how we care for those whom we have called the most vulnerable among us, those at the limits of what is increasingly termed "viable" life in society. As I draw conclusions about the ways in which suffering operates as a formative factor in Schillebeeckx's theology, I will have something to say about the importance of a Christian theology of suffering in negotiating the most controversial issues in the field of ethics today.

NOTES

1. Schillebeeckx, *Christ,* 743.
2. Schillebeeckx typically speaks of "Jesus, parable of God and paradigm of humanity." See, for example, the section heading in *Jesus,* 626.
3. In a discussion of the experience of contingency, Schillebeeckx importantly notes that, "We do not develop the divine out of ourselves, but the divine freely manifests itself in profound human experiences." *Church: The Human Story of God,* 80.
4. Schillebeeckx, "Secularization and Christian belief in God," in *God the Future of Man,* 80.
5. Schillebeeckx defines mysticism according to what he calls the "Thomistic-Carmelite and also Dominican interpretation" as "an intensive form of the theologal life of faith, hope, and love." Elsewhere, he explains, "By 'the religious,' 'the mystical,' 'the theologal' I understand everything in Christian life that has God himself as an explicit object. By 'the ethical,' on the other hand, I understand here directly everything which has as an explicit object the humanization or the furtherance of human beings as human beings. . . . [The] ethical has an autonomous consistency, but . . . on the other hand the ethical as taken up into the mystical dimension of the life of faith is 'transfinalized'; it becomes one expression of the coming kingdom of God." *Church: The Human Story of God,* 68–69; 91–92.
6. Schillebeeckx notes that mysticism is also found in ethics, though it is essentially meta-ethical; "Christian faith transcends the political and personal ethical commitment of Christians, but it is a transcendence by implication and not by exclusion." *Church,* 69.
7. Schillebeeckx, "Church, Magisterium, and Politics," in *God the Future of Man,* 151.
8. Schillebeeckx, "Church, Magisterium, and Politics," 151.
9. Schillebeeckx, "Church, Magisterium, and Politics," 151. Illustrative of this is the way Schillebeeckx speaks about the concrete particularity of Mary's life, in which her historical but decisive human acts "become the poles between which God's redemptive act breaks into human history." *Mary, Mother of the Redemption,* 5.
10. Schillebeeckx asserts, "There is something subtle and killing in a particular kind of virtue. The subtle vice of 'perfection' has not yet disappeared from church life." See *Church: The Human Story of God,* 117.
11. The word "solidarity" today is popularly associated with liberation movements, and most notably with the Solidarity movement in Poland. Pope John Paul II's well-known use of the term is often associated with his strong commitment to the latter, though he extends the concept broadly in church teaching. In fact, Kevin Doran demonstrates that

the development of a philosophy of solidarity in the social teaching of the Catholic Church can be traced from the nineteenth century under a terminology of "social charity," becoming more explicit in the 1930s with Pius XI's *Quadragesimo Anno,* and increasingly evident in encyclicals of subsequent popes and the documents of Vatican II. John Paul's sense of solidarity is firmly rooted in the understanding of *communio* shaped by his own early philosophical development. John Paul II's writings as Karol Wojtyla are strongly influenced by the personalist phenomenology of Max Scheler and Emmanuel Mounier, the school of thought shared, with variations, by Merleau-Ponty, in whose writing Schillebeeckx was steeped. See Kevin P. Doran, *Solidarity: A Synthesis of Personalism and Communalism in the Thought of Karol Wojtyla/Pope John Paul II* (New York: Peter Lang, 1996), 77–121; 25ff.

12. See, for example, *Mary, Mother of the Redemption,* 40–41; see chapter two.

13. Schillebeeckx, *Mary, Mother of the Redemption,* 40. John Paul II speaks of such factors as homelessness, unemployment, international debt, and the refugee crisis as negative signs of our original solidarity. These are just some of the disastrous consequences of the reality of global interdependence separated from its ethical requirements. Such obstacles to the authentic development of peoples are evidence of the moral evil that the Pope defines as "the fruit of many sins which lead to structures of sin." *Sollicitudo Rei Socialis* (1987) 17, 18, 19, 23, 37.

14. John Paul II cautions that solidarity is "not a vague feeling of compassion or shallow distress at the misfortune of so many people. . . . [but rather] a firm and persevering commitment to the common good." In language that evokes what Schillebeeckx would call the role of negative contrast experience in the process of metanoia, he affirms that "This determination is based on the *solid* conviction that what is hindering full development is that desire for profit and thirst for power. . . . These attitudes and 'structures of sin' are only conquered—presupposing the help of divine grace—by a *diametrically opposed attitude:* a commitment to the good of one's neighbour." *SRS* 38.

15. Juan Luis Segundo speaks of "primeval sin" in terms that reflect what Schillebeeckx means by negative contrast: "[It is the] base and foundation for the unity of the human species and for our solidarity with the universe. It is the base of our liberty, which puts up resistance to that liberty. It is the world that makes the Incarnation possible and then tries to suffocate it. It is the flesh of society that needs redemption and then flees from it." Juan Luis Segundo, *Evolution and Guilt* (Maryknoll, N.Y.: Orbis, 1974), 84–85.

16. Cf. the complex evolutionary pattern developed by Segundo in *Evolution and Guilt* and in *Grace and the Human Condition* (Maryknoll, N.Y.: Orbis, 1973).

17. Schillebeeckx is explaining the reality of the experience being communicated in *Hebrews* through such concepts as atonement and bloody sacrifice in conjunction with the levitical priesthood. His purpose here is to make clear "that the unifying factor is provided by what is to be interpreted and not the interpretative element." *Christ,* 632.

18. The reciprocal influence of suffering and Schillebeeckx's appropriation of hermeneutics, critical theory, and modern biblical exegesis is discussed at length in chapter one of this volume.

19. We do not imply here, nor does Schillebeeckx imply, that a suffering individual must desire conversion in order to be healed of the effects of physical or social ills. Rather, the purpose of the biblical image is to point to the deeper meaning to be uncovered in the experience of suffering in light of the dynamic of metanoia. The ethical call to attend to the *human* conditions of salvation will be discussed more fully later in this chapter.

20. Biblical examples include the bent-over woman in Luke's gospel (Lk 13:10–17) and the woman with the hemorrhage (Mk 5:25–34); Schillebeeckx's analysis of the latter is discussed above in chapter three. In Schillebeeckx's words, "The sick woman had been at her wits' end for years, she had tried everything, and it had got worse and worse. Then she heard about Jesus." *Jesus*, 195.

21. Elaborating the eschatological-revolutionary significance of the beatitudes in a context in which Jesus himself believed that "the End was very near, despite various distinctions that have to be made," Schillebeeckx asserts, "Indeed, Jesus did not preach social revolution, although his eschatological message brings the whole pain-ridden history of mankind [*sic*] radically under God's critical judgment and so calls for an about-turn." *Jesus*, 177; cf. *Christ*, 584–85. At the same time, Schillebeeckx is critical of those who were overly concerned to show that Jesus was not a revolutionary; see, for example, *Christ*, 569. Albert Nolan observes that neither a strictly political nor a strictly spiritual reading of Jesus' life is correct; both are anachronistic. "The Jews made no distinctions at all between politics and religion. Issues which we would today classify as political, social, economic or religious would all have been thought of in terms of God and the law." Albert Nolan, *Jesus before Christianity* (Maryknoll, N.Y.: Orbis, 1976, 1992), 114.

22. In a discussion of the New Testament's approach to suffering, Schillebeeckx notes that "Jesus breaks with the idea that suffering has necessarily something to do with sinfulness. This is expressly stated in two texts." The texts are John 9:2f, cited above, and Luke 13:1–5. In the latter, "when Jesus hears that Pilate had murdered some Galileans, . . . he says, 'Do you think that they were worse sinners than all the other Galileans because they suffered thus?' . . . Both New Testament statements finally show that it is possible to draw conclusions from sin to suffering, but not from suffering to sin." *Christ*, 695.

23. Throughout the Church's history of social teaching, social *charity* has been deemed the soul and life principle of social *justice*. Genuine charity has its roots in the divine gift of grace that changes the heart. Before the term "solidarity" arose in papal documents, the term "charity" was used to similar effect. Kevin Doran observes that Leo XIII used the term with specific reference to healing society's ills; John XXIII in *Pacem in Terris* linked "justice" and "charity"; the documents of Vatican II encourage dialogue and mutual charity; and, in Paul VI's *Populorum Progressio*, "universal charity" is used in conjunction with "mutual solidarity" and "social justice" as a threefold obligation derived from the "universal brotherhood of man [*sic*]." Doran, 97–101.

24. Schillebeeckx, *Christ*, 649.

25. Schillebeeckx, *Christ*, 569.

26. For instance, Schillebeeckx posits "*development* in dogma, an interpretative contemporary translation of the 'old' material of the faith" as "essentially the fidelity that follows from man's [*sic*] historicity." Elucidating certain principles within his hermeneutics of history, he continues, "On the basis of the filled distance in time, a text is understood only if it is understood in a *different* way—which does not mean a better or worse way—from the way in which it was understood in its past social and cultural context. Understanding must change in changing situations, otherwise the same thing cannot continue to be understood." See "Toward a Catholic Use of Hermeneutics," in *God the Future of Man*, 20, 31.

27. Schillebeeckx, *Christ*, 562.

28. Schillebeeckx, *Christ*, 562.

29. Schillebeeckx, *Christ,* 563.

30. Schillebeeckx, *Christ,* 553.

31. Schillebeeckx, *Christ,* 559; see 544ff for analysis of the legacy of Greek philosophy as well as the stoic origins of Paul's concept of freedom.

32. Schillebeeckx, *Christ,* 563.

33. Schillebeeckx, *Christ,* 565.

34. Joseph Fitzmyer's exegesis generally corroborates that of Schillebeeckx. He, too, asserts that "Paul does not try to change the existing social structure"; rather, he "tries to advocate a principle, while realizing the futility of trying to abolish the system of slavery." Fitzmyer's use of "principle" does not contradict Schillebeeckx but is employed in a different sense. With Schillebeeckx, he notes that "Paul's own solution was to transform or interiorize the social structure; recall 1 Cor 7:20–24; 12:13." Paul's plea is made "for love's sake; . . . but it took centuries for the Pauline principle to be put into practice, even in the Christian West." See Joseph A. Fitzmyer, S.J., "The Letter to Philemon," in *The New Jerome Biblical Commentary,* ed. Raymond E. Brown, Joseph A. Fitzmyer, and Roland E. Murphy (Englewood Cliffs, N.J.: Prentice Hall, 1990.), 870.

35. Schillebeeckx, *Christ,* 565.

36. Schillebeeckx, *Christ,* 547.

37. Schillebeeckx, *Christ,* 559.

38. Holocaust literature is filled with examples of people whose trust in God (by whatever name) not only sustained them in situations of imprisonment, but rendered their relations with those suffering with them a source of peace and transformation. Dietrich Bonhoeffer speaks of personal relationships as "the most important things in our lives." *Letters and Papers from Prison,* ed. Eberhard Bethge, trans. Reginald Fuller (London: SMC Press, 1953), 82. In the midst of the hatred and human suffering of the concentration camps where she faces her own inevitable death, Etty Hillesum longs to be "willing to act as a balm for all wounds." *An Interrupted Life and Letters from Westerbork* (New York: Henry Holt, 1996), 231.

39. Schillebeeckx, *Christ,* 695.

40. Elizabeth Johnson speaks eloquently of the many dimensions of solidarity in her feminist analysis and re-visioning of the doctrine of the communion of saints. "The *communio sanctorum,"* she observes, "is a most relational symbol." Elizabeth A. Johnson, *Friends of God and Prophets: A Feminist Theological Reading of the Communion of Saints* (New York: Continuum, 1998), 219.

41. Schillebeeckx asserts, "Jesus did not absolutize politics; his most burning concern was the kingdom of God. . . . We can only say that Jesus was not interested in politics, while remaining aware that his proclamation of the kingdom and above all his practice of dealing with the oppressed had political implications." *Christ,* 584–85.

42. Some contemporary "questers" for the historical Jesus would assert that Jesus acted out of an intentional political agenda. John Dominic Crossan, emphasizing the class-consciousness of the day, maintains that Jesus' activity can *only* be seen as revolutionary. See John Dominic Crossan, *Jesus: A Revolutionary Biography* (San Francisco: HarperSanFrancisco, 1994) and *The Historical Jesus: The Life of a Mediterranean Jewish Peasant* (San Francisco: HarperSanFrancisco, 1991). In a more nuanced approach, Marcus Borg speaks of Jesus' witness to the subversive power of God's compassion breaking through human structures. See Marcus Borg, *Meeting Jesus Again for the First Time* (San Fran-

cisco: HarperSanFrancisco, 1994). In a quite different vein, Elisabeth Schüssler Fiorenza's project of feminist biblical hermeneutics proposes a deconstructive and reconstructive process situated within a "rhetorical-emancipatory paradigm." Rather than attributing political motives to Jesus, Schüssler Fiorenza asserts that it is our historical search which is political, because "our understanding of the present shapes our reconstructions of the past, while our reconstructions of the past shape present and future reality." Her method reflects Schillebeeckx's own appropriation of critical theory, hermeneutics, and biblical exegesis in a concrete feminist praxis illustrating the dynamic of negative contrast experience. Elisabeth Schüssler Fiorenza, *But She Said: Feminist Practices of Biblical Interpretation* (Boston: Beacon Press, 1992), 101. For the development of her model of historical reconstruction, see her *In Memory of Her: A Feminist Theological Reconstruction of Christian Origins* (New York: Crossroad, 1983).

43. Marcus Borg distinguishes the "politics of holiness" of the Jewish status quo from the "politics of compassion" of Jesus and his movement. Borg's description of the characteristics of Jesus' movement (joy in Jesus' presence, banqueting with outcasts, associating with women, announcing good news to the poor, etc.) are consonant with Schillebeeckx's reflections; however, while Schillebeeckx speaks of the movement "brought to life" by Jesus, and even of "the movement which he set afoot" (*Jesus,* 19), and though he acknowledges the social and political impact of Jesus' behavior, he maintains that Jesus did not intentionally establish a social or political movement in his lifetime. Borg, on the other hand, attributes to Jesus a comprehensive but clear political intentionality as *founder* of a movement. See Marcus J. Borg, *Jesus: A New Vision* (San Francisco: Harper & Row, 1987), 86–93, 125–42.

44. Schillebeeckx, "Church, Magisterium, and Politics," in *God the Future of Man,* 155–56.

45. For example, in both Canada and the United States, political policies evidence an increasing element of neo-conservatism in the systematic dismantling of social welfare structures. Protests raised on behalf of the poor and disenfranchised are frequently met with rhetoric that blames the victims for their plight; these official voices in turn strengthen an unthinking righteousness on the part of "decent tax-payers" who, believing that they are being taken advantage of by the "lazy" recipients of social support, back legislation that ultimately benefits business and government interests.

46. Schillebeeckx, *Christ,* 592.

47. Schillebeeckx, *Jesus,* 175.

48. Schillebeeckx, *Jesus,* 175; for assessment of a parallel significance in the New Testament, cf. Albert Nolan, *Jesus before Christianity,* 114ff.

49. Schillebeeckx, *Jesus,* 176.

50. Schillebeeckx, *Jesus,* 176.

51. Schillebeeckx, *Jesus,* 176. The underlying concept of the *anawim* is developed in the discussion of Schillebeeckx's *Mary, Mother of the Redemption,* in chapter two.

52. Guatemala's civil war, for example, claimed more than 140,000 dead and "disappeared." At over five hundred excavation sights, the bones of the dead and their communities' memories of horror are being exhumed. The security forces and government-backed death squads that perpetrated many of the gross human rights violations that occurred during the war were substantially armed by the U.S. government and trained at Fort Benning's "School of the Americas"; opposition forces were also responsible for violations.

See Julie Schwab, O.P., "Finding the Way Forward: A Letter from Guatemala," *Amnesty Action* (spring 1998), 6–8.

53. Though the situations in Northern Ireland, the Middle East, and South Africa come readily to mind, I have not included them here because they share (in ways that are distinct and marked by varying degrees of success) concrete current efforts toward reconciliation and peace. Regarding South Africa, Robert Schreiter draws examples from the Truth and Reconciliation Commission. Importantly for this discussion, he notes that "the term 'reconciliation' does not mean quite the same thing in its individual and social incarnations. Individual reconciliation, in its Christian understanding . . . does not appear to have great cultural variance. . . . Social reconciliation, while having many common characteristics across cultural boundaries . . . , is subject to much more cultural variance." (Schreiter cites, for example, cultural differences in how human rights are ranked and in what will restore relationships.) See Robert J. Schreiter, *The Ministry of Reconciliation: Spirituality & Strategies* (Maryknoll, N.Y.: Orbis, 1998), 115.

54. Schillebeeckx distinguishes repentance and conversion as having their own intuitions "which derive from a different experience than that of the oppressed. The theology of the oppressed is not that of the converted. Both have something to say to us." *Christ,* 649–50.

55. Schillebeeckx, *Christ,* 650.

56. Schillebeeckx, *Christ,* 650.

57. Frequently, the church's own magisterium fearfully represses these impulses where they arise, thus contributing to the suffering of diminishment through a lack of trust. Consider, for example, the censorship of theologians in our own age, especially those constructing contextual theologies in solidarity with oppressed and marginalized communities. Schillebeeckx addresses the problems underlying this reality in *Church: The Human Story of God* (e.g., xv, 187ff, 227–28).

58. Schillebeeckx, *Church,* 650–51.

59. Schillebeeckx, *Church,* 651.

60. Schillebeeckx, *Church,* 651. What Schillebeeckx is referring to here entails a narrative theology; for an example of the philosophical/religious significance of narrative, see Don Cupitt, *What Is a Story?*(London: SCM Press, 1991).

61. See, for example, Schillebeeckx's discussion of "earthly salvation as an inner component of Christian redemption," *Christ,* 764ff.

62. Schillebeeckx, in elaborating his first anthropological constant, warns against the dangers of submitting to the forces of technological advancement instead of subjecting the tool of technology to the guidance of the integrated human spirit . See *Christ,* 734–36; see also "Questions on Christian Salvation of and for Man," in Schillebeeckx, *The Language of Faith,* 114.

63. The writings of John Paul II point to the awareness of truth as among the "causes of solidarity." Others include freedom, both external and internal, and love. See Kevin P. Doran, *Solidarity: A Synthesis of Personalism and Communalism in the Thought of Karol Wojtyla/Pope John Paul II* (New York: Peter Lang, 1996),181.

64. Dean Brackley asserts that today's global crisis calls for a new, radical ethos that incarnates Christian values and retains the positive roots of both traditional and liberal models purified of their respective oppressive and individualistic tendencies. Highlighting today's need for nothing short of moral heroism, Brackley's construct embodies the reci-

procity of solidarity and metanoia so essential to the significance of suffering in Schillebeeckx's theology. Society's crisis is fundamentally moral, not structural; "in order to be
viable the radical ethos requires 'new persons' capable of identifying their own interests
with those of the weak and oppressed." Dean Brackley, "A Radical Ethos," *Horizons* 24,
no.1 (1997), 7–36, 33.

65. Though the situations in Northern Ireland, the Middle East, and South Africa
come readily to mind, I have not included them here because they share (in ways that
are distinct and marked by varying degrees of success) concrete current efforts toward
reconciliation and peace. Regarding South Africa, Robert Schreiter draws examples from
the Truth and Reconciliation Commission. Importantly for this discussion, he notes that
"the term 'reconciliation' does not mean quite the same thing in its individual and social
incarnations. Individual reconciliation, in its Christian understanding . . . , does not appear
to have great cultural variance. . . . Social reconciliation, while having many common
characteristics across cultural boundaries . . . , is subject to much more cultural variance."
(Schreiter cites, for example, cultural differences in how human rights are ranked and in
what will restore relationships.) See Robert J. Schreiter, *The Ministry of Reconciliation:
Spirituality & Strategies,* (Maryknoll, New York: Orbis, 1998), 115.

66. The relationship of death and sin is discussed in chapter two, which cites Schillebeeckx's emphasis, echoing Thomas, on death's human origins. God did not make death,
but Christ's death transformed death's meaning forever.

67. Schillebeeckx, "The Death of a Christian," 68. Earlier, Schillebeeckx notes the
emerging awareness in the Old Testament that "a religious tragedy lay at the origin of
death," 66.

68. Schillebeeckx has described death as a decisive, though provisional, phase of
redemption: "Death is something that happens to us; in itself, dying is not an action that
is done by man [*sic*], let alone the greatest act he does: it is something which overcomes
us. Death can therefore only have a positive, Christian, and salutary significance when we
freely accept this alienation from self, which is a fact, as a positively desired detachment
from self for the love of God in union with the dying Christ. In other words, the attitude
of mind in which we die gives death the power to take on the value of an act." "The Death
of a Christian," 75.

69. Schillebeeckx calls the resurrection the "breakthrough . . . of something that was
already present in the life and death of Jesus, namely his living communion or communion
of grace with the living God, . . . which could not be broken by death" (*Church,* 130);
Schillebeeckx also asserts that living communion with God is expressed in human solidarity during earhly life. On the other hand, a life-style that radically contradicts human solidarity rejects God and living communion, forming the foundation for non-eternal life (i.e.,
hell) (137). And, in an example of countless assertions explicitly regarding trust, Schillebeeckx states: "Trust in God issues in a trust and a faith in one's fellow-man—in man
[*sic*]" (*Christ,* 801).

70. Schillebeeckx, "'God is op deze plek en ik wist het niet' (Gen. 28:16): Jezus van
Nazaret, meester in het vergeven" (Albertinum-conferentie, 2 April 1992), 7.

71. This point cannot be made strongly enough today; many object to the language of
sin because they have misinterpreted the Judeo-Christian tradition as ignoring the interpersonal, relational dimension of sin. Indeed, in some cases the problem has not been a misin-
terpretation, but a mis-rendering. See, for example, Nel Noddings, *Women and Evil,*
211–12.

72. Schillebeeckx, "'God is op deze plek en ik wist het niet . . .'"; Schillebeeckx notes that "purely human ethics often makes excessive demands on people. Ethics without God-centred spirituality often becomes 'graceless,' in both senses of the word" (*Church*, 31).

73. Schillebeeckx here draws upon Thomas Aquinas's sense of a *iudicium connaturalitatis*. *Christ*, 591.

74. Schillebeeckx, *Christ*, 592.

75. Schillebeeckx describes Adam's failed vocation as mediator of grace as bringing about our condition of "universal solidarity in sin," over against which we can image the state of "original justice." See *Mary, Mother of the Redemption*, 40–45.

76. See "The Death of a Christian," 67.

77. Philip Kennedy, whose work demonstrates how mysticism is the force of continuity throughout Schillebeeckx's theological "shifts," speaks of the experience of impasse being transformed by the positive element in the negative experience of contrast, so that "an ethical praxis striving to overcome experiences of suffering (the negation of negation) becomes an *immanent* way of knowing God. In brief, the *theoretical* apophatic moment (involving the negation of concepts) of Schillebeeckx's early explanations of faith's cognitivity, has become an experiential, *practical* apophatic moment in his later theology (involving the negation of suffering)." *Deus Humanissimus: The Knowability of God in the Theology of Edward Schillebeeckx*, 359.

78. Dorothy Soelle distinguishes between passive acceptance and that true, mystical acceptance that transforms suffering into labor pains giving birth to the future. See Dorothy Soelle, *Suffering* trans. Everett Kalin (Philadelphia: Fortress, 1975).

79. Schillebeeckx, "The Non-conceptual Intellectual Element," in *Revelation and Theology*, vol. 2, 71.

80. Schillebeeckx does not develop the relational essence of the Trinity, but it is implicit in his work. For a thorough development of this image, see Catherine Mowry LaCugna, *God for Us: The Trinity and Christian Life* (San Francisco: HarperSanFrancisco, 1991).

81. Segundo observes that original sin pictured in an "immobilist view" (Augustine) rather than an evolutionary one ends up in individualism, which results in Christian passivity and the neglect of the communal reality. See Segundo, *Evolution and Guilt*, 64ff.

82. Schillebeeckx, *Church*, 94.

83. Schillebeeckx, *Church*, 94.

84. Schillebeeckx, *Church*, 94.

85. Schillebeeckx, *Church*, 95.

86. Schillebeeckx, *Church*, 96.

87. Schillebeeckx, *Church*, 96.

88. Schillebeeckx recognizes the Jewish roots of this Christian hope when he speaks of the Old Testament awareness that a religious tragedy lay at the origins of death. In this context, he alludes to the sense of a promise of immortality in the soul that is recalled in the contrast experience posed by death's absurdity. See "The Death of a Christian," 66–67.

89. Schillebeeckx, *Church*, 97.

90. Schillebeeckx, *Church*, 31.

91. Schillebeeckx, *Church*, 31.

92. Schillebeeckx, "'God is op deze plek en ik wist het niet,'" 1.

93. Schillebeeckx, "'God is op deze plek en ik wist het niet'"; here Schillebeeckx observes how Thomas Aquinas also names *misericordia* as among the most beautiful of the divine traits. The longing for this quality of mercy is thus inscribed in our being, authored by the creator. It is toward this compassionate divinity that our created being tends and thrives.

94. Schillebeeckx, "'God is op deze plek en ik wist het niet,'" 6.

95. In this retreat conference on metanoia and forgiveness ("'God is op deze plek en ik wist het niet'"), Schillebeeckx provides a pastoral rendering of what he has often written of as cognitive contact with God, or the mystical dimension, involving the experience of contingency, finitude, or absolute limit; see, for example, *Church*, 67–80.

96. Schillebeeckx, *Christ*, 529.

97. Schillebeeckx, *Christ*, 528. Kenan Osborne, in a study that relativizes the place of the sacrament of penance within a total theology of reconciliation, demonstrates reconciliation's anthropological nature as well as its dependence upon God's initiative. Reconciliation is the meaning of the salvation we find in Jesus; it is basic to his public ministry, to the message he preached, and to the meaning of his healing miracles. "Jesus in his humanity is the primordial sacrament of reconciliation." Kenan Osborne, *Reconciliation and Justification* (Mahwah, N.J.: Paulist, 1990), 213ff.

98. See Schillebeeckx's extended explanation in *Christ*, 762ff.

99. Schillebeeckx, *Christ*, 762ff.

100. For Schillebeeckx's explication of "mediated immediacy," "dark night," "dark light," contingency, etc., see *Christ*, 814ff; also *Church*, 69–80; 99–101.

101. Schillebeeckx, *Christ*, 817.

102. Schillebeeckx, *Christ*, 821.

Chapter Five

A Praxis of Solidarity

The praxis of solidarity embodies the dynamic interrelationship of the elements of resurrection faith, political mysticism and metanoia as they have emerged in Schillebeeckx's theology in the light of "the critical and productive *epistemic* power" of human suffering.[1] Reflection upon the nature of this epistemic power leads us to a deeper understanding of what is entailed in the praxis of solidarity. Schillebeeckx maintains that it is the contrastive experience of suffering that gives rise to the clearest moral perception of what is wrong with the human state of affairs and what, therefore, must be done to promote human flourishing. The critical, epistemic and productive force of suffering resides precisely in its "non-theorizable" mediation between the Christian praxis of mysticism and social and political praxis.[2] In speaking thus of suffering's epistemic power, Schillebeeckx immediately cautions against reducing it to either the practical, "purposive" knowledge of science and technology, or to contemplative, "purposeless" knowledge. In fact, the epistemic power of the contrastive experience of suffering "provides the purely contemplative total perception . . . with a critical element. But at the same time it is critical of the dominating knowledge of the sciences and technology."[3] In a world much damaged by the severance of science and contemplation, Schillebeeckx's reflection upon how the experience of suffering becomes the dialectical link between these two forms of knowledge is arresting:

> In fact, much can be said in favor of the thesis that the contrastive experience of suffering (with its implicit ethical demand) is the only experience capable of linking these two intrinsically, since it is the only experience which unites both types of knowledge. For just like contemplative or esthetic experiences, experiences of suffering *overcome* a person. . . . On the other hand, to the extent that the experience of suffering is a contrastive experience, it opens perspectives for a praxis that aims at removing both the suffering itself and its causes. It is on the basis of this inner relationship, a relationship of critical negativity, both with the contemplative type of knowledge and with the type of knowledge which seeks to master nature, that the specific "pathetic" (*pati*) epistemic force of suffering is *practically* critical, i.e., it is

a critical epistemic force which promotes a new praxis anticipating a better future and actively committed to realizing it.[4]

The union of contemplation and action uniquely effected by the contrastive experience of suffering depends upon the prior, positive reality evoked by the human longing for happiness. Here Schillebeeckx points to the fundamental awareness of "the positive vocation of and to the *Humanum.*"[5] This recalls his early sense of our universal human solidarity in grace, which becomes now the basis for a praxis of justice intent on opening up a future. In concrete situations, the forces denying such a future may be overwhelming, and continued praxis, especially on a public, political scale, demands trust in that future and in the One who has guaranteed it. Present action on behalf of that future demands a willingness not to withdraw from the mediatorship for which we were designed.[6] The praxis of solidarity entails this mediatorship; it entails this trust.

The human failure to trust is at the heart of the human agency in evil which the tradition terms "original sin." And, while the origin of the natural forces of evil in the world remains mysterious, we know that in the face of powers beyond our control, the capacity to trust becomes the key to the quality of human response and presence. The mystical centrality of trust that we found at the heart of the experience of suffering in "The Death of a Christian" remains pivotal in understanding the ways in which suffering informs the development of Schillebeeckx's theology. The contemplative realization of trust in the personal encounter with death is precisely what is required in the human praxis of solidarity. The grace of loving detachment with which the Christian entrusts herself to God in the approach to death is the same grace required for courageous action on behalf of justice and against the powerful forces of this world responsible for suffering.[7] Confronting those forces requires solidarity with those who are suffering, especially the voiceless, as well as solidarity with many others on their behalf. In real terms, this requires sufficient trust to enter into communion with one another in action. Communion in solidarity entails the ongoing work of reconciliation, which is a work that cannot be undertaken alone and is never finished. What hinders courageous action on behalf of those who suffer defenselessly is also what hinders humans' genuine communion with one another in a praxis of justice and love. It is fear, which is the opposite of trust, and which is its own suffering.

The fear that keeps people from entrusting their lives to God and to one another—the fear that keeps them from risking true words and true acts on behalf of the future—is the force that allows evil to reign in the world. It is an empty, vacuous force that promotes the darkness thinly cloaked by this world's dominant values and ethos. Here is the palpable reality of the classical understanding of evil as "nothingness" or privation of good. Nothingness has the power to suck lives, communities, the world itself into its destructive vacuum if there is no positive counterforce creating a future out of love and communion. Grace acts as that counterforce, but divine grace is a relational power, which depends upon human mediatorship for its effective presence in the world.

The overwhelming seriousness of human power and responsibility and the basis of compassion for our human failure thus burst upon consciousness simultaneously. The very construct of "original sin" as privation of original justice illumines the ground of compassion—God's and ours. Schillebeeckx never shrinks from asserting our full human responsibility for allowing the darkness of suffering and injustice to envelop so many of our brothers and sisters; he never shrinks from proclaiming the gospel mandate to actively correct injustice. Human failures to mediate justice and love, personal and political, abound. At the same time, the moment that failure is named as complicit in the causes of suffering, the moment in which we name it as sin in all its (negative) relational depths, is a moment of grace—metanoia—the inner turning that gives rise to the moral imperative and issues in a praxis of justice and love. The moment of sorrowful recognition *is* the moment of transformation. This constitutes the reciprocal dynamic of metanoia and solidarity. Moreover, this contemplative, relational praxis of solidarity forms the substance of Schillebeeckx's implicit theology of suffering.

Suffering, unwilled by God as it is, and unwanted by us, nevertheless provides the context for the process of conversion. Amidst the chaos and fragmentation of our world, it is frequently the element which triggers metanoia. In precisely this sense, it provides the context and formative stimulus for the development of Schillebeeckx's theology, which at every point is and remains profoundly incarnational.

Schillebeeckx's enduring rootedness in the doctrines of creation and incarnation enables him to construct a theology of salvation while steadily contemplating the reality of suffering and evil. And it enables him to do so without succumbing to the relentless forces of the age-old theodicy question that continues to amass new literature in its service. Schillebeeckx refuses to entertain the theodicy question because he refuses to countenance the notion that in some way God wills evil or bears some responsibility for its presence. For Schillebeeckx, God is pure positivity, having no shred of evil, no trace of darkness, no nuance of complicity in the presence and workings of evil in the world, even on behalf of some "greater good."[8] God is always and everywhere the force of "anti-evil," and we are assured of this in the concrete manner of God's being among us in the humanity of Jesus.

The story of God revealed in the life of Jesus and elaborated in the endless diversity of the living men and women who follow Jesus evokes a praxis of solidarity that eschews an abstract theodicy in favor of a "practical theodicy" and a "discipleship of presence." Though these are not Schillebeeckx's own terms, they are apt descriptions of the way in which the complex implications of suffering in his theology resolve into a praxis of solidarity. I will address each of them in turn.

"Practical Theodicy"

"Practical theodicy" essentially negates the traditional meaning of the term "theodicy." Kenneth Surin establishes a basis for understanding "practical theodicy" by explaining why theodicy formulations are so dissatisfying. His explanations hinge upon the historical, cultural, and intellectual developments that Schillebeeckx would sum up as the hermeneutical spiral. It is impossible in our age to view evil as a "problem" to be intellectually answered. As Kenneth Surin points out, there is no prevailing sense in our day (as there was, for instance, in the thirteenth century) of a "Divine, cosmic Orderer."[9] Nor are most people, in the face of the concrete enormity of world suffering, tolerant of the abstract conception of evil used by the theodicist. Finally, theodicy involves application of the principles of reason to a problem that defies all rational principles. Evil and suffering are fundamentally mysterious. Ultimately, Surin opts for a practical theodicy, one that operates from the point of view of sufferers and that embraces a *theologia crucis*.[10]

Thus understood, the concept of a "practical theodicy" neatly encapsules Schillebeeckx's response to the reality of suffering as we have seen it evolve in his theology. And, if certain theodicists question the *privatio boni* theory for failing to take seriously evil's concrete destructiveness, Schillebeeckx's own concretely incarnational theology answers their question in a manner that preserves the classical definition of evil without evading or denying the tangible complexity of evil's manifestations.[11] As noted earlier, the fear that hinders the praxis of solidarity promotes evil's palpable existence as "nothingness," *das Nichtige*.[12] The next step is to examine the precise way in which the empty, vacuous force of fear gives substance to "nothing," how it gives flesh to the deep meaning of sin which is, in its origin, the emptiness of loss.

"FEAR IS USELESS, WHAT IS NEEDED IS TRUST"

The crippling force of fear not only diminishes the life of one who is afraid, but also diminishes the life potential of relationship and communion in those places from which one's presence is withdrawn. In countless scenarios characterized by hopelessness and despair, the suffering that we perceive is wrought by the fear responsible for the absence of goodness, truth, and love. This, in its deepest dimension, is the manifest loss of original justice which is what is meant by 'original sin.' Many contemporary theologians grappling seriously with the reality of suffering and the problem of evil express frustration with the dominance of the doctrine of original sin throughout the Christian tradition from the time of Augustine. Many, especially those constructing relationally-based theologies, are working to formulate alternative readings of the tradition.[13] There is an understandable desire to correct and counteract what has too often been a damaging and burdensome overemphasis upon guilt and sin. However, the pervasiveness of evil and the suffering to which it gives rise testifies to something gone seriously awry at the roots of the human condition.[14] Edward Schillebeeckx makes a case for the fundamental goodness of human beings created in grace and called to a life in harmony with the whole created universe. Our original solidarity in grace—"original justice"—is the fundamental truth of our identity. The original sin with which we are so much more familiar has no being except in reference to this deeper origin of God's willing.

We have already seen how Schillebeeckx's early elaboration of the Augustinian and Thomistic tradition on original justice and sin, enhanced by his personal leanings toward Irenaeus, is a fundamentally relational articulation of the doctrine. Recall his formulation in *Mary, Mother of the Redemption* depicting original sin as Adam's failure in the human vocation to mediate grace. The paradigm of sin and redemption wherein the refusal of one human being had power to damage the relational fabric of the race, while the surrender in trust of another had power to restore it metaphorically, expresses humanity's capacity for goodness and grandeur, not its depravity.[15] Suffering and evil illumine the scope of human responsibility and the magnitude of human freedom negatively realized. In "The Death of a Christian," Schillebeeckx evokes the images of fear in the Genesis accounts of the human refusal to remain walking with God in the garden. From the creation account throughout the drama of salvation history, fear has operated to harden boundaries, heighten the compulsion to control, increase possessiveness, promote isolation and its attendant loneliness, and place human beings in enmity with one another and with God. In short, fear hinders the communion entailed in a praxis of solidarity. Fear translates into the failure or inability to trust, and as such is a lack, an emptiness, a void. Fear, which prevents or inhibits the active presence of goodness, makes room for evil, which manifests itself in untold suffering. An ancient tract from a sermon by St. Peter Chrysologus, a fifth-century bishop, illumines the role of fear and trust vis-à-vis suffering and salvation, indirectly providing a most compassionate rendering of the doctrine of original sin:

> When God saw the world falling to ruin because of fear, he immediately acted to call it back to himself with love. When the earth had become hardened in evil, God sent the flood. . . . He called Noah . . . and showed that he trusted him; he gave him fatherly advice about the present calamity, and through his grace consoled him with hope for the future. . . . The sense of loving fellowship thus engendered removed servile fear, and a mutual love could continue to preserve what shared labor had effected.[16]

The fear that prevents love's substantiation and allows evil's vacuousness to hold sway is clearly named in all its destructive potential by this early shepherd of the Church. It is counteracted by the trust that has its origin in God—that "risky trust" so often expressed by Schillebeeckx. God trusted Noah, and thus Noah's own trust in God was strengthened to the point that he could work together with God for a new human future. And that mutual trust extended to others in a shared practical presence that provided a concrete basis for hope.

Though Schillebeeckx does not elaborate on original justice and original sin in his later theology, he points to the latter as the mysterious root of the evil of suffering.[17] And he subsumes the primordial vision of original justice into the more profound expression of eschatological hope in the divine promise vindicated by Jesus' resurrection.[18] And it is here, in the life, death, and resurrection of Jesus, that the centrality of trust in Schillebeeckx's theology is most fully revealed. Here, too, are both the dimensions and implications of trust vis-à-vis the pervasiveness of suffering.

If fear gives way to the empty power of nothingness, then it can only be counteracted by the presence of goodness and love dependent upon trust. Trust counteracts fear by risking entry into the unknown. We have seen how, for Schillebeeckx, trust is the essence of the communion between Jesus and God, which remains unbroken through suffering and death and which issues in the resurrection. Jesus' intimacy throughout his life with the God whom he knew as "Abba" and "Father" was expressed through his intimacy with men and women. In his own being, Jesus witnessed to God's trust in humanity, God's will for creation's flourishing. And he bore in his own being the effects of humanity's resistance, absorbing the consequences of God's own risk.

The relational centrality of trust in Jesus' life and mission is paradigmatic for the lives of those who follow Jesus. Those who would follow enter into a covenant, which entails loving communion, openness to ongoing reconciliation, and a mutual obedience that is, in its depths, obedience to the divine source of the promise. Schillebeeckx's christology demonstrates Jesus' trust in God enfleshed in his life and ministry, in relationships with men and women, in his unflinching proclamation of God's reign in the presence of those who employed power, prestige, and the cloak of religious righteousness to oppress the poor. God's risky trust invested in all of humanity is fully reciprocated in Jesus and vindicated in the resurrection. We have only to recall the events of the paschal mystery to soberly realize the human risk entailed in the *sequela Jesu* today. To follow Jesus is to live out of the same quality of trust which marked his life. Such trust is essential for bold denouncing of injustice, resistance of oppression, and announcing of good news for the poor in today's arenas of power. Such trust is essential for entering into the solidarity with the "other" that is the basis for the living proclamation of justice and love.

Once again, and as always, the questions arise: "What happens after all efforts for constructive action are defeated? What about those situations in which fear seems to conquer love in unremitting violence, and suffering seems never-ending? What of those sufferings which originate in the disasters of nature, or physical diseases that are incurable?" The trusting relationship with God that is rooted in ongoing metanoia both challenges and enables a contemporary discipleship of presence in precisely those places where suffering seems beyond hope.

A "Discipleship of Presence"

It takes little imagination to realize the risk incurred by a discipleship of presence amidst some of our world's most extreme situations of poverty, violence, and disaster. That risk takes a different form for those engaged in the overlapping realms of business and politics. To speak and act truly and to remain in solidarity with those who suffer, regardless of the consequences, is to risk martyrdom of one kind or another. It has always been thus.[19] The moral imperative arising from the vision of human flourishing leads to the kind of sacrifice undertaken not for its own sake, but for the sake of fuller and deeper life for all.[20] It is integral to our sharing in the life of Jesus, who saves us not by death, but by a life lived in trust unto and through death.

Schillebeeckx has no illusions about the potential for martyrdom inherent in discipleship in the contemporary world. In 1983, at the height of the Cold War, he spoke starkly of the praxis of the gospel translated into political action in terms of the "risky trust of unilateral disarmament."[21] Acknowledging all of the arguments regarding balance of power and insurance of safety, Schillebeeckx challenged the concern for "our" safety at the expense of the world's starving populations from whom we withhold resources while pouring billions into arms production. Emphasizing Jesus' own praxis of peace, Schillebeeckx noted that, on the basis of the development of a "teleological ethos of responsibility" in the aftermath of World War II, Popes John XXIII, Paul VI, and John Paul II have denounced all aspects of the arms race.[22] Schillebeeckx is clear: "It is better for us to be martyrs because we refuse to help to prepare for a possible nuclear war than for us to be victims of such a war because we fail to oppose it actively."[23] The question of martyrdom posed in this way brings us to the incarnational principle upon which Schillebeeckx's entire theology hinges: God's cause is the human cause. If, indeed, we are not willing to risk martyrdom for the cause of humanity, do we believe in the God revealed to us in Jesus Christ?[24]

The martyrdom entailed in translating gospel praxis into politics has counterparts wherever believers risk taking a stance on behalf of those who are vulnerable or marginal by any of society's standards. In every place where goodness and peace, justice and love seem thwarted by the powers of evil and sin; in every place where suffering flies in the face of a compassionate God, the only response possible is presence. In powerlessness, the other side of solidarity is revealed in the courage of silent witnessing: standing against the chaos, trusting in the power and meaning of the human presence of God.

Human beings who suffer and grieve do not care about "theodicy," and Schillebeeckx has always known this. Their questions about the suffering, evil, and sin in the world do not cry out for answers, but for hope, which they can only experience through solidarity. Human beings in crisis long for presence, especially the presence of a ministering disciple.[25] And this is where the point of view of the sufferer becomes the paramount test of the incarnational principle. The most concrete test case of the principle that values the human above all else emerges in the needs of the most vulnerable in our midst, those at life's beginning and end, those who, at any stage of life are, from society's point of view, "sick beyond hope."

Those who are "sick beyond hope" include the man or woman who is terminally ill, the child who is physically and/or mentally incapacitated, the Alzheimer's victim who no longer recognizes her family, the schizophrenic son whose violence cannot be contained. The list is endless. These scenarios evoke not only the suffering of those named, but also the suffering of those in relationship to them. And each of these scenarios is exacerbated when it occurs in situations of poverty. There are other varieties of suffering, such as those involving abuse and addiction, and those that are the direct results of political oppression and the violence of war. We leave these, for now, in the categories calling for resistance and for the social, political praxis of justice. The praxis of solidarity that is the crucial substance of Schillebeeckx's implicit theology of suffering has different manifestations in accord with the vastly different types of individual and communal suffering. The scenarios we list here are representative of all those situations where the prevailing "hopelessness" demands a "discipleship of presence." The praxis of solidarity appears here as faithful waiting: attentive love in a "now" that belies the very promise that sustains us. When all is said and done, the primacy of the human and the epistemological priority of suffering requires the contemplative, relational presence that both depends upon and evokes metanoia. The call to suffer with the suffering is the call to conversion of the deepest kind. It is the call to live the depths of the incarnation, to both believe in and become God's human presence.

In the depths of the most hopeless suffering, God is present in the human "other" who chooses to remain holding the sufferer's hand. When all is said and done, Schillebeeckx's theology is summed up in this: In the midst of Jesus' existential sense of abandonment on the cross, God remains holding his hand. When all seems lost, the living God has not let go.

We do not know from history what the last word to suffering and evil will be. But we know from faith what God's last word is. The point of Schillebeeckx's theology is that God's last word must be enfleshed in our human refusal to abandon the sufferer.

The end of the story does not leave us passively holding one another's hands. The hermeneutical spiral continues. The willingness to companion those who suffer is not an individual vocation, but a communal one. The choice to remain present demands the mobilization of society's ethical will to provide the structures to maintain the care and presence required by all of society's suffering members, especially those who have no personal ties, those who inhabit our streets, those who have been abandoned by our unredeemed institutions. The relationship of radical trust in God that makes such presence possible is at the heart of Schillebeeckx's theology, as it is at the heart of the gospel. That trust, rooted in Jesus' embodiment of God's own risky trust in humanity, remains central in spite of every experience to the contrary.

In a Christmas meditation, Schillebeeckx points out that the world into which Jesus was born was a cruel world, and that reality has not changed. Nevertheless, what the world requires for salvation in every age is *more humanity.* [26] That is the meaning of the incarnation, cast into vivid relief by the history of suffering. God's being is revealed to us in the humanity of Jesus. "It was and is God's free decision to see and define himself as a 'God of human beings' . . . identifying himself with vulnerable people who in their vulnerability can also be wounding."[27]

We have already seen that the challenge to the trust out of which solidarity is woven is precisely that the vulnerable and the wounded amongst us can also be wounding. Human beings, Schillebeeckx has noted, are not only grace to one another, but also threat. But this is the reality in which Jesus has already gone before us. In this world's places of power, which sometimes include our churches, there seems to be no room for genuine, good, and true humanity:

> Humanity is too threatening for the powerful; it reveals their weak spot, their vulnerability and ultimate helplessness. Their power which crushes people and structurally forces their backs to the wall is really disguised powerlessness which, precisely because it is powerless, arms itself with terror and annihilation, with torture and even with nuclear weapons, with a Herod-like massacre of children.[28]

In this fragment of Schillebeeckx's preaching we have a concrete manifestation of evil's fear-based essence of "nothingness." Its devastating impact is known in and through the powerhouses of the world; it subtly infects even our humanitarian systems of ethical decision-making.

If Schillebeeckx's theology resolves into the choice of solidarity with those who suffer, it does not rest with patient waiting. It soon becomes evident that we must fight even for the right to remain patiently holding the sufferer's hand. In those situations where the powerful determine what makes life worth living, solidarity with sufferers demands relentless re-education in the understanding of the *humanum.*

CONCLUDING REFLECTIONS

"Really only those who have suffered, in *person* and in *others,* know what concern for fellow human beings and their society, what concern for more humanity, require of us."[29] This is the essence of what Schillebeeckx elsewhere refers to as "the critical, epistemic, and productive power of suffering." It summarizes the final authoritative significance of suffering for Schillebeeckx's theology. The hermeneutical spiral through which we have imaged the growth and development of Schillebeeckx's project has carried us from the dogmatic starting point of his early theology, through an increasingly experience-centered theology with social, political implications, to the epistemological priority of suffering for theology. The matrix of that spiral is Edward Schillebeeckx's personal rootedness in the divine ground of being which he comes to know as the horizon of the eschatological promise. The dialectical tension between the promise and the reality of suffering shapes Schillebeeckx's appropriation of multiple intellectual disciplines according to what he deems evangelically fruitful.

At the beginning of this study, I noted that Schillebeeckx does not give voice to the suffering "other" in the way that an African, Asian, feminist, womanist, or Latin American liberation theologian does. Though he is a white, male, European theologian, it is precisely as such that he has prepared the way for these new voices to be heard. And he could only do that by being faithful to the historical particularity of his own life. In the concrete substance of that particularity, Schillebeeckx bridges the riches of the Christian tradition, the developments of the modern era, and the postmodern reality that no one quite has a handle on yet, because it is of its nature fragmentary. In doing so, Schillebeeckx does much more than provide a foundation. His theology is a dynamic, still-developing rung of the spiral circling into the present and coming generation of theologians. Thinkers from all of the standpoints mentioned are consciously constructing theologies from the starting point of the epistemological priority of suffering. The critical and productive force of theology forged from the standpoint of the sufferer is borne out in the work of not only the varieties of feminist, liberation, and other contextual theologies, but also in the fields of philosophical hermeneutics, biblical exegesis, and social ethics as these fields evolve into their post-modern manifestations.[30]

With reference to the postmodern, it is important to point out the implications of the critical, productive epistemic force of suffering for the specifically deconstructionist strands of postmodernism. The concreteness of suffering flies in the face of the idea that everything is play, that reality is unrelievedly open-ended, and that all action must be postponed in contemplation of an infinite variety of possibilities. However much disintegration and flux actually characterize our world, suffering's concreteness demands a concrete response rooted in the reciprocal dynamic of solidarity and metanoia. Suffering demands relational presence supported, ultimately, by a living community of faith. And here we must take note of Schillebeeckx's prizing of wisdom gleaned from suffering over knowledge gleaned from philosophy or science.[31] "(W)e have come once again to recognize that the authority of reason has to subject itself to the criticism of the 'authority of suffering humanity.'"[32] Theologically, this means that communities of suffering people become the subjects of a new theology that enters into mutually critical correlation with the tradition. In the 1980s, Schillebeeckx clearly had in mind Latin American liberation theology; today, theologies arising out of multiple contexts fit this description. Most immediately, however, in our own North American and Western European societies, another scenario is raising up subjects of a theology straining for form and voice. We come, finally, to the concrete scenario of the most vulnerable among us, those hovering at the margins of what society deems to be supportable life. Those at life's beginning or end, as well as those at any stage of life whose physical and/or mental incapacity render them only marginally "functioning," usually do not have a voice, let alone the capacity to be the subjects of a "contextual" theology. And this is precisely where solidarity with sufferers becomes central to gospel praxis. In our day, critical ethical decisions are being made by secular government, scientific, and social authorities, which do not take sufficiently into account the point of view of these suffering subjects. And large numbers of people, including "Christian believers," lack both the capacity and the support for maintaining this point of view. It is the task of the theologian not only to take this point of view into account, but to give a voice to these voiceless ones and to assist those who companion them in suffering to uncover the meaning of their journey. It is the task of cultivating wisdom and inviting conversion.

Schillebeeckx indicates in his system of anthropological coordinates the dangers of unrestrained technological advance without a corresponding advance in human wisdom. The current state of affairs vis-à-vis scientific capability to enhance, lengthen, terminate, or otherwise manipulate life poses moral questions that challenge the core of human meaning. The most controversial ethical issues of life today require the foundations of a profound theology of suffering. Schillebeeckx provides the material for such a theology as well as a method in the dynamic of negative contrast, which is the moral imperative at the root of metanoia. But even that is not an answer. It is an invitation to trust enough to enter upon true discipleship.

We can arrive at no ultimate conclusion but only draw near to one by returning again and again to Schillebeeckx's starting point in the concrete reality of suffering, while continuing to proclaim God's promise of a true and happy humanity. In that place of tension, solidarity can effect the transformation of suffering through conversion in the hearts of human agents. Still, all reflection is inadequate; in the end, we are always left with the question of that dark residue of suffering that seems forever removed from the ground of hope that sustains meaning. For those human beings whose dignity is destroyed, for all of those whose spirits are quenched by the brutality of oppression, there are no words that have meaning. In the face of all those persons whose deepest suffering is the isolating loss of reflective and relational capacity, we stand powerless and silent. But we remain in a discipleship of presence, extending a sorrowful embrace. Where suffering is in vain, its victims depend upon those still free to act in hope or wait in the fruitful silence of reverent solidarity. Ultimately, in silence or in speech, in waiting or in activity, we are all dependent upon God, whose initiative finds fulfillment beyond the limits of our time or judgment, and whose intentions for our unity, wholeness, and flourishing will not be thwarted.

NOTES

1. Schillebeeckx, "Questions on Christian Salvation," in *The Language of Faith*, 124.
2. Schillebeeckx, "Questions on Christian Salvation," 124. It is important here to take emphatic note of Schillebeeckx's deliberate use of the word *praxis* in relation to mysticism as well as social action. Erroneous popular usage often regards "praxis" as synonymous with "practice." Explaining Schillebeeckx's prioritizing of "orthopraxis" as insurance of "orthodoxy," William Hill elaborates: "Christian life practice cannot exist in isolation from theory, and without it would lack all criteria for truth. Still it is the more fundamental dimension of human existing from which theories are reflectively derived and is far more than the mere practical implementation of theory. Praxis means precisely this dialectical interacting of theory and concrete action." William J. Hill, O.P., "Human Happiness as God's Honor: Background to a Theology in Transition," in Schreiter and Hilkert, eds., *The Praxis of Christian Experience: An Introduction to the Theology of Edward Schillebeeckx*, 1–17, 3.
3. Schillebeeckx, "Questions on Christian Salvation," 124–25.
4. Schillebeeckx, "Questions on Christian Salvation," 124–25. Certain feminist theologians today would caution us to remember that many people are overcome by experiences of suffering in ways that leave no room for reflection or any practical, critical effect. Rebecca Chopp speaks of radical suffering, the effect of radical evil that leaves human beings bereft of any sense of dignity or selfhood. Chopp's perspective in *A Praxis of Suffering* is interpreted by Wendy Farley in *Tragic Vision and Divine Compassion* (Louisville: John Knox, 1990), 53. On the same point, Dorothy Soelle speaks of "mute suffering," the "suffering *in extremis*" that imposes silence; see Soelle, *Suffering* (Philadelphia: Fortress, 1975), 61–62. Schillebeeckx shows signs of his own sensitivity where he speaks of those who must rely upon others, "because oppression robbed them of the capacity for speech." *Christ*, 648. Schillebeeckx would take issue, however, with the term "radical suffering" or "radical evil," believing as he does that in the depths of every human person, even where unknown to them, God lives hidden in a place evil cannot touch. Mercy remains at the heart of reality.
5. Schillebeeckx, "Questions on Christian Salvation," 125.
6. In his early theology, Schillebeeckx reflects on Adam's failure in the human vocation to mediate grace. See *Mary, Mother of the Redemption*, 40–42; cf. also chapter two of this volume.. In his later christology, Schillebeeckx speaks of redemption in terms of God's solidarity with suffering people in Jesus, who entered into relationship with us "while we were still sinners." See, for example, *Christ*, 637–40.
7. Schillebeeckx defines redemption as freedom from self for the loving service of others, which is the essence of abiding in God. "Ethics, and above all love of one's neighbour, is the public manifestation of the state of being redeemed." *Christ*, 495.
8. Richard Swinburne, for example, employs examples of Christian theodicy throughout the centuries in the service of his argument that God imposes evil and suffering in

order to bring about a greater good that could not otherwise be wrought. See Swinburne, *Providence and the Problem of Evil* (Oxford: Clarendon Press, 1998), 32ff. His notion of a great design in which God actually has a reason for allowing suffering is utterly incompatible with the perspective of Edward Schillebeeckx. Schillebeeckx is consistently adamant about God's unequivocal "no" to evil and suffering from his early to his late works.

9. See Surin's essay, "Theodicy?" in Kenneth Surin, *The Turnings of Darkness and Light: Essays in Philosophical and Systematic Theology* (New York: Cambridge University Press, 1989), 73–90.

10. Surin, "Theodicy?" 73–90.

11. Examples of quite distinct perspectives on this point are found in John Hick, *Evil and the God of Love;* Kathleen M. Sands, *Escape from Paradise: Evil and Tragedy in Feminist Theology* (Minneapolis: Fortress, 1994); and Marjorie Hewitt Suchocki, *The Fall to Violence: Original Sin in Relational Theology* (New York: Continuum, 1995).

12. Karl Barth's concept of *"das Nichtige"* evokes Schillebeeckx's sense of contrast. It signifies true, irreconcilable evil which can be perceived only in contradistinction to Jesus Christ; in the moment of recognition, it is overcome by Christ's power. See John Hick's analysis in *Evil and the God of Love,* 127ff.

13. See, for example, Sands and Suchocki; and Delores S. Williams, "A Womanist Perspective on Sin," in *A Troubling in My Soul: Womanist Perspectives on Evil and Suffering,* ed. Emilie M. Townes (Maryknoll, N.Y.: Orbis, 1993), 130–49.

14. Gil Bailie explores the problem in a contemporary cultural analysis relying on the philosophy of René Girard; see Bailie, *Violence Unveiled: Humanity at the Crossroads* (New York: Crossroad, 1997).

15. Sebastian Moore corrects damaging traditional usage of the language of "restoration" and the distorted notions of redemption underlying it. See Dom Sebastian Moore, "Getting the Fall Right," *The Downside Review* 116/404 (1998): 213–26.

16. From a sermon by St. Peter Chrysologus, bishop (Sermo 147: PL 52, 594–95), "Love Desires to See God," found in *The Liturgy of the Hours* (New York: Catholic Book Publishing Co.) vol. 1, 235.

17. *See* Schillebeeckx, "Doubt in God's Omnipotence: 'When bad things happen to good people,'" in *For the Sake of the Gospel,* 88–102; 93–94.

18. Speaking of the entwinement of protology and eschatology, Schillebeeckx asserts, "The story of creation is therefore also an eschatological statement." Schillebeeckx, "Some Thoughts on the Interpretation of Eschatology," in *The Language of Faith,* 49; see 43–58.

19. Elizabeth Johnson shows how the tradition of martyrdom bears witness to the power of relationship within the communion of saints to witness to God's will to human flourishing through and beyond death. See her *Friends of God and Prophets,* 71–93.

20. "True humanity is also concerned with the way of suffering through and for others." Schillebeeckx, "Christian Identity and Human Integrity," in *The Language of Faith,* 185–97; 194.

21. Schillebeeckx, "Eager to Spread the Gospel of Peace," in *The Language of Faith,* 199–209.

22. Schillebeeckx, "Eager to Spread the Gospel of Peace," 201.

23. Schillebeeckx, "Eager to Spread the Gospel of Peace," 208.

24. Schillebeeckx, "Eager to Spread the Gospel of Peace," 209.

25. Scott W. Gustafson, "From Theodicy to Discipleship: Dostoyevsky's Contribution to the Pastoral Task in *The Brothers Karamazov,*" *Scottish Journal of Theology* 45 (1992): 209–22.

26. Schillebeeckx, "Christmas Meditation: 'Being made man' (Matthew 2. 13–21)," in *For the Sake of the Gospel,* 45–49.

27. Schillebeeckx, *For the Sake of the Gospel,* 48.

28. Schillebeeckx, *For the Sake of the Gospel,* 48.

29. Schillebeeckx, "Christmas Meditation," 48–49.

30. See David Tracy, "Evil, Suffering, and Hope: The Search for New Forms of Contemporary Theodicy," *CTSA Proceedings* 50 (1995): 15–36.

31. Schillebeeckx, "Christmas Meditation," 46.

32. Schillebeeckx, "The Teaching Authority of All: A Reflection about the Structure of the New Testament," in *The Language of Faith,* 225–36; 233.

Selected Bibliography

EDWARD SCHILLEBEECKX:
PRIMARY SOURCES

1. Books and Collected Writings

Note: Years in parenthesis are dates of original publication.

Christ: The Experience of Jesus as Lord (1977). Translated by John Bowden. New York: Crossroad, 1980.

Christ: The Sacrament of the Encounter with God (1959). Translated by Paul Barrett New York: Sheed & Ward, 1963.

Church: The Human Story of God (1989). Translated by John Bowden. New York: Crossroad, 1990.

For the Sake of the Gospel (1988). Translated by John Bowden. New York: Crossroad, 1990.

God Among Us: The Gospel Proclaimed. Translated by John Bowden. New York: Crossroad, 1983.

God and Man. Translated by Edward Fitzgerald and Peter Tomlinson. New York: Sheed & Ward, 1969.

God Is New Each Moment. Translated by David Smith. Edinburgh: T&T Clark, 1983.

God the Future of Man (1967). Translated by N. D. Smith. New York: Sheed & Ward, 1968.

I Am a Happy Theologian: Conversations with Francesco Strazzari. Translated by John Bowden. NewYork: Crossroad, 1994.

Interim Report on the Books Jesus and Christ (1978). New York: Crossroad, 1980.

Jesus: An Experiment in Christology (1974). Translated by Hubert Hoskins. New York: Crossroad, 1979.

Mary, Mother of the Redemption (Antwerp, 1954). Translated by N. D. Smith. New York: Sheed & Ward, 1964.

Mary: Yesterday, Today, Tomorrow. With Catharina Halkes (1992). New York: Crossroad, 1993.

Ministry: Leadership in the Community of Jesus Christ. New York: Crossroad, 1981.

On Christian Faith: The Spiritual, Ethical, and Political Dimensions. Translated by John Bowden. New York: Crossroad, 1987.

Revelation and Theology I. Translated by N. D. Smith. New York: Sheed & Ward, 1967.
Revelation and Theology II: The Concept of Truth and Theological Renewal. London: Sheed & Ward, 1968.
The Church with a Human Face: A New and Expanded Theology of Ministry. Translated by John Bowden. New York: Crossroad, 1985.
The Eucharist. London: Sheed & Ward, 1968.
The Language of Faith: Essays on Jesus, Theology, and the Church (1978). Introduction by Robert J. Schreiter. Nijmegen, Netherlands: Concilium, 1995.
The Mission of the Church. Translated by N. D. Smith. New York: Seabury, 1973.
The Schillebeeckx Reader. Edited by Robert J. Schreiter. New York: Crossroad, 1984.
The Understanding of Faith: Interpretation and Criticism. (1955) London: Sheed & Ward, 1974.
Vatican II: The Struggle of Minds and Other Essays. Dublin: Gill & Son, 1963.
World and Church. New York: Sheed & Ward, 1971.

2. Other Articles and Unpublished Conferences

"Can Christology Be an Experiment?" *Proceedings of the Catholic Theological Society of America* 35 (1980): 1–14.
"Cultuur, Godsdienst en Geweld: 'Theologie als onderdeel van een cultuur.'" *Tijdschrift voor Theologie* 36 (1996): 387–404.
"'God is op deze plek en ik wist het niet' (Gen. 28:16): Jezus van Nazaret, meester in het vergeven." Albertinum-conferentie, 2 April 1992.
"God, Society, and Human Salvation." In *Faith and Society: Acta Congressus Internationalis Theologicus Lovaniensas 1976.* Edited by Marc Caudron. Gembloux, Belgium: J. Ducolot, S.A., 1978, 87–99.
"God the Living One." *New Blackfriars* 62 (1981): 357–70.
"Identiteit, eigenheid en universaliteit van Gods heil in Jezus." *Tijdschrift voor Theologie* 30 (1990): 159–75.
"In Search of the Salvific Value of a Political Praxis of Peace." Lecture delivered at Fordham University, New York (6 June 1982). Mimeographed.
"Speaking about God in a Context of Liberation, Emancipation, and Redemption." Lecture delivered at the Dominican School of Philosophy and Theology at Berkeley (January 31, 1983). Mimeographed.
"The Right of Every Christian to Speak in the Light of Evangelical Experience." In *Preaching and the Non-Ordained.* Edited by Nadine Foley. Collegeville, Minn.: Liturgical Press, 1983, 11–40.
"Universalité unique d'une figure religieuse historique nommée Jésus de Nazareth." *Laval theologique et philosophique* 50 (1994): 265–82.

SECONDARY SOURCES FOR EDWARD SCHILLEBEECKX

Abdul-Masih, Marguerite. "Experience and Christology in the Thought of Edward Schillebeeckx and Hans Frei." Ph.D. diss., University of St. Michael's College/Regis, Toronto, 1995.

Bergin, Helen F. "The Death of Jesus and Its Impact on God: Jürgen Moltmann and Edward Schillebeeckx." *Irish Theological Quarterly* 52 (1986): 193–211.

Borgman, Erik. "Theologie tussen universiteit en emancipatie: de weg van Edward Schillebeeckx." *Tijdschrift voor Theologie* 26 (1986): 240–58.

Borgman, Erik. "Van cultuurtheologie naar theologie als onderdeel van de cultuur: De toekomst van het theologisch project van Edward Schillebeeckx." *Tijdschrift voor Theologie* 34 (1994): 335–60.

Bowden John. *Edward Schillebeeckx: In Search of the Kingdom of God.* New York: Crossroad, 1983.

Callewaert, Janet. "The Role of Creation Theology in the Contemporary Soteriology of Edward Schillebeeckx." Ph.D. diss., Catholic University of America, Washington, D.C., 1988.

Dupré, Louis. "Experience and Interpretation: A Philosophical Reflection on Schillebeeckx's *Jesus* and *Christ.*" *Theological Studies* 43 (1982): 30–51.

Galvin, John. "The Death of Jesus in the Theology of Edward Schillebeeckx." *Irish Theological Quarterly* 50 (1983–84): 168–80.

———. "The Uniqueness of Jesus and His 'Abba Experience' in the Theology of Edward Schillebeeckx." *Proceedings of the Catholic Theological Society* 35 (1980): 309–14.

Fackre, Gabriel. "Bones Strong and Weak in the Skeletal Structure of Schillebeeckx's Christology." *Journal of Ecumenical Studies* 21/2 (1984): 248–77.

Fuller, Reginald. "The Historical Jesus: Some Outstanding Issues." *Thomist* 48 (1984): 368–82.

George, William. "The Praxis of the Kingdom of God: Ethics in Schillebeeckx's *Jesus* and *Christ.*" *Horizons* 12 (1985): 44–69.

Haight, R., and M.C. Hilkert. "Liberationist and Feminist Themes in Edward Schillebeeckx's *Church: The Human Story of God.*" *CTSA Proceedings* 46 (1991): 114–17.

Hilkert, Mary Catherine. "Hermeneutics of History in the Theology of Edward Schillebeeckx." *The Thomist* 51 (1987): 97–145.

———. "Towards a Theology of Proclamation: Edward Schillebeeckx's Hermeneutics of Tradition as a Foundation for a Theology of Proclamation." Ph.D. diss., Catholic University of America, Washington, D.C., 1984.

Jacko, Dorothy. "Salvation in the Context of Contemporary Historical Consciousness: The Later Theology of Edward Schillebeeckx." Ph.D. diss., University of St. Michael's College, Toronto, 1990.

Johnson, Elizabeth A. "Mary and Contemporary Christology: Rahner and Schillebeeckx." *Église et Théologie* 15 (1984): 155–82.

Kennedy, Philip. *Deus Humanissimus: The Knowability of God in the Theology of Edward Schillebeeckx.* Fribourg, Switzerland: University Press, 1993.

———. *Schillebeeckx.* Collegeville, Minn.: The Liturgical Press, 1993.

Kuikman, Jacoba H. "Christology in the Context of Jewish-Christian Relations: The Contribution of Edward Schillebeeckx." Ph.D. diss., University of St. Michael's College/Regis, Toronto, 1993.

Malan, D. J. "The Implications of Edward Schillebeeckx's Theology of Liberation for Anthropology and Creation." *Skrif en Kirk* 14/2 (1993): 249–62.

McAuliffe, Patricia. *Fundamental Ethics: A Liberationist Approach.* Washington, D.C.: Georgetown University Press, 1994.

———. "A Liberationist Ethic: Some Fundamental Elements and Their Logic." Ph.D. diss., University of St. Michael's College, Toronto, 1990.

————. "Schillebeeckx's Negative Contrast Experience and Its Application to the Scandal of World Suffering." M.A. Thesis, Regis College, Toronto, 1985.

Nijenhuis, John. "Christology without Jesus of Nazareth Is Ideology: A Monumental Work by Schillebeeckx on Jesus." *Journal of Ecumenical Studies* 17/1 (1980): 125–40.

Portier, William L. "Edward Schillebeeckx as Critical Theorist: The Impact of Neo-Marxist Social Thought on His Recent Theology." *The Thomist* 48 (1984): 341–67.

————. "Ministry from Above, Ministry from Below: An Examination of the Ecclesial Basis of Ministry According to Edward Schillebeeckx." *Communio* 12 (Summer 1985): 173–91.

————. "Mysticism and Politics and Integral Salvation: Two Approaches to Theology in a Suffering World." In *Pluralism and Oppression: Theology in a World Perspective,* ed. Paul Knitter. Annual Publication of the College Theology Society, 1988, vol. 34. Lanham, Md.: University Press of America, 1991.

————. "Schillebeeckx's Dialogue with Critical Theory." *The Ecumenist* 21/2 (1983): 20–27.

Scheffczyx, Leo. "Christology in the Context of Experience: An Interpretation of Christ by Edward Schillebeeckx." *The Thomist* 48 (1984): 383–408.

Schoof, Mark. "Dutch Catholic Theology: A New Approach to Christology." *Cross Currents* Winter (1973): 415–27.

————. "Masters in Israel: VII, The Later Theology of Edward Schillebeeckx." *Clergy Review* 55 (1970): 943–58.

Schoof, Ted. "E. Schillebeeckx: 25 Years in Nijmegen." *Theology Digest* 37/4 (1990): 313–31; 38/1 (1991): 31–43.

Schreiter, Robert J. "An Orientation to His Thought." In *The Schillebeeckx Reader,* ed. Robert J. Schreiter. New York: Crossroad, 1984.

Schreiter, Robert J. and Hilkert, Mary Catherine, eds. *The Praxis of Christian Experience: An Introduction to the Theology of Edward Schillebeeckx.* New York: Harper & Row, 1989.

Vandervelde, George. "Creation and Cross in the Theology of Edward Schillebeeckx." *Journal of Ecumenical Studies* 20/2 (1983): 257–71.

Wiseman, James. "Schillebeeckx and the Ecclesial Function of Critical Negativity." *The Thomist* 35 (1971): 207–46.

THOMAS AQUINAS: PRIMARY SOURCES

On Evil (De malo). Translated by Jean Oesterle. Notre Dame, Ind.: University of Notre Dame Press, 1995.

On the Truth of the Catholic Faith (Summa Contra Gentiles). 5 volumes. Translated by Pegis, Anderson, Bourke, and O'Neil. New York: Doubleday, 1955–1957.

Summa Theologiae. Blackfriars Edition. 3 volumes. New York: Benziger, 1947.

SECONDARY SOURCES FOR
THOMAS AQUINAS

Chenu, Marie-Dominic. *Toward Understanding St. Thomas.* Translated by A.-M. Landry and D. Hughes. Chicago: Regnery, 1964.

Clarke, W. Norris, S.J. "A New Look at the Immutability of God." In *God Knowable and Unknowable,* edited by Robert J. Roth, S.J. New York: Fordham University Press, 1973.
———. "Person, Being, and St. Thomas." *Communio* 19 (1992): 601–18.
Davies, Brian. *The Thought of St. Thomas Aquinas.* Oxford: Clarendon Press, 1992.
Dodds, Michael J. *The Unchanging God of Love: A Study of the Teaching of St. Thomas Aquinas on Divine Immutability in View of Certain Contemporary Criticisms of this Doctrine.* Fribourg, Switzerland: Editions Universitaires, 1986.
———. "Thomas Aquinas, Human Suffering, and the Unchanging God of Love." *Theological Studies* 52 (1991): 330–44.
Donceel, Joseph F. *The Searching Mind: An Introduction to a Philosophy of God.* Notre Dame, Ind.: University of Notre Dame Press, 1979.
Fitzpatrick, Edmund J. *The Sin of Adam in the Writings of St. Thomas Aquinas.* Mundelein, Ill.: St. Mary of the Lake Seminary, 1950.
Hill, William. *Knowing the Unknown God.* New York: Philosophical Library, 1971.
———. "Two Gods of Love: Aquinas and Whitehead" and "Does Divine Love Entail Suffering in God?" In *Search for the Absent God.* Edited by Mary Catherine Hilkert. New York: Crossroad, 1992.
Journet, Charles. *The Meaning of Evil.* Translated by Michael Barry. London: Geoffrey Chapman, 1963.
LaCugna, Catherine M. "The Relational God: Aquinas and Beyond." *Theological Studies* 46 (1985): 347–63.
Maritain, Jacques. *St Thomas and the Problem of Evil.* Milwaukee, Wisc.: Marquette, 1942.
McCabe, Herbert, O.P. *God Matters.* London: Geoffrey Chapman, 1987.
O'Brien, T. C. "Original Justice." Appendix to *Summa Theologiae,* by St. Thomas Aquinas. Vol. 26, no. 8. New York: McGraw-Hill, 1965.
———. "*Sacra Doctrina* Revisited." *Thomist* 41 (1977): 475–509.
O'Meara, Thomas F. "Thomas Aquinas and Today's Theology." *Theology Today* 55, no. 1 (1998): 46–58.
Pegis, Anton Charles. *St. Thomas and the Problem of the Soul in the 13th Century.* Toronto: St. Michael's College, 1934.
Pieper, Josef. *Guide to Thomas Aquinas.* Translated by Richard and Clara Winston. San Francisco: Ignatius Press, 1991; Pantheon, 1962.
Weisheipl, James A., O.P. *Friar Thomas D'Aquino: His Life, Thought and Works.* Washington, D.C.: Catholic University of America, 1974.

GENERAL SOURCES

Achtemeier, Paul J. *Romans: Interpretation.* Atlanta, Ga.: Knox, 1985.
Allik, Tina. "Narrative Approaches to Human Personhood: Agency, Grace, and Innocent Suffering." *Philosophy and Theology* 1 (1987): 305–33.
Anselm of Canterbury. *Trinity, Incarnation, and Redemption.* Edited and translated by Jasper Hopkins and Herbert W. Richardson. New York: Harper & Row, 1970.
———. *Why God Became Man (Cur Deus Homo).* Edited and translated by Jasper Hopkins and Herbert Richardson. Lewiston, N.Y.: The Edwin Mellen Press.

Aquino, Maria Pilar. *Our Cry for Life: Feminist Theology from Latin America.* Maryknoll, N.Y.: Orbis, 1993.

Armstrong, Hilary. "Negative Theology." *Downside Review* 95 (July 1977): 176–89.

Augustine. *Confessions.* Edited by Henry Chadwick. Oxford: Oxford University, 1993.

Bailie, Gil. *Violence Unveiled: Humanity at the Crossroads.* New York: Crossroad, 1997.

Barth, Karl. *Christ and Adam.* New York: Collier, 1962.

———. *The Epistle to the Romans.* Translated by Edwyn Hoskyns. New York: Oxford University Press, 1932.

———. *The Humanity of God.* Richmond: John Knox Press, 1960.

Bauckham, Richard. "Theodicy from Ivan Karamazov to Moltmann." *Modern Theology* 4:1 (January 1988): 83–97.

Beker, J. Christiaan. *Suffering and Hope: The Biblical Vision and the Human Predicament.* Philadelphia: Fortress, 1987.

Benjamin, Walter. *Reflections.* Translated by Edmund Jephcott. Edited by Peter Demetz. New York: Schocken Books, 1986.

Berkhof, Hendrikus. *Christian Faith.* Translated by Sierd Woudstra. Grand Rapids: Eerdmans, 1979.

Boff, Leonardo. *Liberating Grace.* Maryknoll, N.Y.: Orbis, 1979.

———. *Trinity and Society.* Translated by Paul Burns. Maryknoll, N.Y.: Orbis, 1988.

Bonhoeffer, Dietrich. *Creation and Fall.* Translated by John C. Fletcher. London: SCM Press, 1959.

———. *Letters and Papers from Prison.* Edited by Eberhard Bethge. Translated by Reginald H. Fuller. London: SMC Press, 1953.

———. *Life Together.* Translated by J. W. Doberstein. New York: Harper & Row, 1954.

Borg, Marcus J. *Jesus: A New Vision.* San Francisco: Harper & Row, 1987.

———. *Meeting Jesus Again for the First Time.* San Francisco: HarperSanFrancisco, 1994.

Borgman, Erik. "Negative Theology as Postmodern Talk of God." In *The Many Faces of the Divine,* edited by Hermann Häring and J. B. Metz. London: SCM; Maryknoll, N.Y.: Orbis, 1995; vol. 2, Nijmegen, Netherlands: Concilium, 1995, 102–11.

Brackley, Dean. *Divine Revolution: Salvation & Liberation in Catholic Thought.* Maryknoll, N.Y.: Orbis, 1996.

———. "A Radical Ethos." *Horizons* 24/1 (1997): 7–36.

Brown, Neil. "Experience as a Moral Source: A Literary Commentary on Official Catholic Ethics." *Irish Theological Quarterly* 61 (1995): 182–90.

Buber, Martin. *Good and Evil.* New York: Charles Scribner's Sons, 1953.

Buck-Morss, Susan. *The Origin of Negative Dialectics.* New York: The Free Press, 1977.

Burrell, David B. "Incarnation and Creation: The Hidden Dimension." *Modern Theology* 12, no. 2 (1996): 211–20.

Camus, Albert. *Resistance, Rebellion, and Death.* Translated by Justin O'Brien. New York: Vintage, 1960.

Catherine of Siena. *The Dialogues.* Translated by Suzanne Noffke, O.P. New York: Paulist, 1980.

Chopp, Rebecca. *The Power to Speak: Feminism, Language, and God.* New York: Crossroad, 1989.

———. *The Praxis of Suffering: An Interpretation of Liberation Theology and Political Theologies.* New York: Orbis Books, 1986.

Coleman, John A. *The Evolution of Dutch Catholicism, 1958–1974.* Berkeley: University of California Press, 1978.

Comstock, Gary. "The Truth of Religious Narratives." *International Journal for the Philosophy of Religion* 34 (1993): 131–50.

Constantelos, Demetrios. "Irenaeos of Lyons and His Central Views on Human Nature." *St. Vladimir's Theological Quarterly* 33 (1989): 351–86.

Cook, Michael L., S.J. *Christology as Narrative Quest.* Collegeville, Minn.: Liturgical Press, 1997.

Cronin, Kieran. "Illness, Sin, and Metaphor." *Irish Theological Quarterly* 61 (1995):191–204.

Crossan, John Dominic. *The Historical Jesus: The Life of a Mediterranean Jewish Peasant.* San Francisco: HarperSanFrancisco, 1991.

———. *Jesus: A Revolutionary Biography.* San Francisco: HarperSanFrancisco, 1994.

Cupitt, Don. *What Is a Story?* London: SCM Press, 1991.

D'Angelo, Mary Rose. "Abba and 'Father': Imperial Theology and the Jesus Traditions." *Journal of Biblical Literature* 111/4 (1992): 611–30.

Dickey-Young, Pamela. "Encountering Jesus Through the Earliest Witnesses." *Theological Studies* 57 (1996): 513–21.

DiNoia, J. A., O.P. *The Diversity of Religions: A Christian Perspective.* Washington, D.C.: Catholic University of America, 1992.

Doran, Kevin P. *Solidarity: A Synthesis of Personalism and Communalism in the Thought of Karol Wojtyla/Pope John Paul II.* New York: Peter Lang, 1996.

Donovan, Mary Ann, S.C. "Alive to the Glory of God: A Key Insight in St. Irenaeus." *Theological Studies* 49 (1988): 283–97.

Dostoevsky, Fyodor. *The Brothers Karamazov.* Translated by Richard Pevear and Larissa Volokhonsky. New York: Vintage Classics, 1991.

Eliade, Mircea. *Myth and Reality.* New York: Harper & Row, 1963.

———. *Myths, Dreams, and Mysteries: The Encounter Between Contemporary Faiths and Archaic Reality.* London: Collins, 1968.

Enns, Diane. "'We-Flesh' Re-Membering the Body Beloved." *Philosophy Today.* Fall (1995): 263–79.

Farley, Edward. *Good and Evil: Interpreting a Human Condition.* Minneapolis, Minn.: Fortress, 1990.

Farley, Wendy. *Tragic Vision and Divine Compassion: A Contemporary Theodicy.* Louisville: John Knox, 1990.

Fasching, Darrell J. *Narrative Theology After Auschwitz: From Alienation to Ethics.* Minneapolis: Augsburg Fortress Press, 1992.

Fitzgerald, Constance, O.C.D. "Impasse and Dark Night." In *Women's Spirituality: Resources for Christian Development,* ed. JoAnn Wolski Conn. New York: Paulist, 1986, 287–311.

Fulkerson, Mary McClintock. "Sexism as Original Sin: Developing a Theacentric Discourse." *Journal of the American Academy of Religion* 59, no.4: 653–75.

Gadamer, Hans-Georg. "Rhetoric, Hermeneutics, and the Critique of Ideology: Meta-Critical Comments on *Truth and Method.*" In *The Hermeneutics Reader,* edited by Kurt Mueller-Vollmer. New York: Continuum, 1994.

———. *Truth and Method.* 2nd ed. Translation revised by Joel Weinsheimer and Donald G. Marshall. New York: Continuum, 1994.

Gelpi, Donald. *The Turn to Experience in Contemporary Theology.* New York and Mawah, N.J.: Paulist, 1994.

Gustafson, Scott W. "From Theodicy to Discipleship: Dostoyevsky's Contribution to the Pastoral Task in *The Brothers Karamazov.*" *Scottish Journal of Theology* 45 (1992): 209–22.

Gutiérrez, Gustavo. *On Job: God-Talk and the Suffering of the Innocent.* Translated by Matthew J. O'Connell. Maryknoll, N.Y.: Orbis, 1987.

Habermas, Jürgen. "The Entwinement of Myth and Enlightenment: Max Horkheimer and Theodor Adorno." In *The Philosophical Discourse of Modernity.* Cambridge: MIT Press, 1990.

———. "On Hermeneutics' Claim to Universality." In *The Hermeneutics Reader,* edited by Kurt Mueller-Vollmer. New York: Continuum, 1994.

Haight, Roger. "The Case for Spirit Christology." *Theological Studies* 53 (1992): 257–87.

———. "Jesus Research and Faith in Jesus Christ." In *Finding God in All Things: Essays in Honor of Michael J. Buckley, S.J.,* edited by Michael J. Himes and Stephen J. Pope. New York: Crossroad, 1996.

Hall, Douglas. *Lighten Our Darkness: Toward an Indigenous Theology of the Cross.* Philadelphia: Westminster, 1976.

Harrison, Beverly Wildung. "The Power of Anger in the Work of Love." *Union Theological Seminary Quarterly Review* 36, supplement (January 1981): 41–57; reprinted in *Weaving the Visions,* edited by Judith Plaskow and Carol P. Christ. San Francisco: Harper & Row, 1989, 214–25.

Hauerwas, Stanley. *Naming the Silences: God, Medicine, and the Problem of Suffering.* Grand Rapids: Eerdmans, 1990.

Hewitt, Marsha. "The Politics of Empowerment: Ethical Paradigms in a Feminist Critique of Social Theory." *The Annual of the Society of Christian Ethics.* (November 1991).

Heyward, Carter Isabel. *The Redemption of God: A Theology of Mutual Relationship.* Washington, D.C.: University of America Press, 1982.

Hick, John. *Evil and the God of Love* (1977, 1966). London: Macmillan, 1985.

Hilkert, Mary Catherine. "Cry Beloved Image." In *The Embrace of God: Feminist Approaches to Theological Anthropology,* edited by Ann O'Hara Graff. Maryknoll: Orbis Books, 1995, 190–205.

———. *Naming Grace: Preaching and the Sacramental Imagination.* New York: Continuum, 1997.

Hill, William. "Christian Panentheism: Orthopraxis and God's Action in History." *Proceedings of the Catholic Theological Society* 35 (1980): 113–23.

Hillesum, Etty. *An Interrupted Life and Letters from Westerbork.* Translated by Arnold J. Pomerans. Foreword by Eva Hoffman. Edited by Jan G. Gaarlandt. New York: Henry Holt & Company, 1996.

Holland, Scott. "How Do Stories Save Us? Two Contemporary Theological Responses." *Louvain Studies* 22 (1997):328–51.

Horkheimer, Max, and Theodor Adorno. *Dialectic of Enlightenment.* Translated by John Cumming. New York: Continuum, 1993.

Irenaeus. *Against the Heresies.* Translated by Dominic Unger. New York: Paulist, 1992.

———. *The Writings of Irenaeus.* Translated by A. Roberts and W.H. Rambaut. In *Ante-Nicene Christian Library,* vol. 5, edited by A. Roberts and J. Donaldson. Edinburgh: T&T Clark, 1867.

Jeanrond, Werner. *Text and Interpretation as Categories of Theological Thinking.* Translated by Thomas J. Wilson. New York: Crossroad, 1988.

————, and Christoph Theobald, editors. *Who Do You Say That I Am?* Maryknoll, N.Y.: Orbis; London: SCM; Nijmegen, Netherlands: Concilium, 1997.

Jennings, William James. "'He Became Truly Human': Incarnation, Emancipation, and Authentic Humanity." *Modern Theology* 12, no. 22 (1996): 239–54.

John Paul II. *On the Christian Meaning of Human Suffering (Salvifici Doloris).* Apostolic Letter, February 11,1984. Washington, D.C.: U.S. Catholic Conference, 1984.

————. *Sollicitudo Rei Socialis.* 1987.

Johnson, Elizabeth A. *Friends of God and Prophets: A Feminist Theological Reading of the Communion of Saints.* New York: Continuum, 1998.

————. *She Who Is: The Mystery of God in Feminist Theological Discourse.* New York: Crossroad, 1992.

————. Presidential Address. "Turn to the Heavens and the Earth: Retrieval of the Cosmos in Theology." *Proceedings of the Catholic Theological Society of America* 51(1996).

Jones, L. Gregory. *Embodying Forgiveness: A Theological Analysis.* Grand Rapids, Mich.: Eerdmans, 1995.

Jüngel, Eberhard. *God as the Mystery of the World.* Translated by Darrell L. Guder. Edinburgh: T&T Clark, 1983.

————. *Theological Essays II.* Edinburgh: T&T Clark, 1994.

Käseman, Ernst. *Perspectives on Paul.* Philadelphia: Fortress, 1971.

King, Ursula. *Women and Spirituality: Voices of Protest and Promise.* University Park, Pa.: Pennsylvania State University Press, 1993.

Knitter, Paul. *No Other Name?* Maryknoll, N.Y.: Orbis, 1985.

Kuitert, H.M. *The Reality of Faith: A Way between Protestant Orthodoxy and Existential Theology.* Translated by Lewis Smedes. Grand Rapids, Mich.: Eerdmans, 1968.

Kuschel, Karl-Josef. "World Religions, Human Rights and the Humanum." In *The Ethics of World Religions and Human Rights,* edited by Hans Kung and Jürgen Moltmann. Nijmegen, Netherlands: Concilium, 1990.

LaCugna, Catherine M. *God for Us: The Trinity and Christian Life.* San Francisco: HarperSanFrancisco, 1991.

————, ed. *Freeing Theology: The Essentials of Theology in Feminist Perspective.* San Francisco: HarperSanFrancisco, 1993.

Lamb, Matthew. *Solidarity with Victims: Toward a Theology of Social Transformation.* New York: Crossroad, 1982.

Lane, Dermot. "Anthropology and Eschatology." *Irish Theological Quarterly* 1 (1995): 14–31.

Lasalle-Klein, Robert. "The Body of Christ: The Claim of the Crucified People on U.S. Theology and Ethics." *Journal of Hispanic/Latino Theology* 5, no. 4 (1998): 48–77.

Lash, Nicholas. *Easter in Ordinary: Reflections on Human Experience and the Knowledge of God.* Charlottesville: University Press of Virginia, 1988.

Leonard, Ellen. "Experience as a Source for Theology." *Proceedings of the Catholic Theological Society of America* 43 (1988): 44–61.

Levinas, Emmanuel. *Collected Philosophical Papers.* Translated by Alphonso Lingis. The Netherlands: Nijoff Publishers, 1987.

Levine, Michael P. "Pantheism, Theism and the Problem of Evil." *International Journal for the Philosophy of Religion* 35 (1994): 129–51.

Lohfink, Gerhard. *Jesus and Community.* Translated by John P. Galvin. New York: Paulist, 1984.

Maas, Franz. "Meister Eckhart: The Postponement of Unity as a Sphere of Life." In vol. 2 of *The Many Faces of the Divine,* edited by Hermann Häring and J. B. Metz. London: SCM; Maryknoll, N.Y.: Orbis, 1995; Nijmegen, Netherlands: Concilium, 1995; 70–79.

Macann, Christopher. *Four Phenomenological Philosophers: Husserl, Heidegger, Sartre, Merleau-Ponty.* N.Y. & London: Routledge, 1993.

McDonagh, Enda. "Orthopraxis and Moral Theology." *Proceedings of the Catholic Theological Society of America* 35 (1980): 15–26.

McFague, Sallie. *The Body of God: An Ecological Theology.* Minneapolis, Minn.: Fortress, 1993.

———. *Models of God: Theology for an Ecological, Nuclear Age.* Philadelphia: Fortress, 1987.

McGill, Arthur Chute. *Suffering: A Test of Theological Method.* Philadelphia: Westminster, 1982.

Merleau-Ponty, Maurice. *Phenomenology of Perception* (1962). Translated by Colin Smith. London: Routledge, 1995.

———. *The Primacy of Perception and Other Essays on Phenomenological Psychology, the Philosophy of Art, History and Politics.* Edited by James M. Eddie. Evanston, Ill.: Northwestern University Press, 1964.

Metz, Johannes Baptiste, and Jürgen Moltmann, eds. *Faith and the Future: Essays on Theology, Solidarity, and Modernity.* Maryknoll, N.Y.: Orbis, 1995.

Mieth, Dietmar. "What Is Experience?" In *Revelation and Experience,* edited by E. Schillebeeckx and Bas van Iersel. Nijmegen, Netherlands: Concilium, 1979.

Moltmann, Jürgen. *The Crucified God.* New York: Harper & Row, 1974.

Moore, Sebastian. "Getting the Fall Right." *Downside Review* 116 /404 (1998): 213–26.

———. *The Crucified Jesus Is No Stranger.* London: Darton, Longman, & Todd, 1977.

———. "Reflexions on Death." *Downside Review* 69 (1952): 14–24.

———. "Reflexions on Death II." *Downside Review* (1952–53): 373–83.

Moule, C.F.D. *The Origin of Christology.* Cambridge: Cambridge University Press, 1977.

Murphy-O'Connor, Jerome. *Becoming Human Together: The Pastoral Anthropology of St. Paul.* Dublin: Veritas Publications, 1978.

Neufield, Franceen (Vann). "The Cross of the Living Lord: The Theology of the Cross and Mysticism." *Scottish Journal of Theology* 49 (1996):131–45.

Nolan, Albert. *God in South Africa: The Challenge of the Gospel.* Grand Rapids, Mich.: Eerdmans, 1988.

———. *Jesus before Christianity.* Maryknoll, N.Y.: Orbis, 1976, 1992.

O'Hara-Graff, Ann. "The Struggle to Name Women's Experience: Assessment and Implications for Theological Construction." *Horizons* 20/2 (1993): 215–233.

Osborne, Kenan B. *Reconciliation and Justification.* Mahwah, N.J.: Paulist, 1990.

———. *The Resurrection of Jesus: New Considerations for Its Theological Interpretation.* New York and Mahwah, N.J.: Paulist, 1997.

Padovano, Anthony. *Original Sin and Christian Anthropology.* Washington: Corpus Books, 1969; Catholic Theological Society of America, 1967.

Pelikan, Jaroslav. *Jesus Through the Centuries: His Place in the History of Culture.* New York: Harper & Row, 1987; originally published by Yale University Press (New Haven, 1985).

Peukert, Helmut. *Science, Action, and Fundamental Theology: Toward a Theology of Communicative Action.* Translated by James Bohman. Cambridge: MIT Press, 1984.

Power, David, and F. Kabasele Lumbala, eds. *Spectre of Mass Death.* London: SCM Press; Maryknoll, N.Y.: Orbis, 1993; vol. 3, Nijmegen, Netherlands: Concilium, 1993.

Portalie, Eugene, S.J. *A Guide to the Thought of St. Augustine.* Translated by Ralph J. Bastin, S.J. Chicago: Henry Regnery, 1960.

Richard, Robert L. *Secularization Theology.* New York: Herder & Herder, 1967.

Ricoeur, Paul. *Figuring the Sacred: Religion, Narrative, and Imagination.* Translated by David Pellauer. Edited by Mark I. Wallace. Minneapolis: Fortress, 1995.

———. *The Conflict of Interpretations.* Edited by Don Ihde. Evanston, Ill: Northwestern University, 1974.

———. *The Symbolism of Evil.* Translated by Emerson Buchanan. Boston: Beacon, 1967.

Roberts, Dom John. "The Injustice of Sin." *Downside Review* 71 (Summer 1953):233–42.

Robinson, John A. T. *The Body: A Study in Pauline Theology* (1952). London: Bloomsbury Street, 1963.

Rondet, Henri. *Original Sin: The Patristic and Theological Background.* Translated by Cajetan Finnegan. New York: Alba House, 1972.

Sands, Kathleen M. *Escape from Paradise: Evil and Tragedy in Feminist Theology.* Minneapolis, Minn.: Fortress, 1994.

Saward, John. "Towards an Apophatic Anthropology." *Irish Theological Quarterly* 41 (1974):222–34.

Scharlemann, Robert P., ed. *Negation and Theology.* Charlottesville: University Press of Virginia, 1992.

Schnackenburg, Rudolf. *Baptism in the Thought of St. Paul.* Oxford: Basil Blackwell, 1964.

Schneiders, Sandra. *The Revelatory Text: Interpreting the New Testament as Sacred Scripture.* San Francisco: HarperCollins, 1991.

Schreiter, Robert J. *Reconciliation: Mission and Ministry in a Changing Social Order.* Maryknoll, N.Y.: Orbis, 1992.

———. *The Ministry of Reconciliation: Spirituality & Strategies.* Maryknoll, N.Y.: Orbis, 1998.

———. *The New Catholicity: Theology between the Global and the Local.* New York: Orbis, 1997.

Schoonenberg, Piet. *Man and Sin.* Translated by Joseph Donceel. Notre Dame, Ind.: University of Notre Dame Press, 1965.

Schüssler Fiorenza, Elisabeth. *But She Said: Feminist Practices of Biblical Interpretation.* Boston: Beacon, 1992.

———. *In Memory of Her: A Feminist Theological Reconstruction of Christian Origins.* New York: Crossroad, 1983.

———, and David Tracy, eds. *The Holocaust as Interruption.* Edinburgh: T&T Clark, 1984; Nijmegen, Netherlands: Concilium.

Schüssler Fiorenza, Francis. "Critical Social Theory and Christology: Towards an Understanding of Atonement and Redemption as Emancipatory Solidarity." *Proceedings of the Catholic Theological Society of America* 30 (1975): 63–110.

Scott, Michael. "The Morality of Theodicies." *Religious Studies* 32 (1996): 1–13.

Segundo, Juan Luis. *Evolution and Guilt.* Maryknoll, N.Y.: Orbis, 1974.

———. *Grace and the Human Condition.* Maryknoll, N.Y.: Orbis, 1973.

Sheldrake, Philip, S.J. *Spirituality and History: Questions of Interpretation and Method.* Maryknoll, N.Y.: Orbis, 1998 (London: SPCK, 1991; revised edition, 1995).

Shults, F. LeRon. "A Theology of Chaos: An Experiment in Postmodern Theological Science." *Scottish Journal of Theology* 45 (1992): 223–35.

Sia, Marian F., and Santiago Sia. *From Suffering to God: Exploring Our Images of God in the Light of Suffering.* New York: St. Martin's Press, 1994.

Sobrino, Jon. *The True Church and the Poor.* Maryknoll, N.Y.: Orbis, 1984.

Soelle, Dorothy. *Suffering.* Translated by Everett R. Kalin. Philadelphia, Fortress, 1975.

———. *The Strength of the Weak: Toward a Christian Feminist Identity.* Translated by Robert and Rita Kimber. Philadelphia: Westminster Press, 1984.

Springsted, Eric O. *Simone Weil and the Suffering of Love.* Cambridge, Mass.: Cowley, 1986.

Suchocki, Marjorie Hewitt. *The Fall to Violence: Original Sin in Relational Theology.* New York: Continuum, 1995.

Surin, Kenneth. *Theology and the Problem of Evil.* London: Basil Blackwell, 1986.

———. *The Turnings of Darkness and Light.* New York: Cambridge University Press, 1989.

Stein, Edith. *On the Problem of Empathy.* Vol. 3, *The Collected Works of Edith Stein.* Translated by Walraut Stein. Washington, D.C.: ICS Publications, 1989.

Swidler, Leonard and Paul Motzes, eds. *The Uniqueness of Jesus: A Dialogue with Paul Knitter.* Maryknoll, N.Y.: Orbis, 1997.

Swinburne, Richard. *Providence and the Problem of Evil.* Oxford: Clarendon Press, 1998.

Talbert, Charles. *Learning through Suffering: The Educational Value of Suffering in the New Testament Milieu.* Collegeville, Minn.: Liturgical Press, 1991.

———. *Reading Corinthians: A Literary and Theological Commentary on 1 and 2 Corinthians.* New York: Crossroad, 1987.

Talvacchia, Kathleen. "Learning to Stand with Others through Compassionate Solidarity." *Union Seminary Quarterly Review* 44 (1993): 177–94.

Taylor, Mark, ed. *The Mystery of Suffering and Death.* New York: Doubleday, 1974.

TeSelle, Eugene. *Augustine the Theologian.* New York: Herder & Herder, 1970.

Thistlewaite, Susan, and Mary Potter Engel, eds. *Lift Every Voice: Constructing Christian Theologies from the Underside.* San Francisco: Harper & Row, 1990.

Tobin, Thomas H. *The Spirituality of Paul.* Wilmington, Del.: Michael Glazier, 1987.

Townes, Emilie M., ed. *A Troubling in My Soul: Womanist Perspectives on Evil and Suffering.* Maryknoll, N.Y.: Orbis, 1993.

Tracy, David. *Dialogue with the Other: The Inter-Religious Dialogue.* Grand Rapids, Mich: Eerdmanns, 1990; Louvain, Belgium: Peeters Press, 1990.

———. "Evil, Suffering, and Hope: The Search for New Forms of Contemporary Theodicy." *Proceedings of the Catholic Theological Society of America* 50 (1995): 15–36.

———. *Plurality and Ambiguity: Hermeneutics, Religion, Hope.* San Francisco: Harper & Row, 1987.

————— and Hermann Häring, editors. Vol. 1 of *The Fascination with Evil.* New York: Orbis, 1998; Nijmegen, Netherlands: Concilium, 1998.

Trible, Phyllis. "Eve and Adam: Genesis 2–3 Reread." In *Womanspirit Rising,* edited by Carol Christ and Judith Plaskow. New York: Harper & Row, 1979.

Valevicius, Andrius. *From the Other to the Totally Other: The Religious Philosophy of Emmanuel Levinas.* New York: Lang, 1988.

Vandervelde, George. *Original Sin: Two Major Trends in Contemporary Roman Catholic Interpretation* (Amsterdam, 1975). Washington D.C.: University Press of America, 1981.

Von Loewenich, Walter. *Luther's Theology of the Cross* (1929). Translated by Herbert J. A. Bouman. Minneapolis, Minn.: Augsburg Press, 1976.

Walsh, James, S.J., and P.G. Walsh. *Divine Providence and Human Suffering.* Wilmington, Del.: Michael Glazier, 1985.

Webb, Dom Bruno. "God and the Mystery of Evil." *Downside Review* 75 (Autumn 1957): 338–58.

Webster, John. " 'The Firmest Grasp of the Real': Barth on Original Sin." *Toronto Journal of Theology* 4 (1988): 19–29.

Weil, Simone. *The Need for Roots: Prelude to a Declaration of Duties towards Mankind.* London: Routledge & Kegan Paul, 1952.

—————. *Waiting for God.* Translated by Emma Craufurd. New York: G. P. Putnam's Sons, 1951.

Weisberger, A. M. "Depravity, Divine Responsibility and Moral Evil: A Critique of a New Free Will Defence." *Religious Studies* 31 (Spring 1995): 375–90.

White, Stephen K., ed. *The Cambridge Companion to Habermas.* New York: Cambridge University Press, 1995.

Wiesel, Elie. *Night.* Translated by Stella Rodway. New York: Bantam Books, 1982.

Wyschogrod, Edith. "Man-Made Mass Death: Shifting Concepts of Community." *Journal of the American Academy of Religion* (LVIII/2): 165–76.

—————. *Saints and Postmodernism: Revisioning Moral Philosophy.* Chicago: University of Chicago Press, 1990.

Yandell, Keith E. "Tragedy and Evil." *International Journal for the Philosophy of Religion* 36 (1994): 1–26.

Young, Frances. "God Suffered and Died." In *Incarnation and Myth: The Debate Continued,* edited by M. Goulder. Nijmegen, Netherlands: Concilium, 1979.

Index

Abba experience, 14, 95, 96, 97
absolute reality, 87–89
Adam, 51, 52, 58, 66, 145, 160n75, 163, 166
Adam, Karl, 11
Adorno, Theodor, 27, 28, 29, 30, 31, 32
Africa, 139, 140
African Americans, 117n65
alienation, 28, 44n72, 136
Ambrose, 149
Amos, 134
anawim, 57–58, 71n32, 135, 137, 158n54
anthropological constants, of humanum, 79–84, 86
appearance narratives, 103–4, 105, 106, 107, 108, 109; by women, 106, 108, 122n121
Aquinas. *See* Thomas Aquinas
arms race, 168
art, 30
Augustine, 50, 51, 54, 55, 75, 76, 166

Balkans, 139
Beatitudes, 57, 58
being human, 80, 88, 124
belief. *See* faith
Benjamin, Walter, 31
biblical exegesis, 4, 13, 35–39, 65
bioethics, 79
Bloch, Ernst, 27, 28–29

Borgman, Erik, 11, 12, 26
Bultmann, Rudolf Karl, 18, 19, 20

Camus, Albert, 27, 146
Chalcedon, 13, 88
charity, 154n11, 155n23
Chenu, Marie Dominique (Marie-Dominic), 11, 12, 17, 27, 28, 55
China, 135, 139, 140
Christ: The Experience of Jesus as Lord (Schillebeeckx), 34, 37, 46n112, 76
Christ: The Sacrament of the Encounter with God (Schillebeeckx), 13, 14–15
christology, 13, 20, 36, 37, 38, 46n112, 89, 103, 113n7; and soteriology, 76, 86, 87
Church: The Human Story of God (Schillebeeckx), 66
civil rights movement (U.S.), 126
civil structures. *See* political structures
cognition, cognitivity. *See* knowing
communication, 32, 33, 46n104
compassion, 83, 149, 164
Congar, Yves, 17, 27
conversion: of disciples, 103, 104, 106–7, 109; and suffering, 164, 172
Corinthians, 105
creation, 14, 21, 51, 52, 54, 78, 149; and suffering, 112
creation story, 52, 166. *See also* Adam; fall from original grace

189

Hermeneutics, The" (Schillebeeckx), 32
Nichtige, das, 165, 174n12
Noah, 166, 167
nonbelief, 87, 137
nothingness, 93, 163, 165, 170

obedience, 56, 58, 59, 60, 62, 71n32, 75, 97; and metanoia, 112, 131–32; and trust, 4, 75, 125
oppressed, 30, 44n72, 111–12, 131, 133–34, 135–36, 138, 140, 156n38
original justice, 49, 50–53, 54, 58, 59, 63, 69n14, 70n23, 141–44, 148, 166, 167
original sin, 4, 6n4, 49, 53–56, 58, 59, 70n23, 72n37, 72n40, 72n42, 160n81, 163, 165, 166, 167; and death, 63, 66, 72n51, 73n54, 101; and grace, 49, 54, 58–59, 144, 146, 160n75
orthodoxy, 23, 25, 43n57
orthopraxis, 27, 34, 103
other, 8–9, 29, 51, 89, 109, 124, 125, 126, 145, 169, 171; and solidarity, 128, 139, 140

pain, 49, 50, 69n7
Pannenberg, 18, 20, 21
paradise, 51
para-religious consciousness, 82–83
paschal event, 39, 40, 123, 126, 143. *See also* Easter experience; Last Supper
passion narrative, 100–101, 103, 120nn95–96
passive contrast experience, 100
Paul, 61, 105, 106, 130–31, 133
Paul VI, 168
penance, 161n97
personal relationships, transformation of, 130–32, 156n38
Peter, 106–7, 108
Peter Chrysologus, St., 166
Pharisees, 57, 132
phenomenology, 13; defined, 10
Philemon, 130–31
pluralism, religious, 21–22, 87, 88
political action, 143

political mysticism, 5, 7n9, 123, 126, 127, 132–33, 143, 152
political responsibility, 5, 130
political structures: contemporary, 133, 157n45; and early Christians, 128–32, 155n26, 156nn41–42; Hebrew Testament on, 134. *See also* secularism, secularization
political theology, 67
politics: defined, 123; and grace, 130
poor, 44n72, 71n32, 81–82, 134–41
Portier, William, 26, 34
postmodernist thought, 28, 29, 171
praxis, 16, 19; and theory, 18, 28, 33, 82, 162, 173n2
prayer, 90, 151
privileged culture, 81
protest, 5, 31, 32, 83, 133–34
Protestants, 19
Psalms, 101

Q community, 92

Rahner, 17
reality, 19, 20, 21, 22, 24, 151
reason, 3, 28
reconciliation, 5, 31, 149, 150–52; and metanoia, 136, 140, 148; and mysticism, 5, 151; and salvation, 149, 150, 152, 161n97; social, 151, 158n153, 159n65; and solidarity, 135–36, 140, 163
redemption, 30, 31, 60, 149; of Christ, 59; and death, 66; defined, 173n7; and grace, 60; and Mary, 57, 58, 71n26; objective/subjective, 58, 59; and sin, 166; and suffering, 151
redemptive memory, 31
religious consciousness, 82–83
resistance, and negative dialectics, 28–30
responsibility, 21, 24, 79, 81; ethic of, 45n83, 81, 145–46
resurrection, 39; and Jesus' relation to God, 103, 112, 143; and suffering, 109
resurrection faith, 102, 104–6, 112; and bodily appearances, 103, 104–5, 106,

About the Author

Kathleen McManus, a Dominican of Blauvelt, New York, is assistant professor of theology at the University of Portland. She has a background in preaching and pastoral ministry and holds a doctorate in systematics from the University of St. Michael's College in Toronto. Her teaching interests include Christology, theological anthropology, and women's contextual theologies, especially in Latin America. She is currently researching the implications of a theology of suffering for ethics in situations where human life is threatened or diminished.